Intellectuals
and Left Politics
in Uruguay,
1958-2006

para Anita –
a pesar de todos los pesares

Intellectuals and Left Politics in Uruguay, 1958-2006

Stephen Gregory

sussex
ACADEMIC
PRESS

BRIGHTON • PORTLAND

2 4 6 8 10 9 7 5 3 1

First published 2009 in Great Britain by
SUSSEX ACADEMIC PRESS
PO Box 139
Eastbourne BN24 9BP

and in the United States of America by
SUSSEX ACADEMIC PRESS
920 NE 58th Ave   Suite 300
Portland, Oregon 97213-3786

British Library Cataloguing in Publication Data
A CIP catalogue record for this book is available from the British Library.

Library of Congress Cataloging-in-Publication Data
Gregory, Stephen, 1948–
Intellectuals and left politics in Uruguay, 1958–2006 : frustrated dialogue
/ Stephen Gregory.
p. cm.
Includes bibliographical references and index.
ISBN 978-1-84519-265-5 (h/c : alk. paper)
1. Uruguay—Politics and government—20th century. 2. Uruguay—
Intellectual life—20th century. 3. Intellectuals—Uruguay—Political
activity. 4. New Left—Uruguay—History. I. Title.
F2728.G74 2008
959.506′4—dc22

                                                      2008029922

The author gratefully acknowledges a 2007 Publication subsidy from the Australian
Academy for the Humanities, which greatly facilitated the publication of this book.

Typeset & Designed by SAP, Brighton & Eastbourne.
Printed by TJ International, Padstow, Cornwall.
This book is printed on acid-free paper.

CONTENTS

ACKNOWLEDGEMENTS

This book could not have been completed without the professional and good-humoured help over many years of the staff in the Interlibrary Loans and Document Delivery sections of the Social Sciences and Humanities Library at the University of New South Wales. Without such services, it would be impossible to complete a project such as this in Australia, so far from the major repositories of Latin American materials.

I am also grateful to the Special Study Programme of the Faculty of Arts and Social Sciences at the University of New South Wales, which provided funds and time for me to do the initial research for this book.

Votes of thanks to individuals go, first, to Jim Levy and Diana Palaversich, supervisors of the original doctoral thesis on which about half of the present book was based. Their constant support, encouragement and critical intelligence made writing that thesis both more congenial and more challenging. I am also grateful to Peter Ross, Jeff Browitt and Jim, again, who read and made detailed comments on different versions of the entire manuscript. Susan Keen, John Perkins, Elena Sheldon and Jim (once more) made cogent and valuable comments on drafts of individual chapters or sections.

I also thank Jeff Browitt for being interested enough to support my application for a Publication Subsidy from the Academy for the Humanities, Canberra. My gratitude to the Academy is more formally recorded elsewhere.

I should also like to acknowledge the help of Orosmán García Gopar, who went to great lengths to search for books for me in Montevideo.

I also take this chance to record my gratitude to Anthony Grahame at Sussex Academic for his irreplaceable help in transforming my computer printout into a publishable text.

Finally, and more personally, I would like to thank Anita Lezcano, to whom I dedicate this book. Anita shared with me her memories of the pleasures and pains, the terrors and excitements, of her life before, during, and after the Uruguayan dictatorship that began in 1973. She may well neither agree nor identify with anything in the pages that follow, but they would not be what they are if her story had not been what it was.

Any deficiencies that remain after the good offices of all these people are, as always, my own.

NOTE ON TRANSLATIONS AND REFERENCES

Translations are not generally accompanied by the original in a note or parenthesis. Words or phrases in Spanish are included only in cases of untranslatable puns, neologisms or possible confusion.

The desire to make it possible to read the chapters of this book separately has involved a minimum of cross-referencing and repetition. Also, full referencing for books and articles begins again at the start of each chapter, short titles being used in the text once a complete reference has appeared in a footnote.

All books are published in Montevideo unless otherwise stated. Place of publication for a serial is given if the text does not clarify that it is Uruguayan and if it is not well known to professional Latin Americanists.

The following are abbreviations and acronyms used throughout the notes and bibliography. The list does not include parties and organisations whose acronyms are given in the text.

CEDAL	Centro Editor de América Latina
CLAEH	Centro Latinoamericano de Economía Humana
EBO	Ediciones de la Banda Oriental
FCU	Fondo de Cultura Universitaria
INDAL	*either* Información Documental de América Latina [Caracas] *or* Information Documentaire d'Amérique Latine [Heverlee-Louvain]
n.p.	No page number(s)
no publ.	No publisher given
Suppl.	Supplement
UP	University Press

"And when words seem slippery, in the end there is only violence. We are on its threshold. We belong to a generation which lives Uruguay as a problem, which no longer accepts what has been done, and which, alienated from the usual routines for salvation, has been compelled to ask itself the radical question: what the hell is all this?"

Alberto Methol Ferré (1958)

"'There's nothing like Uruguay' began as a proud vision of the country and ended up as the advertising slogan for a brand of cooking oil. Sic transit gloria mundi."

CARLOS MARTÍNEZ MORENO (1971)

"If a better Left is to come, it will only be after people have greeted on the streets the triumph or failure of this one. David always found a way to beat Goliath."

JOSÉ 'PEPE' MUJICA (2002)

INTRODUCTION

Uruguay as a Question

It cannot be said the recent social and political situation lacks problems capable of awakening the greatest interest in the 'intelligentsia'.

Roberto Ares Pons (1955)

The period covered by this book is the roughly fifty years beginning in 1958, from the victory of the National Party in that year's elections to the first period of the Frente Amplio government that took office in March 2005. The Nationals' government in the late 1950s was the first change of ruling party in Uruguay for over ninety years, while the election win by the centre-left in 2004 was the first time a party other than the 'traditional' Colorado or National parties had won power since Uruguay's independence from Spain. Not only did the left gain power nationally for the first time; Uruguay turned from a two-party into a multi-party system. 1958 and 2004 are, then, indicators of a remarkable transformation undergone by Uruguayan society in the second half of the twentieth century, a process interrupted only by the other unprecedented event in recent Uruguayan history: the military coup of 1973 and the subsequent twelve-year dictatorship.

These years saw the disintegration of the dominant way Uruguayans saw themselves, a view laid down in the early years of the century under the modernising social reformism called simply 'Batllismo', after the legendary President José Batlle y Ordoñez who initiated it. Its main elements were. acceptance of a modicum of individual happiness and security guaranteed by the state; the sense that Uruguay was different from (or superior to) its Latin American neighbours; consensus in the form of a generally shared respect for social and political institutions and the law; and the belief that Uruguayans were exemplary educated citizens.[1]

In the 1950s, once wars abroad stopped artificially prolonging Uruguay's prosperity, there began a crisis in the country's modernisation and indus-trialisation process. As de Torres Wilson pithily worded it: 'Uruguay, a country without problems, suddenly became a problematic country'.[2] During the 1960s, burgeoning foreign debt coupled with economic stagnation, capital flight, major bankruptcies and galloping inflation; labour unrest due to unemployment, declining real wages and an unwieldy state administration's failure to deliver much-needed social services; political corruption at all levels, and an initially successful (and surprisingly popular) urban guerrilla campaign looked like eroding the country's institutions as well as its somewhat complacent idea of itself. Indeed, it might tenably – if contentiously – be argued that by 1969 Uruguay (and not Chile in 1970) was the Latin American country most likely to emulate the Cuban experience of 1959.

In fact, however, from 1968 the government took a sharp and often brutal turn to the right and clamped down on all forms of opposition (not only the armed insurgency), continuing the counter-revolutionary movement begun in Brazil in 1964 which was to be unleashed throughout Latin America during the 1970s and frequently resulted in military coups (most infamously in Argentina and Chile). Uruguay was not to escape this fate. The armed forces, having been called upon for what became universally condemned internal security purposes, refused to return to barracks, demanding instead greater involvement at all levels of government decision-making and eventually assuming power themselves in June 1973, where they remained for nearly twelve years.

Partly through assassinations and 'disappearances' (although not as widely as in Argentina and Chile) but mostly through exile, imprisonment and censorship, the military eliminated all political opposition and began a movement towards market economics that enmeshed Uruguay into global capitalism but did not solve internal problems. Following redemocratisation in 1985, Colorado and National party governments largely pursued neoliberal economic orthodoxy, although they did open up regional cooperation with Uruguay's incorporation into Mercosur in 1990–1991. Regional economic difficulties in the late 1990s led eventually to implosion in Argentina in 2001 and a major recession in Uruguay a year later. In the meantime, a restructured centre-left, having inherited the mantle from the Frente Amplio of the early 1970s, gained control of Montevideo in 1989 and made electoral headway in each successive national ballot afterwards. Finally, after the Uruguayan population indicated its disinclination to continue with unchecked neoliberalism, the Frente Amplio finally won power outright in the October 2004 ballot.[3]

This study employs the words 'intellectuals' and 'intelligentsia' as catch-all terms to refer to those people who work in the arts, social sciences, journalism and such liberal professions as the law and secondary or tertiary teaching, and who seek through words or deeds to influence the organisation of the society in which they live.[4] To these could be added three of the four criteria used by Nicola Miller: namely, that they should be national and not just local in their frame of reference and intended influence, and independent of church and state. Some of my examples, however, might fall foul of her other demand that they primarily seek intellectual persuasiveness over political influence.[5] Some of the intellectuals studied here write only as an adjunct to their political work.

In addition, Uruguayan commentators writing during the period covered by this book assumed that such intellectuals were dissidents. In a prophetic, even precocious essay, Roberto Ares Pons argued that intelligentsias only arise at 'moments of instability caused by the decadence of an old order and the appearance of new ways of living', and were made up of educated members of the lower middle class whose non-conformism was a '*sine qua non*' among the intelligentsia.[6] Graceras defined the intelligentsia as 'all those intellectual groups that critically analyse society and advocate political change'.[7] Similarly, Angel Rama enthused that in the social changes undergone in Uruguay in the 1960s, the role of intellectuals was especially important: they 'clarified consciences, explained reality, helped to train new generations, prepared people for change and instilled the moral values necessary to oppose the corruption of the political and economic elite'.[8] The changing nature of this dissidence and of the relationship between intellectuals and progressive politics in Uruguay over the last fifty years is the main theme of this book.

Castañeda and Santi have argued that the intellectual, whether primarily a writer, journalist, artist or activist, has articulated the social and political demands of society wherever the institutions of civil society are weak or threatened,[9] while others have optimistically assumed – as do many of the intellectuals themselves – that their influence on society is all but assured.[10] Such a view could not survive long in Uruguay after the 1973 coup. Indeed, the pages that follow can be read in the context of the gradual demise of the intellectuals' role as 'legislators' and their relegation to mere 'interpreters'.[11] Neoliberal economics and the growth of an all-pervasive popular culture over the last years of the twentieth century have created both a new public as well as a series of different cultural artifacts. This has meant that the intellectual elite now has to compete in an open cultural market to appeal to a semi-literate but ever more informed audience that increasingly recognises itself in the images of mass culture. The story of this gradual dethronement of the intellectuals from their Olympian position as mediators and mentors of their societies falls outside the scope of this book,[12] but what follows can be seen as a Uruguayan case study of the last period when intellectuals could attempt to influence the path taken by a particular nation towards modernisation on terms of their own choosing, and then of their first entry into an era which questioned many assumptions about intellectuals' social function.

In essence, the book will argue that in the 1960s Uruguayan intellectuals helped to unify a fragmented left, and helped to broaden its constituency with a new kind of politics built on the need to revive the principles of consensus and dialogue in an increasingly polarised society. This endeavour foundered because the social and political rifts in Uruguayan society became so great that they permitted only a militarist solution from which all forms of dialogue were excluded. After the authoritarian period had put an end to the conditions in which such a dialogue was possible, redemocratisation has seen the relationship between intellectuals and politics take two paths, one following closely the progress of the political centre-left, the other staying resolutely independent of it.

Part One, *Towards Intellectual and Political Unity*, concentrates on how progressive intellectuals contributed to the unification of the left during the intensifying social and political strife in Uruguay up to the coup in 1973. The first chapter illustrates the effects of fragmentation and impotence on leftist intellectuals. Eschewing such predictable polemics as those found in newspapers put out by the Communist and Socialist parties, the chapter concentrates on the cut and thrust of comments by individuals in articles, reviews or letters pages, mostly in *Marcha*. It looks at exchanges arising from what were two occasions for frustration and self-delusion for the Uruguayan left: 'ruralism' and the 1958 elections, and *tercerismo*, the possibility of a 'third way'. Chapters 2 and 3 begin the analysis of progressive intellectuals' more direct involvement in the Uruguayan political scene. I start by looking at the document that rallied just about all the major intellectual figures in Uruguay around the banner of the centre-left coalition, the Frente Amplio, just prior to the national elections of November 1971. These chapters use interviews, formal documents and manifestos to retrace the tortuous path followed by various groups on the left and dissidents from the progressive sections of the major parties in their many efforts to build a working dialogue with each other, efforts that remained frustrated until the creation of the Frente Amplio early in 1971.

I then examine the ways in which the principle of dialogue was embedded in both the Frente's internal organization and its political platform, and claim that this was especially attractive to intellectuals who were searching for more direct ways of reaching and influencing their public. While the Tupamaros and the radical left inspired by the example of Che Guevara generated most publicity, I argue here that it was the creation of the Frente Amplio that first illustrated the left intelligentsia's ability to devise realistic proposals that would address Uruguay's political and social problems and appeal to a wider public. The chapter closes with an account of the Frente's modest showing in the national elections of November 1971, suggesting that while it had enabled and strengthened dialogue among its member groups, the Frente's attempt to reinvigorate productive dialogue with and in the nation at large foundered on a badly polarised political scene in which any space for dialogue was steadily being eroded.

A brief **Interlude** sketches how, during the twelve-year dictatorship, the military attempted to replace the artists and thinkers they had banned, censored and exiled by becoming their own 'organic' intellectuals. They failed, in the end paradoxically enabling the completion of the process they had tried to stop in 1973.

Part Two, *Political Unity; Intellectual Dispersal,* follows how, in a social and political context quite removed from the one preceding the dictatorship and in a culture less accepting of modernist elitism, the energies of the post-1985 progressive intelligentsia are dispersed, as the left itself becomes more entrenched, better organised, and closer to assuming power.

Chapter 4 shows how the incipient counterculture was incubated but not fully expressed during the authoritarian years, finally flowering in a libertarian outburst in the mid-1980s that eschewed conventional politics. This combined with a first contact with the poststructuralism brought in by visitors and returning exiles to produce a utopian celebration of diversity.

The final two chapters take up the tale left at the end of chapter 3, chapter 5 examining intellectuals who are also political activists or Frente Amplio members from the centre and radical sections of the party. It illustrates the extent to which they accompany their counterparts throughout the Southern Cone who have abandoned the revolutionary utopianism of the 1960s in favour of a reinterpretation of democracy for a post-authoritarian era.

Chapter 6 follows those intellectuals who have chosen to negotiate between the Frente and its new and growing constituency by offering a sympathetic critique and interpretation of its reform agenda from the fields of political history and sociology. These intellectuals can find themselves in dangerous terrain when called upon by those in power to lead the task of publicly thinking through the painful history of the recent past. Such difficulties illustrate how enmeshing with immediate political realities can relate directly to the more general question of national identity. The book closes with an account of Hugo Achugar and Abril Trigo, two important politically independent intellectuals. They are emblematic of a new Uruguay in that they have lived and worked at least in part outside Uruguay, thus ensuring that their inquiries into the topics of the nation and the national culture interrogate where they do not entirely undo much conventional thinking on such matters.

My use of the term dialogue has nothing to do with the currently fashionable concepts of it derived from either Richard Rorty or Mikhail Bahktin. Rather, it refers to the principles of conciliation and negotiation through reasoned argument and discussion, or, in more idealised terms, to the aim of the public or politically involved intellectual as being that of generous-spirited, lucid conversation among equals, these being either their colleagues or a receptive and responsive audience. Dialogue in this light penetrated a collection of essays that appeared in Montevideo in 1960 at the outset of the period under consideration here. Sergio Visca's *Un hombre y su mundo* [*A Man and His World*] was typical of the writings of a group of Uruguayan intellectuals who bemoaned what they saw as the declining spiritual integrity of a society plagued by crass materialism. Sergio Visca saw lack of empathy as a national trait, describing the Uruguayan as 'the anti-socratic rational animal, [...] the anti-conversationalist [anti-locutor]', and lamented this 'monodialogism' so harmful to individual and collective life in Uruguay.[13] He clearly hoped to aid in reversing this trend: the author was just one individual who wanted 'to strike up a dialogue with other Uruguayans'. This involved a Sartrean act of generosity, a stepping outside of oneself that could only be realized 'through active contact, sincere dialogue, with the not-I [no-yo]'.[14]

A similar notion of dialogue informed the ideas of consensus, shared benefits and solidarity that made up the legacy of the ideology (and later, the mythology) of 'Batllismo' outlined above. By the early 1970s, this 'dialogue without struggle' typical of a society characterised by peaceful coexistence between antagonists was under threat by the pressure of events.[15] Consequently, a rather more 'militant' idea of dialogue would be needed, as was foreseen in the mid-1960s. While making allowances for the other's opinions in an exchange intended to clear up misunderstandings and reach agreement on essentials, one should be prepared to 'close down or refuse [all communication with the other] when common objectives are lacking, when our opponents defend interests totally opposed to our own'.[16]

This book traces the left wing intelligentsia's attempts to found a 'militant dialogue', examining what happened to that dialogue when it was eventually confronted with an 'opponent' whose purposes were indeed 'totally opposed to' the intellectuals' own, and finally how the progressive intelligentsia coped when dialogue became freely available once more but no longer conformed to their preconceptions of it.

My starting point is what would turn out to be a prophetic event in 1952. The essay competition on 'Problems of Youth in Our Country', jointly organised by the leftist weekly *Marcha* and the Uruguayan Young Christian Association, was peculiar in that, as Rama pointed out,[17] the judges[18] were in the position of either assessing their peers or effectively being themselves assessed by representatives of the generation which, in succeeding them, would critically evaluate the intellectual legacy it inherited. The contribution by Juan Flo, a future Professor of Aesthetics at the country's most prestigious university, is a touchstone for what sparked many progressive intellectuals over the next twenty years.[19] It challenged his intellectual predecessors and contemporaries to find adequate answers to Uruguay's problems. It is simultaneously a critical essay and a demand. Its polemical and controversial qualities caused problems for the judges who violently disagreed about its merits and ended up nominating it as the competition's only 'honourable mention'.

Flo realised that, at the age of 21, he was himself part of the problem of youth in Uruguay. His generation was part of the very reality against which it rebelled while naively trying to reform it, a contradiction he then attributed to *Marcha* itself. For Flo this aloofness was compounded by a highly critical, Olympian aesthetic fastidiousness: 'We have ended up transformed ... into a critical generation that loathes kitsch and bombast, not realizing that nothing backs up our urge for moderation, that life and the world have slipped through our fingers along with what we saw as trivial'.[20] Anticipating Angel Rama's title for his book about those sitting in judgment on his essay, Flo impugned them for infecting him and his younger colleagues with the same noxious bug: that of being hypercritical observers instead of active agents grasping life with both hands, accepting responsibility for the consequences. Criticism might be essential to a society's intellectual life (Flo's own essay was a fine example of how necessary it was), but its effect was nefarious if it led only to quietism or paralysis.

Having surveyed this 'landscape where everything is appearance', Flo ended by confronting his mentors and sponsors:

> In short, we can state that, since our problem is specifically cultural, it seems practical to interrogate principally those who through vocation threaten to solve all such problems. We can also state that no private, separate problem can be detached from general circumstances, from this large problem of our failure.
>
> What shall we do, then?
>
> If it were possible to make predictions, we would say that our destiny is to save ourselves as exceptions or individuals, that none of us, since we exist only as potential, will be able to justify this ashen life we lead.[21]

Flo had no grand schemes to offer, only a perplexed question and a despairing and dim notion of the future. Unbeknownst to Flo, of course, the cultural problem would become a political one, and how to save oneself would not remain a personal matter.

It was undoubtedly Flo's sense of life as simulacrum, his rejection of totalising solutions, the caustic and ironic tone, the anxious probing of current cultural values, his questioning of the nation itself and, most importantly, his refusal to set himself outside or above the problem he both interpreted and experienced as his own, that led Rama to describe his essay as the first clear marker of a new attitude.[22] The relevance of Flo's question for this study lies more in its linking of words to deeds, in its implicit demand that intellectual reflection lead to (or be in itself) a guide for social change. Yet Flo's interrogation of *Marcha*'s – and his own – intellectual assumptions still took for granted the possibility of dialogue between questioner and respondent. However suspicious he may have been of some of the results, Flo implicitly accepted or at least hoped that this relationship could be an active and creative one. The chapters that follow are, in effect, an analysis of the intelligentsia's attempts to find a convincing reply to Flo's question – 'What shall we do, then?' – and I shall refer back to it at key moments in what follows.

PART
One

Towards Intellectual and Political Unity

1

From Alienation to Integration

Intellectuals, Politics and Polemics

Between the pressure or penetration of contemporary imperialism, on the one hand, and the resulting demand for a Latin American Union, on the other, under what conditions will the renewed problem of national independence present itself to current – and future – generations?

Arturo Ardao (1967)

In 1957, the historian and essayist Carlos Real de Azúa summarised the presuppositions about Uruguay's unquestioned cultural advantages during the first third of the century as follows: the arts and sciences were '"superior" activities of the spirit' carried out in a situation that guaranteed freedoms of all kinds. As a result, the nation's intellectuals felt able to live in a kind of 'limbo' that alienated them from everything really close to them:

> Our status as a small, ethnically Europeanised country, with no extremes or tragedies of climate, size or race (we were not a 'republic of Indians') put us proudly on the margin of the traits (understood as burden instead of potential) that characterised everything Latin American.[1]

Only six years later, however, after he and his colleagues who had been born around 1920 had 'demolished' that blinkered complacency, the same writer could see an emerging younger generation so stunned and disillusioned by what was going on around them that they seemed to be scrambling about in search of something to believe in and worth aiming for.[2] Not too far away they could find both, for as a younger commentator realised, they had felt the heady news emanating from the feverish early period of the Cuban Revolution, 'the best' of them militating in 'what could vaguely be called the left' because of their 'discontent with the current state of our society' and their 'desire to transform it for the better'.[3] As Aínsa observed, any disagreement between older and younger intellectuals in the 1960s grew out of their sense of solidarity against what they saw as a reactionary enemy.[4] Historical circumstance brought two intellectual generations together and helped them to learn how to talk to one another. The problem over the next ten years or so would be how to persuade others on the left with which they felt such increasing solidarity to do likewise.

Politics might turn out to be an obstacle to intellectual dialogue over much of the decade to come, but it was also that dialogue's main theme. As far back as 1931, Zum Felde had written that intellectuals and politics had been linked in Uruguay since independence,[5] an observation that could be repeated fifty-seven years later.[6] Almost mid-way between the two, Real de Azúa had stated categorically that from the early period of the country's formation onwards, due to the all but zero possibility of professionalisation, to the weakness of its institutions, the ubiquitousness of political control and the lack of financial return on literary activity, the Uruguayan writer would be dependent on politics in any of his activities as 'parliamentarian, bureaucrat, journalist, diplomat or revolutionary'.[7]

Prior to the 1930s, under the Batllista reformist state, intellectuals had shared to a large extent the values of the majority of their society and had gone about the task of constructing a national mythology,[8] leading to the self-satisfaction described by Real de Azúa in this chapter's opening paragraph. Achugar has argued that even though there was, as might be expected, some conservative opposition to the cultural hegemony of the interventionist Batllista state, no concerted attempts to find any real alternative modes of participation were made until the end of the 1920s.[9] As Trigo put it, 'the country became Batll-istified'.[10]

The 1933 coup by Gabriel Terra shattered this apparent consensus by revealing the fragility of institutions and social values that both the intelligentsia and the general populace had perhaps too complacently taken for granted.[11] Virtually all Uruguay's major intellectual figures opposed the coup and the suspension of democratic rights,[12] initiating a rift between them and the political mainstream that would be the keynote of the relationship between intellectuals and the governing elite for decades to come. As Varela points out, this critique of ethics in politics received a leftwards push by the coincidence in time between the opposition to Terra and the Uruguayan contribution to the world wide intellectual resistance to the rise of fascism in Europe and the equally international move to rally support for the Spanish republic against the nationalist uprising led by Franco in 1936.[13] The hastily formed anti-fascist and pro-Spanish Republic 'Popular Fronts' made up the first doomed attempts at forging some kind of unity on the Uruguayan left.[14]

To the feeling of marginalisation implied here can be added the sense of alienation and unreality glimpsed in de Torres Wilson's evocation of

Montevideo at the end of the 1930s as 'a large balcony on to the universe'. Compared with the 'dramas' of the Spanish civil war and the Second World War, the realities of Uruguay were bound to look diminished.[15] For his part, Roberto Ares Pons suggested what became almost a litany for those he named the paternalist Batllista bureaucracy's 'intellectual proletariat': the disproportion between their educational level and their real possibilities in Uruguayan society as it was, a frustration that found an outlet in cultural or intellectual activity of one sort or another,[16] but would ever more quickly migrate towards politics as the 1960s wore on.

Juan Flo's 1952 question about what intelligent, well-educated young Uruguayans were to do with themselves and the country hovered over the two debates discussed below. Both of these robust exchanges took place in the pages of *Marcha*, underlining that independent leftist publication's importance in providing a space for argument between opponents who otherwise might not have been able to face off against one another. The members of the progressive intelligentsia show themselves to some extent in their worst light. Prisoners and victims of the left's impotence and fragmentation, they engage (or indulge) in everything from rhetorical overkill to character assassination. The topics are potentially serious, even grave; the debates themselves frequently less so. Largely as a result of this, these polemics can also be said to illustrate the range of positions gathered under the general heading of the Uruguayan Left, and of the difficulties that would have to be overcome if ever they were to be brought together under the same political banner.[17]

The Shock of 1958

Real de Azúa makes the crucial point that nearly all Uruguay's intellectuals at mid-century were based in or near the capital, Montevideo,[18] while Rama adds that they were the first group of writers in Uruguayan history to come predominantly from the middle classes,[19] which had been the main beneficiaries of the progressive social policies initiated during the Batlle era. Perhaps the quintessential example of this exclusionary view is Benedetti's much-quoted sentence 'Uruguay is the only office in the world that has qualified for definition as a republic',[20] clearly implying that the entire country could be seen accurately through the eyes of a lower middle class office clerk.[21] As later commentators from the interior such as the novelist Mario Delgado Aparaín have pointed out,[22] the ensuing tendency to see the nation as merely an extension of Montevideo seriously distorted where it did not invalidate much analysis of the nation as problem. This animosity between capital and interior is bound up with the first of the intellectual polemics examined here.

The somewhat feverish altercation between December 1958 and March 1959 had its origins in the historic victory of the Partido Nacional in the presidential elections of November 1958, winner for the first time in nearly a hundred years over its rival, the Colorados. An event worthy of celebration no doubt, it probably did not deserve the self-congratulatory crowing given it by Alberto Methol Ferré,[23] who began what turned out to be the battle's first salvo as follows: 'The whole of Uruguay is perplexed, knocked out [. . .] for the first time Montevideo understands nothing, absolutely nothing of what's happening in the country'.[24] This scarcely veiled attack upon the supposed long-time hegemony of Montevideo in Uruguayan politics would have come as no surprise to those familiar with Methol Ferré's pedigree. He had been for sometime involved with progressive intellectuals in the National Party and the Catholic Church who gathered around the long discarded ideal of regional and continental federation, and from the early 1950s became an 'accomplice' (as he calls himself here) in Benito Nardone's 'Federal League of Ruralist Action' (popularly shortened to 'Ruralism'), which would henceforward become the chief focus of the *Marcha* debate.[25]

Benito Nardone, the son of working-class Italian migrants, grew up on the streets of the Montevideo coastal suburb of Palermo. He had been an occasional contributor to anti-Batllista Colorado newspapers but was working as a minor functionary in the state railway's statistics section when he was picked in 1937 to run the newspaper *Diario Rural* to support the bid for a Senate seat in the following year's elections by Domingo Bordaberry, a discontented leader of the well-established Rural Federation. More importantly, in the 1940s, Bordaberry also handed over to him the running of his country radio station. For more than a decade, Nardone was to use these two organs to broadcast an eclectic and heady mixture of diatribes against the urban-based pro-industrialisation policies emanating from Montevideo, attacks on the big banks and financial operators who manipulated exchange rates to damage the rural sector, and hatred of communists, trade-unionists and bureaucrats who soaked up the wealth earned by the farmer's sweat. He melded all this together in a racy, colloquial and demagogic style that seemed to understand the clouded minds, entrenched prejudices and worst fears of masses of rural workers and small farmers.[26] As Líber Seregni has remarked, Nardone was important because he was the first in Uruguay to see the role modern electronic media could play in national politics, and also led the way in bringing rural workers closer to the political mainstream.[27]

In 1950 he and Bordaberry, after spending two fruitless years trying to make the Rural Federation more representative of the interests of their growing numbers of supporters, broke away to form the Federal League of Ruralist Action, leadership of which Nardone assumed when Bordaberry died shortly afterwards. In addition to his work in the newspaper and on the radio, Nardone initiated a face-to-face campaign style of 'Open Councils' [cabildos], a legacy from Spanish colonial times briefly revived in the early nineteenth century by Artigas, whose mythical reputation Nardone was learning to exploit. By the mid-1950s, he was all but worshipped by an audience whose standard of living was plummeting along with the prices fetched by their products and who felt doubly marginalised: by the policies of the national government in the capital and by their own traditional rural organisations, which were dominated by large landowners whose interests lay as much in the financial and industrial centres as anywhere else. It was this side of Nardone's activities that deceived progressive intellectuals such as Methol Ferré and Ares Pons into believing – for a while at least – that Ruralism might be the foundation of a different Uruguay that looked westwards from its interior to the rest of the Southern Cone rather than eastward from Montevideo across the Atlantic to Europe.

Up to this point Nardone had studiously avoided formally affiliating the League with any political party. As the 1958 presidential elections approached, however, he took to Montevideo a detailed proposal for constitutional reform that would return considerable political influence and economic power to the rural sector. Mindful of the extensive country vote Nardone could probably command, factions from both major parties expressed interest. After some haggling, Luis Alberto de Herrera, the wily, eccentric and experienced political wheeler-dealer at the head of the National Party, offered Nardone a leading place on their election ticket. It turned out to be a shrewd move. Although the constitutional changes were rejected at the polls, the votes of Nardone's supporters together with the Nationals' ability to present the electors with a united party, in conjunction with the hard-pressed nation's clear desire for a change at any price, sufficed to give the party its first victory in presidential elections for 93 years. As though symbolising the potential meaning of this win, on the day following the announcement of the result, an old, lone farmer was able to ride slowly on his horse the entire length – several kilometres – of Montevideo's main thoroughfare without anyone uttering a word of complaint.

Unfortunately, Nardone's ambition and talent for vote-catching were far greater than his capacity as politician on the national stage. Despite some early success, particularly in the area of economic policy, Nardone became increasingly associated with anti-communist and right-wing vigilante movements in the early 1960s. The alliance with Herrera's faction proved unstable and Nardone's fortune began to wane. His faction's share of the vote declined in the 1962 elections and dwindled almost to nothing following Nardone's death in 1964. In essence, Nardone was a reincarnation in modern garb of the rural 'caudillo', although he was the first to have been born and brought up in the suburbs of the capital and the first to have fought long and hard – and to have won – using the modern weapons of the mass media instead of guns and machetes. But like most of the other 'caudillos' before him, his ideology – such as it was – died with the man who personified it.[28]

Bemoaning the Colorado government's squandering and the increasing unreality of its politics, Methol Ferré ended his salute to the Nationals' election victory by positing Nardone as a 'more lofty' successor to the earlier President Berreta,[29] both expressing the arrival on the political scene of the rural middle class. The triumphalist, ecstatic article finished with a gloss on the 'parish' of its title: after the 'interregnum' (belittling thereby over ninety years of Colorado rule), Uruguay had returned to its real home in Latin America. In *Marcha*'s next issue, Methol Ferré continued in the same vein,[30] boldly asserting that it would now be agriculture – the primary sector – that would save everyone else, even those who had voted against it.

It was unlikely this sort of pontificating would go unanswered for long, especially in a leftist publication such as *Marcha*, and Methol Ferré was joined in the same issue by the Communist-leaning sociologist Carlos Rama with a somewhat frenetic and overblown article whose title asked whether there could be a Uruguayan brand of fascism.[31] However attractive this might appear in the wake of the 1973 military coup, Rama cannot be said to have been gifted with any kind of prescience. His piece was written very much in the context of the shock felt (and feared) by the Left at the Colorados' loss. Rama saw Nardone's 'Ruralism' as a spirited and effective defense of the rural oligarchy's privileges, and interpreted the election results in general as indicating the Uruguayan middle classes had abandoned the centre and taken refuge in extremes of left or right, and that they would now be on the lookout for scapegoats. Rama closed his rather hysterical article by likening 1958 Uruguay to 1930s Europe,[32] and advocated 'intense and productive dialogue among all fractions and trends on the left' to combat the whole dire situation, a fervent hope that found an echo in the readers' letters page a week later[33] and would become a litany repeated by many across the whole of the next decade.

Rama received some support a week later in a rather defensive article by Eduardo Galeano, then linked to the Socialist party, who tried to make the best of the fact that, in the electorate's rush to get the corrupt Colorados out at any cost, the left had at least not lost votes to the right. He then commented shrewdly that the change of government itself indicated a transition from 'a vote by tradition to a vote by conviction', and foresaw that such a move would in the end favour the Left.[34]

Meanwhile, Methol Ferré went on unabashed. In the first of his last two pieces, he saw Nardone's definitive contribution to the Nationals' victory as the vindication of the peasantry against the wasteful unproductiveness of centralised government officials, conceived as an intellectual proletariat given to vacuous moralism.[35] Methol's final offering likened 'Ruralismo' to the relieving of the siege of Montevideo, with Nardone as a new General Otorgués, and closed by throwing down the gauntlet to *Marcha*'s whole readership: Uruguay had to return to its own Interior, in order to find the past that would enable it to face a future for which nothing currently available had prepared it.[36] This resounding challenge got a rejoinder in the same issue from Galeano, who returned to the fray to rescue Marxism, accusing Methol Ferré of mystifying reality by reducing class struggle to a deceptive wrangle between social sectors, and predicting that his optimism would shortly prove to be just so much pinkish hot air.[37] Galeano was proved right: while retaining his faith in the potential of the Ruralist movement, Methol Ferré had to publish a bitter retraction of his view of Nardone two years later in the same paper.[38]

Methol Ferré had felt too confident in himself and his cause to bother to debate: his articles were as if written in advance, as though all issues were settled and all objections too trivial or obviously misguided to be worth comment. His most eloquent supporter, although a friend and sympathiser with Methol Ferré's expectations of 'Ruralism', was not so convinced a disciple and therefore could respond to others' criticisms. Roberto Ares Pons, a history teacher, had also been involved in the journal *Nexo*, and was equally sure that Uruguay's future lay both in a revival of its agricultural sector and its close alliance with its neighbours in the Southern Cone.[39] However, as he would reveal, he had voted Socialist in the 1958 elections.

The title of Ares Pons' first piece answered Rama's question directly: fascism in Uruguay was impossible.[40] He rejected the (for him) now outdated terms Right/Left, preferring to contrast a 'tendency toward stagnation' with 'perennial creation and renewal'. Ares then argued that fascism was only possible in the developed capitalist world, not in the underdeveloped countries where only dictatorships were feasible, implying that neither was likely in Uruguay. He went on to argue that Nardone was at the head of a trade union style organisation representing small landowners and tenant farmers, and moreover wanted to limit the role of the State, not expand it. He admitted that Ruralism's program was 'confused' but, whether progressive or reactionary, was essential to Uruguay's development.

Rama responded to both Methol Ferré and Ares Pons[41] by admitting the importance of the rural awakening but attributed it to the process of industrialisation and modernisation, which countries without empires had always had to pay for themselves. He predicted Ruralism's anti-modernist turn to the right, and foresaw an austerity programme, measures to enhance the export of primary products and restrain urban standards of living, leading to increased impoverishment of the majority, who were then unlikely to tolerate their situation, the whole country resembling others such as Honduras or Nicaragua, so that centralised executive power would be necessary to suppress dissent.[42] He closed by asking pertinently what National party progressives like Methol Ferré and Ares Pons would do when the government showed its true colours.[43]

Ares Pons again rejected Rama's unhistorical use of anachronistic, fossilised terminology, and summarised the progressive elements of Ruralism as unifying a dispersed peasantry and putting their issues at the centre of the entire country's political and economic agenda.[44] He then accused the traditional left (students, trade unions, political parties and groups) of being out of touch with the interior (which would prove true even in 1971 as the Frente Amplio faced the elections), and argued that Nardone's movement should be given time to show whether it could deliver the much needed modernisation of the agricultural sector.[45] However, a week later, a highly prescient reader followed Rama's line in seeing Uruguay heading into a crisis no government could solve except by extremely repressive policies that would fan social discontent. Getting even closer than Rama to anticipating future events, he went on to argue that the left could ill afford to be fooled by reactionary lions like Ruralism, now matter how prettily dressed up in moderate or even progressive sheep's clothing.[46]

In a way, the most revealing and important aspect of the last article in the debate is Rama's omission of question marks in his title, imitating a previous title of Ares's: for him fascism in Uruguay *was* possible.[47] Dismissing Nardone as a nobody who had powerful forces behind him, Rama prophesied again that present social and political conditions would override long-standing traditions favourable to democracy. While the latter might see out the immediate influence of Ruralism, they would not be enough to prevent a military takeover fifteen years later, although nobody in 1958 could see such an outcome.

Rama referred here to the whole debate somewhat deprecatingly as 'rather esoteric', while many years later, Trigo saw in it only Rama's 'Manichean neo-positivism' opposite a 'naive traditionalism' pushed along more by individual desire than Ruralism's 'slippery demagogy'.[48] Both comments sell the debate short. It needs to be remembered that it took place when the left parties taken together had never totalled more than 10 per cent of the vote in any national elections. It is not surprising, then, that they viewed the incoming government by a party more openly committed than the Colorados to unrestricted market economics as a frightening move to the right. The debate does, of course, also illustrate the fragmentation of left-wing groups and how far they still were from achieving the already acknowledged need for a non-exclusive union of progressive forces in Uruguayan politics. The predilection for airing their ideological squabbles in public forums such as *Marcha* would, as we shall see in the course of this book, eventually pay off in the form of an uninterrupted commitment to dialogue in all its forms.

3 intellectuals w/ different POV's

This exchange also reveals how much traditional Uruguayan leftist rhetoric tended to be focussed on the capital, and by extension on the city, with the result that it both alienated many of those it wanted to reach, thereby allowing any movement such as Nardone's that did not use such language to be seen in a progressive light. This in turn caused the confusion registered at several moments in the debate, as well as reproducing a thoroughly conservative opposition between city and provinces which would obscure for both right and left what was the principal issue at stake for all: how to modernise a rural-based economy in a country whose internal market was so small that it could not generate sufficient wealth to pay for the process if it was to be carried through with any vestige of the social justice expected by the prevailing 'Batllista' mentality.

A Third Position?

The continuing difficulties of dialogue among progressive intellectuals is shown even more clearly in the acrimonious debate in the 1960s about the so-called 'Third Position'[49] in an environment where economic difficulties were fast exacerbating the expression of all political differences. In a nutshell, the 'Third Position' approach to world affairs had rejected the Allies versus Axis dichotomy in the 1940s (despite the sympathy for the latter of the likes of Perón in Argentina as well as National party leader Luis de Herrera and Colorado Terra in Uruguay), and was closely associated with Argentine Peronism even though most Uruguayan sources give the impression that their version was home grown. Profitable neutrality in the Second World War then grew into a determination to reject both US imperialism and Soviet expansion in the Cold War.[50] A 1951 article in *Marcha* (itself always sympathetic to this outlook through its editor Carlos Quijano) summed up the matter well: one could have any philosophical approach to life, be of any political persuasion, the key to the 'Third Position' being the rejection of the Cold War polarisation of the world into two hostile camps.[51] With its emphasis on independent thinking and a circumscribed freedom, the 'Third Position' seems calculated to appeal to some of the 45 generation's core values, and also to be a political posture well fitted to the ethical demands of the individualist – or 'Batllista' – version of freedom and responsibility found in an existentialism still popular among the intellectual elite in Uruguay.

While it gave rise to the Non-Aligned Movement in the world at large, in Latin America the attractive options potentially offered by the 'Third Position' were erased by the face-off from the mid-1960s onwards between the influence of the Cuban revolutionary example on the one hand, and the even more determined counterrevolutionary offensive largely organised and financed by the United States on the other. It was precisely in this context, when it was becoming increasingly urgent for intellectuals on the left to define themselves in relation to revolutionary potential, that Solari produced his book on *tercerismo*, the ideological slant that had for a decade or more been a guide for many attracted to the left but positioned outside the Communist and Socialist parties.

Still the standard work on the 'Third Position' in Uruguay, despite being preceded and, to some extent, anticipated ten years earlier by a 1955 essay by Ares Pons,[52] Solari's book offered an historical account and a critical analysis of the movement, followed by an appendix of a selection of nine articles from *Marcha* and four short pieces and a manifesto taken from student publications, all produced between 1946 and 1954.[53]

The crux of what would be Solari's thesis comes in the preface. Having declared that, to some extent, he himself was a 'tercerista', a circumstance which obliged him to stick as closely as possible to the documentary evidence, he continued with what seems simply a legitimate sociological concern: since it was 'almost impossible' to find a Uruguayan intellectual who was not either for or against the 'Third Position', it followed that an inquiry into this stance would say something important about intellectuals in general, especially those 'who consider themselves as belonging on the left' (*T*, 7–8). However, Solari later mounted a swingeing attack on them. Supporters of the 'Third Position', he argued, neither held power nor had much chance of securing any, so the 'Third Position' was for them more a safe statement of principles than 'a plan for political action' (*T*, 115).[54] How, Solari pointedly wanted to know, was it possible to be 'efficient' if you 'renounce all links with power' (*T*, 103), thus confronting directly nearly thirty years of Uruguayan intellectuals' aloofness from mainstream politics.

The sceptical and challenging conclusion widened the scope of his accusations still further, effectively arguing that the 'Third Position' generated the warm, morally satisfying glow of being against nasty abstractions like imperialism and corruption, but without ever having to do anything in particular about them (*T*, 125). If in the preface the advocates of the 'Third Position' stood for intellectuals as a social group, in a paragraph worth quoting in full their deficiencies became the failure of a whole society:

> The drama of the 'Third Position' is the drama of Uruguayan society. Without any doubt, there has not been an effort of greater analytical reach or better intentions to overcome the ever worsening social situation. Because none of the sometimes just criticisms that can be made of it can get round the fact that the 'Third Position' is the only serious alternative to communism amid the quietism of the traditional parties. The failure of the 'Third Position' to find an image of Uruguay that can be turned into an instrument of action, whether or not its own fault, is one more indicator of

a society that has lost its own character, its commitment to a clearly defined collective enterprise that could be the base of the transformation so many groups hope for and which the most superficial analysis shows to be indispensable. (*T,* 132)

Solari ended the analytical section of his book with a more assertive and more desperate reformulation of his earlier question: 'What makes realism such a difficult adventure for the Uruguayan intelligentsia?' (*T,* 133) – a question that goes to the heart of the drama of what it has frequently meant to be a leftist intellectual anywhere in the West during the twentieth century, and more locally, takes us back to the question the Introduction presented as posed by Juan Flo in 1952: what can well educated, left-leaning young people do about Uruguay today?

In effect, Solari impugned the progressive – which, for him, was virtually all – intellectuals with being unable to construct practicable, relevant projects which might be translated into realistic programs well adapted to Uruguayan conditions and capable of persuading a disillusioned populace and reluctant politicians that they are worth the effort required to implement them. Moreover, he implied, intellectuals were perhaps content to put up pie-in-the-sky abstractions so that they could delude themselves into believing they were doing something. In short, a failure of nerve, imagination and communication, a particularly galling accusation after the two main parties on the left, the Socialists and the Communists, had both tried to expand their support base in the 1962 national elections by creating broad fronts. For Solari's attitudes here continue a trend in his thinking begun in 'Requiem for the Left', an influential if controversial essay on the national poll of that year,[55] and extended in the section on intellectuals in his later study of post-war Uruguayan society. Here he had stated baldly that all Uruguayan intellectuals 'are or claim to be on the left' and 'against everything'; he argued that their politicisation was inevitable but ineffective, and concluded that since intellectuals and politics were in opposing camps, the chances of the country finding a way out of 'stagnation' were remote.[56] Clearly, Solari had seen nothing in the intervening two years to change the gist of his 1965 argument; if anything, his pessimism had deepened.[57]

As Ruben Cotelo has pointed out, the summer of 1965/66 was, in contrast to what was to come, fairly slow, and therefore a good time for a lengthy polemic,[58] which is what Solari's *Tercerismo* elicited. At times barbed and personal, at others turgid and academic in the bad sense, the exchange between Arturo Ardao, co-founder of *Marcha* (one of the centres of *tercerista* thinking identified by Solari) and author of several of the texts quoted in his book as well as a professor of intellectual history at the same university, and Carlos Real de Azúa, a teacher of social and cultural history, ran from December 1965 to March the following year.[59] While Ardao had arguably an even more personal stake in the 'Third Position' than even Solari admitted to, it may have been unknown to anyone that in 1963 Real de Azúa himself had completed a massive study of *tercerismo* as an international phenomenon, but considered that post-1959 events had rendered it superfluous.[60] Ardao's long series of articles amounts to a wholesale rejection of Solari's book, but his arguments now seem rather petty-fogging, in that they tend to dwell on such issues as whether or not Solari's book was really an essay, whether *tercerismo* began as early as the Second World War, whether or not it could be properly described as an ideology, and whether Solari's selection of documents was genuinely representative. It was only when Real de Azúa joined in (via the pages of the Montevideo daily *Epoca*) in January 1966, and Ardao had to fight on two fronts simultaneously (graphically reproduced by the compositors at *Marcha* by having his replies to Solari and Real de Azúa start separately on the same page in different type), that the debate began to live up to Cotelo's assessment of it: proof that Solari's study 'touched a raw nerve in the area of political ideas in [Uruguay], especially on the independent left' (*TP*, 814).

Real de Azúa's disagreement with Ardao stemmed not so much from his position on *tercerismo* but from his contention that Ardao's whole mode of argument was much too self-assured and dogmatically rigid in its assessment of what such slippery concepts as nationalism, imperialism and so on are about (see especially *TP*, 948). In response, Ardao questioned Real de Azúa's bona fides by bringing up the issue of his past political allegiances (see Ardao's omitted article referred to in note 58), which occasioned Real de Azúa's admission and defence of certain right-wing positions (including Francoist 'Hispanismo' and 'Ruralism') he had mistakenly adopted earlier (*TP*, 947–958). It is in this highly charged emotional and political context that Real de Azúa was able to extract from the debate its relevance both to Solari's general questioning of the purpose and practice of the left intelligentsia's activities, and, of course, to the continuing relevance of Juan Flo's thirteen-year-old but still unanswered question about what they were to do and how.

Recalling his earlier remarks about the lack of professionalism in Uruguay's intellectual life, Real de Azúa maintained here that it was easy to see that the country would be better off if the people best qualified to turn their enthusiasm, good intentions, intelligence and creativity to the state of the nation had conditions more conducive to good work to do it in. He then came back to Solari's taunting around the issue of realism, asking how it could become possible for intellectuals to command a perspective on social reality that would not either erode their capacity for disinterested analysis or implicate them somehow in the processes being studied (*TP*, 905). Real de Azúa, then, went even further than Solari in suggesting the dire consequences for Uruguayan society of intellectual irresponsibility and superficiality. So while Ardao could congratulate himself on being faithful to *Marcha*'s ideological position, his adversary could pointedly ask him where he was in 1962 when it was a question of actually trying to do something about it:

> [Ardao] never seems to have felt the need that has beset myself and others: to find, not in the year 2000, but here and now, a way out, an opening, a '*take off*' [English in original], out of the stagnation, the degradation, the slow death of the Uruguay in which we live. (TP, 957)

The best Ardao could do in response was go back over old ground: he had no answer (965–972); Real de Azúa took the point and retired from the battle.[61] If Gatto can argue that Ardao's position seems in retrospect 'more pure and precise' than Real de Azúa's,[62] it may only be that Ardao came at the matter as a philosopher determined to stay at the level of ideas, while Real de Azúa was a political historian on his way to a more committed if still independent position on the intellectual left. He in effect took Solari's side in the debate, but in the manner of one more personally involved in trying to answer the questions Solari posed.[63]

Four years later, in November 1969, some people's feathers were still ruffled. Carlos Rama, who clearly liked debates and was, like Solari, a sociologist, gave at the Ninth Latin American Sociology Congress in Mexico a paper entitled 'Uruguay in Crisis'.[64] In the section on Uruguayan sociology, he mentioned just himself and Solari, whose career was summarised in terms requiring quotation in full:

> Aldo Solari, author in 1953 of an excellent *Uruguayan Rural Sociology*, republished in 1958 with an added section favourable to the 'Rural League of Federal Action'.
>
> In the 1962 elections, he supported the 'Unión Popular', a group gathered around the Socialist Party and parts of the National Party. This coalition failed, and Solari wrote 'Requiem for the Left', where he expressed his disillusion with the left to which he ceased to belong. In 1965 he wrote for the Congress for Cultural Freedom his *El tercerismo en el Uruguay*, where he criticised positions taken in the National Students' Federation and *Marcha*, which was answered by Professor Arturo Ardao.
>
> Since then he has been a member of the Latin American Institute for International Relations, an adjunct of the Congress for Cultural Freedom and, in collaboration with it, organised in Montevideo the colloquium on Elites in Latin America.[65] Finally, in 1967 he left the country.[66]

It is difficult to imagine a more thorough attempt at character assassination.

Rama engaged in a tactic typical of political squabbles: disqualify the messenger by pronouncing him guilty by association, so as to be justified in ignoring the message. The guiding structure here is that of the good man corrupted: his first book was 'excellent', but the tainting of its republication through its connection with a reactionary group was a sign of things to come. He may briefly have recovered enough to align himself with the left, but after that he not only abandoned the left but betrayed them even further by turning round to attack them. He compounded this by working openly for the Congress for Cultural Freedom, which by 1969 had been revealed as a front organisation for the CIA's anti-communist propaganda machine, a fact undoubtedly not lost on Rama's audience.[67] The tone of finality in the last sentence suggests that it was only to be expected that such a perfidious and unreliable character would leave the country for good, abandoning its people to their fate.[68] Rama's self-defensive dismissal of Solari only served to legitimise a polarisation symptomatic of a situation in which the left as a whole – not only Rama's or any other particular section of it – felt so marginalised that any participation in intellectual debate was likely to be transformed into an occasion to secure, however tenuously, one's own survival. Such a situation could, in the long run, only erode away the very conditions that made dialogue possible at all.

In retrospect, the 'Third Position' itself seems the product of a failed attempt by a progressive intellectual elite to find some alternative to the political orthodoxy surrounding it. In that sense it was a step on the journey traced out in more detail in the next two chapters, one in which the left had to come terms both with itself and the social realities in which it operated. In this general context, the 'Third Position' was empowering during the short period when its tenets, however construed, seemed viable, but became disenabling once historical realities exceeded its capacity to account for them. The disagreement and confusion generated by the 'Third Position', Solari's use of it as a base from which to mount his own attack on the feebleness of the left intelligentsia, as well as the subsequent accusations against him, can all be seen as responses by a left increasingly frustrated with its own impotence at a time when a worsening social and political situation demanded a substantial intervention.

Real de Azúa had remarked in 1958 that the less purchase culture can get on social and political realities too extreme to accommodate it, the greater the responsibility that falls on the people who produce it to find something more influential to do.[69] By 1963, after the Nationals had been returned to power in the 1962 elections, the situation he saw seemed even less hopeful, precisely because the left in which he and so many others were investing all their desire for change seemed still frustratingly mired in its old habits. Consequently, it was going to be even more difficult, he believed, for younger intellectuals to find 'a way both efficient and elegant of vomiting on the country as it is, of constructively loathing' the powers that ruled it.[70] In 1967 one group of young Marxists realised they had been landed with 'a heavy inheritance of eclecticism and lack of commitment', and, echoing Juan Flo's critique of *Marcha* examined above in the Introduction, accused their predecessors of a hyper-critical approach that rendered suspicious any program or platform that might lead to action. However, Real de Azúa, while accepting their strictures, might well have been pleased to find that one of the reasons they wanted to found yet another journal was their recognition that the kind of infighting that led someone like Rama to do what he did to Solari simply had to stop:

> We know that [. . .] without real exchanges of views, without dialogue, it is not possible to be persuasive, and we do not forget that non-Marxist thinking can give us questions, even answers, we should acknowledge. That sense of dialogue is the one we will seek to preserve, even welcoming pieces that do not agree with our own point of view [provided they] canvass issues that invite real investigation.[71]

Anticipating the 'without exclusions' attitude that would eventually characterise the traditional left's approach to the formation of what would become the Frente Amplio in 1971, these Marxists had the intention of being more generous to their ideological opponents in the interest of elucidating common problems.

By the early 1970s some could see that this was what happened when the prevailing liberal consensus went into decline.[72] One major element in this was purely economic: as the country's fortunes went further into decline, Uruguayan society could find less and less for its increasingly well educated middle and lower-middle classes to do. While the state bureaucracy and the expansion of public education, especially in the humanities, absorbed significant numbers of people, resources and real wages in these areas fell, so that the reward for education became impoverishment, leading to a propensity for a general politicisation of intellectuals, teachers and students.[73] For Germán Rama, such a situation paralleled a process of state industrialisation that had catered little or not at all for scientific research and technological development, thus simultaneously denying the entire notion of vocational education[74] and producing a fertile ground for negative criticism, since there was little other use to which knowledge could be put.[75] This distanced the intellectual even more from the political mainstream, further disinclining the government from investing in high-level research and other intellectual work.[76] In addition, of course, although Uruguay's social stratification and general development seems to have been sufficient for a while to absorb an intellectual sector playing a specific role, the chances of actually earning a living from purely intellectual pursuits such as writing were just about zero; so much so that the intellectual was defined in some quarters as someone 'who lives by doing something else'.[77]

The ability to see how they themselves were disadvantaged by a system that looked increasingly on the verge of collapse understandably made intellectuals, and the better educated in general, more sharply aware of how the deficiencies of the political structures and institutions (as well as of the individuals enmeshed in them) were hampering the development of society as a whole. It is to be expected, then, that the period 1955–1970 would see the rise and slow growth of research in the social sciences.[78] Unfortunately, apart from writing, this situation virtually left intellectuals with only two political options: to ally themselves with the already fragmented left or become more or less independent, increasingly discontented snipers from the margins. Both could exacerbate the tendency to indulge in utopian wishful thinking or rarefied ideology, leading commentators like Debray, who favoured the Tupamaros'[79] choice of armed revolution as the engine of social and political change, to condemn 'the intellectual or literary dilettantism of the in-groups of the Uruguayan left', quoting one Tupamaro as saying, in desperation, 'where the only unifying factor is a theory, it takes only one disagreement to produce a schism'.[80] The fate of the 'Third Position' and the quarrels it caused would seem to support this contention.

As the crisis mounted during the 1960s, divisions and alliances among cultural workers were made less on intellectual grounds and more on the basis of political similarities or differences,[81] the need for a dose of Solari-style pragmatism becoming ever more urgently clear. It seems reasonable to argue that the alienation of both the intelligentsia and youth in general from the traditional parties was a factor in the latter's inability to project an imaginative and creative response to the deepening social and political crisis precipitated by the nosedive taken by the Uruguayan economy.[82] As we have seen, its marginalisation also prevented the intelligentsia from accomplishing this much-needed task. Such lack of a ground on which to base a dialogue reinforced both positions, producing the ironic result that progressive intellectuals risked abetting the very status quo they were so eloquent in condemning. At this point, Varela washes his hands of them, accusing them of dreaming about the future while being alienated from the present, of being 'progressive in words but conformist in their actions'.[83] For, as Rama laconically summed up the situation, one peculiarity of the Uruguayan case was that 'the waged masses, in conditions of guaranteed freedoms, chose left-wing union leaders but in national elections massively supported the traditional parties'.[84] In other words, the public's wages and work conditions were one thing, but their general political allegiances quite another. This was hardly unique to Uruguay, but there would be no palliative to this bleak outlook in that country until the advent of the Frente Amplio in 1971. But before then, the left as a whole was going to have to learn what the young editors at *Praxis* intended to practice: how to live with themselves and talk to others, because there were clearly a large number of people out there who would need a lot of persuading.

2

From FIDEL to the Frente

The Uruguayan Left Searches for
Someone to Talk To

All our good points and all our bad points revolve around the word democracy.
Mario Benedetti (1962)

Put simply, this and the following chapter tell two stories which gradually become intertwined. Both are intimately connected to this book's principal theme of dialogue: one shows how, with the aid of intellectuals (mostly not of the literary kind), those on the Uruguayan left learnt to talk productively among themselves; the other goes on to examine how they then tried to talk to the community at large. Chapter 2 covers the tortuous trail from the frustrated attempts to unite the Uruguayan left in the early 1960s to the largely successful campaign to create a unified centre-left ten years later. The other story, more prominent in chapter 3, seeks to show how the structure, program and practice of the Frente Amplio transposed its solutions to the left's communication difficulties on to the need to rearticulate a dialogue between mainstream politics and the population in a society ever more fragmented and polarised by increasing violence and repression. Intellectuals of various kinds (journalists, political and social commentators, writers of imaginative literature) from all points on the left of the political spectrum were involved in both parts of this process as major players or active if critical supporters.

The left's search for an expanded public to talk to required first that it find new or better ways for the ideologically (and often bitterly) divided groups that comprised it to enter into a dialogue with each other, which proved to be a formidable task in itself. Both the left's attempt to find new ways of talking to itself and its need to appeal to a different and larger constituency became vehicles by which an alienated but politically energised

28

intelligentsia could reinsert itself into the political mainstream. In effect, the problem was to create an electorate that would vote for a program that offered a viable alternative to the *status quo* that seemed to be disintegrating around it. That the whole enterprise was only partially successful and ended up engulfed by the polarisation that resulted in the coup of June 1973 does not detract from the boldness and magnitude of the endeavour to reanimate an entire society's ability to dialogue with itself and thus hold itself together.

My account will be centrally concerned with the declared intentions, promises and statements emanating from congress deliberations and party-political platforms. This would seem to be a hazardous procedure. Debray contends that '[t]he fantastical reflections of the revolution that appear in propaganda leaflets and colour photographs present the glamorous obverse of its true course', for, he adds laconically, '[i]f revolution were simply a matter of manifestos, congresses and press releases, it would be hard to see why it is making such slow progress, for there are plenty enough of those things'.[1] For his part, Real de Azúa stated baldly that manifestos, conference resolutions and the like were often deceptive because they permitted so much pretence.[2] However, my implied argument in this and the following chapter is that it is precisely by submerging themselves anonymously in (or, at the very least, getting behind) collective enterprises such as the recommendations from the Congreso del Pueblo in 1965 and the programme and structure of the Frente Amplio in 1971 that the Uruguayan left-wing intelligentsia of the time put into practice most fully their need to enter into a dialogue with their public about what it actually meant to be Uruguayan.

If the Introduction presented one author who wanted to use the essay form to talk to other Uruguayans about what it was like to be him, Real de Azúa's classic anthology of twentieth-century Uruguayan essays illustrates how a long line of writers and thinkers had been regularly asking similar questions about themselves and the nation for over fifty years.[3] Eloquently summed up in the title of one such inquiry, *Uruguay as a Problem*,[4] the fundamental theme of many such offerings was how the real effects of modernisation as it actually happened in Uruguay, the continent and the world exposed the limitations of the Batllista model for modernising their country that nearly all Uruguayans, including most of Batlle's political opponents and their descendants, had come to rely on. The responses to this situation ranged from the historical and philosophical revisionism of Ardao and Real de Azúa[5] to (in Uruguayan small market terms) best-selling, readily accessible and more personal critiques by Carlos Maggi and Mario Benedetti,[6] who were both among the generation of literary writers which matured in the 1940s and, joined by their younger successors in the 1960s, brought these questions to fiction, poetry, theatre and film. When Benedetti famously declared that around 1960 the Uruguayan reading public 'woke up', he meant that they began to look for a national literature about national themes, as opposed to the Uruguayan cultural snob's usual preference for things irrelevant, outmoded or foreign, preferably French.[7] However, it was also true that those readers only became attentive to such local writing as, over the next ten years, it was more apparent to greater numbers of people that the state of things around them was going from bad to worse and that none of the political options then available had much effect on it.[8] It would be simplistic to say that the original Frente Amplio's task in 1971 was to turn this readership into a constituency, but it would not be wrong to suggest that it set out to combine the left-of-centre political forces at hand into a coalition that could offer at least possible answers to the worries that with growing urgency impelled a determined minority into militancy with, say, the trade unions or the Tupamaro guerrillas and their sympathisers, and a larger proportion of the population toward the progressive ends of the traditional parties or the literary intelligentsia's diagnoses and prescriptions. The results may be condemned as 'shadow-boxing',[9] but they were as close as Uruguayan intellectuals on the left got to answering both Juan Flo's question about what to do and Solari's doubts about their capacity to engage in something other than impractical, self-deluded wishful thinking.

Real de Azúa's book-length essay on the state of party politics, dated 18 July 1971 and written during the heady months leading up to the traumatic national elections, formed part of a collective volume of oppositional history designed to intervene in that campaign.[10] The essay's frequent sarcasm thus demonstrated the antipathy between Uruguayan intellectuals and politics its author described, the ruling elite's marginalisation of writers and thinkers being reciprocated by the latter's ridiculing of the former.[11] Five months later, any similar resignation and frustration felt by others must have been alleviated somewhat when, on 26 November 1971, just two days before the poll, there appeared in the pages of *Marcha* the following paragraph:

> At a time so decisive for the destiny of our country, the undersigned writers, aligned with Frente Amplio's movement for renewal, enthusiastically exhort intellectuals and the general public to participate in the elections on November 28 and support our Frente's programme and immediate measures for government, and to go on, firmly united after the election, attentive to the new tasks that await us, and firm in the commitment we have made to the nation.[12]

There follows an impressive list of 170 names which include the three best known Uruguayan novelists of the time (Mario Benedetti, Carlos Martínez Moreno and Juan Carlos Onetti), major poets such as Juan Cunha, Ida Vitale and Idea Vilariño, leading figures from the social sciences (Manuel Claps, Carlos Rama and Real de Azúa himself) and the humanities (Hugo

Achugar, Angel Rama, Mercedes Rein and Jorge Ruffinelli), as well as a whole host of literary figures, some older (Mario Arregui, Francisco Espínola, Sylvia Lago and Clara Silva) who already had secure reputations in Uruguay's intellectual life, but most of them younger (such as Híber Conteris, Gley Eyherabide, Jorge Musto) who had just begun to make a name for themselves during the previous decade. The gallery of signatories placed the veteran cultural historian Alberto Zum Felde (born in 1888) alongside writers born in the 1940s (Eduardo Galeano being the best known of these), and mingled intellectuals associated with the Communist Party (such as Alfredo Gravina and Ruben Yánez) with inheritors of the 'Batllista' tradition within the Colorado Party like Carlos Maggi.

Whatever the Frente Amplio was to achieve in the political arena, it had, at least initially, galvanised virtually all of Uruguay's leading intellectuals and writers into burying their ideological hatchets, abandoning their inter-generational squabbles and preparing themselves to help build a political consensus radically different from the one that was perceived to be breaking down all around them. The brief text emphasised the importance of post-election unity (thus stressing that the Frente was not just another phony coalition cobbled together for voting purposes only), and implicitly put it forward as a viable alternative to the two dominant traditional parties. Moreover, the strategic use of the first person plural (*'our* Frente') not only implied unity but marked an unheard of sense of intimacy and affection in the relationship between the personal and the political which had imbued the rhetoric surrounding the Frente Amplio from its beginnings, and which would characterise the way many of its adherents (not just the intellectuals) would go about their work within it.

For cultural workers, the task was difficult but attractive in that it assigned to them specific responsibilities relevant to their expertise and area of activity. Writing in the Communist Party's journal, one artist pointed to the intellectuals' potential to be sensitive to the hopes and frustrations of the masses, to identify those progressive currents in creative thought most in tune with collective interests and needs, and to begin to reverse the attacks on all forms of oppositional cultural expression emanating from the regime's supporters, the intellectuals' enthusiastic approval of it being a conspicuous mark of the Frente's difference from other political parties. He saw the artists' and intellectuals' jobs as breaking down the isolation of the rural interior where the Frente was barely making headway, to expose the regime's ideological incoherence and to plan the nation's cultural future.[13] After the 1971 elections, the theatre director Ruben Yáñez offered a broader and more realistic perspective. The many artists who had offered their services to the Frente for nothing were a promising, much needed sign, for the problem was to help the population at large to overcome the uncon-scious ideological prejudices and habits which had over time led them to believe that the state of society and its history were somehow fixed for ever and not subject to change. That was not going to be easy because the majority of the population clearly still felt that ideology to be at least partially if not wholly true, and the main task for intellectuals and artists was going to be to give them the tools needed to dismantle the scaffolding that imprisoned their capacity to think differently.[14]

The principal reasons for this nearly unanimous endorsement by the intelligentsia lay, first, in the Frente's potential as an answer to the basic problems which Solari had identified as the perennial scourge of Uruguay's modern political life: a party system that could cushion social tensions by being a point of entry into society for the vast majority but was not equipped to cope with the social consequences of a major economic crisis and promote change when necessary.[15] Secondly, the Frente might solve some of the intelligentsia's frustrations in a context where deepening social paralysis strengthened intellectuals' opposition to the status quo,[16] since the image the Frente's organisational structure projected was to prove especially compelling to people accustomed to the cut and thrust of debate amongst equals. Julio Castro, a highly regarded, non-aligned journalist who had for years been advocating left-wing unity at *Marcha*, believed the Frente would relate to its members and supporters not through the imposition of a point of view or the award of favours but through shared ideas and attitudes. Allegiance to it meant taking up not only an ideological position but also a moral stance.[17]

Another commentator perceived the same issue as an essential part of a general healing process, feeling that the Frente's main task was the reconstruction of the state since the Pacheco government's policies had sowed such social discord that the country's sense of community and belonging had shattered. So dire was the situation that only neologisms could express it: Uruguayans had to 'un-be [anti-ser] many things before being able to be so many other things', and the Frente's methods could reverse this process because it wanted to hear what the public had to say and not just talk at it.[18] Real de Azúa called upon the language of the 1960s counter-culture to express his notion of the kind of community offered by the Frente, which he described as 'the daily practice of a radicalisation of certain social sectors, the result [. . .] of a definitive alienation from the system out of which they have fashioned an authentic counter-society'.[19] It is not difficult to understand how the chance to participate in a new communal awareness and in a free and open therapeutic dialogue which might help cure the ever growing rifts in their society would prove appealing to a progressive intelligentsia used to feeling disaffected, frustrated and ignored.

Such a situation had been a long time coming. Unfortunately, productive dialogue with a sense of shared goals can hardly be said to have characterised interaction between groups on the left during the previous decade. However, they can be seen to be groping towards it even in their repeated failure to come to grips with what Solari had defined as the principal difficulty for any organisation which simultaneously advocated a radical break with the prevailing trends but avoided attempting to foment a revolution doomed to failure: 'the intensity of the consensus around the idea that political solutions should be moderate is such that any party that wants to play the electoral game must adapt to it as a price for getting votes beyond a tiny minority'.[20] By 1971, the various left-wing parties and groups had been impaling themselves and each other on the thorns of this issue for well over ten years.

Frictions and Fractions (I): Towards the Disaster of 1962

Between the heyday of the 'Third Position' in the 1950s and the tussle about it in the mid-1960s, the social and political situation in Uruguay deteriorated considerably.[21] On the international front, the fall of the Arbenz government in Guatemala in 1954 and the 1965 invasion of the Dominican Republic (not to mention the escalating Vietnam War) had done a lot to strengthen distrust of the United States, while the Cuban Revolution of 1959 aroused hopes for radical change throughout the continent.[22] Uruguay's giant neighbours to north and south suffered ominous military coups: Brazil in 1964 and Argentina two years later. At home, between 1960 and 1967 the average annual inflation rate was just over 50% while real wages had fallen in 1968 to a mere 34.7% of what they had been in 1957.[23] The hopes placed in the National Party's historic election win in 1958[24] after nearly a century of uninterrupted Colorado rule had all been frustrated, as had those invested in the fledgling left-wing alliances of 1962 and 1966. From the mid-1960s, the trade union movement began to assume the role of a *de facto* para-political opposition, while the Tupamaros were beginning their campaign of exposing the ineptitude and corruption of the political and financial elites.

The potential for violence in this situation, largely if not completely held at bay prior to 1967, was released during 1968 after Vice-President Pacheco assumed office following the sudden death of the elected incumbent, Oscar Gestido, in December of the previous year. Aided by constitutional changes which had strengthened the powers of the presidency, Pacheco froze wages and prices (in practice, more the first than the second), initiated a campaign designed to halt the activities not only of the Tupamaros but of perfectly legal organisations such as trade unions, student groups and left-wing parties, and censored the opposition press, while circumventing parliament whenever he could by the dubiously legal repeated use of Prompt Security Measure legislation, which all but allowed him to govern by decree. The increasing fragmentation and factionalism within political parties caused further disaffection and cynicism and an awareness of the traditional political institutions' inability to deal with the economic crisis, while voluntary or enforced emigration continued throughout the period at levels between significant and massive, while the 1970 electoral victory of Salvador Allende's Unidad Popular coalition in Chile offered the enticing prospect of revolutionary social change being voted in at the ballot box. All efforts to promote a viable left alternative to existing political options would take place against a background that made explaining the need for it quite straightforward.

Vain attempts to unite the Uruguayan left go back as far as the 1930s, provoked locally by the need to oppose the Terra dictatorship (1933–42). Indeed, an Anti-imperialist League had been formed in 1929 which had brought together such figures as Emilio Frugoni, founding leader of the Socialist Party, and Carlos Quijano who, in his politically active pre-*Marcha* days, had created in the previous year a doomed Agrupación Nacionalista Demócrata Social, as well as Julio César Grauert, a leading member of the Batllista faction of the Colorado Party, who was to be assassinated by Terra's police in October 1933, eight months after the coup.[25] However, it is Basilio Muñoz's attempt to revive the heroic insurrectionist moments of nineteenth-century Uruguayan history by organising an armed revolt against the Terra regime which produced the first call for a united democratic front, and, incidentally, was influential much later in the formation of the Tupamaros guerrilla organisation.[26] On 27 January 1935, Muñoz issued a manifesto proclaiming his 'revolution' independent of all existing political groups and inviting well-meaning people from all parties to unite with him in a call for new, free elections.[27] Muñoz appended to his signature the motto 'Victor or Vanquished'. Unfortunately, it turned out to be the latter, and rather quickly too, the uprising being put down on February 4. Similar calls were then made from abroad and supported by Quijano in the pages of his clandestine newssheet *Acción*. Following the example of the multi-party anti-fascist and pro-Spanish Republic movements formed in Europe during the 1930s, a number of similar endeavours were made in Uruguay, with the added impetus of the need to oppose the Terra regime. These culminated in 1938 with a massive pro-democracy rally in July and the decision by the Socialist and Communist parties to present a single candidate, the Socialist leader Frugoni, for the presidency in the November national poll. It would require a much more slowly maturing crisis than that of the 1930s before these two parties would join so closely together again, but from the early 1960s they started trying.

The 1962 elections consolidated, although with a decreased majority, the National Party's historic victory in 1958 when it had won government from the Colorados for the first time in 93 years. Although 1962 saw an important regrouping and redistribution of influence among the factions of the two major parties, I shall limit myself here to the smaller parties on the left. Of historical significance in that regard is the foundation of the Partido Demócrata Cristiano out of the already existing centre-right Unión Cívica in alliance with a few breakaway groups from the National and Colorado parties. It would later, after several transformations, be instrumental in forming the Frente Amplio. Also anticipating the process that would lead to the creation of the Frente, in March 1962 a large number of concerned citizens signed a 'declaration' urging the formation of a 'real alternative' that would be – here using adjectives that would appear almost by reflex action throughout the decade – 'popular and nationalist', 'progressive and anti-imperialist'. In addition, and testifying to the ongoing influence of the 'Third Position', the new party should be completely independent of both Cold War power blocs and look to Uruguay's similarities with its Southern Cone neighbours instead of meekly cringing before the pedestal of Europe. Among the several columns of signatures are a number of people who figure in this book in one guise or another: Aldo Solari, Ruben Yáñez, Carlos Quijano, Julio Castro, Carlos Real de Azúa, Hugo Alfaro, Luis Benvenuto and Juan Rial.[28] Unfortunately, this call would not receive the response that a similar one, also by unaligned independents, would get in late 1970.

A large step towards future unity was made by the two oldest organisations on the left, the Communist and Socialist parties, both of which changed their names and form of presentation for the 1962 elections, each attracting to them both smaller independent leftist groups as well as dissident progressive elements from the major parties. The Communist Party formed the nucleus of the Frente Izquierda de Liberación (with its timely acronym FIDEL), which apparently anticipated the Frente Amplio by attracting significant numbers of supporters from the world of culture,[29] while the Socialist Party became the centre of the much less stable Unión Popular. This coalition comprised the Agrupación Nuevas Bases (mainly the progressive ex-Nardone supporters such as Roberto Ares Pons and Alberto Methol Ferré, who featured in one of the debates highlighted in Chapter 1), Senator Enrique Erro's group of renegades from the Nationals (including Raúl Sendic, who would help found the Tupamaros a year later), 'Independents' such as the writers Mario Benedetti, Carlos Martínez Moreno and José Pedro Díaz, some 'Batllista' dissidents from the Colorado Party, plus most of the Socialists themselves.[30] In August 1962, it called for the formation of another 'national, popular and anti-imperialist movement', adding another ingredient that would leave its narrow left confines to become a public rhetorical marker: 'anti-oligarchy'.[31] The response to this call would also be meagre.

Both Communists and Socialists had been making calls for some kind of unity since the mid-1950s, attempts that always fell foul of a long history of ideological and tactical differences.[32] For example, the Communist Party had been making overtures about the formation of a broad left front without exclusions since 1956 and did so again at its 18th Congress in 1962.[33] The Socialist Party consistently rejected these calls, although it circulated internally in mid-1959 a document which asked whether they should try to offer the electorate a wider range of options than the one it could manage on its own,[34] and went as far as formally vetoing the possibility of incorporating the Communists in any wider movement of its making at its 32nd Congress in January 1960. Its General Secretary explained that associating with the Communists would make any left coalition too easy a target for conservative propaganda, thereby discouraging broad popular support from the outset and dissuading other groups from joining, not to mention major ideological and theoretical differences in the ways the two parties interpreted the Uruguayan political situation and planned their response to it.[35] At its 33rd Congress in 1962, it reaffirmed the 1960 resolution but in a form that seemed to allow a greater openness as to what groups might be incorporated into a wider movement in the future. This decision led to the exclusion of a number of the groups that had already formed the Unión Popular, leading some of them (such as the MRO) to join FIDEL. At the same time, the Socialist Party was advocating radical changes to the constitution and received widespread support on the left (including the Communists) in the task of collecting the required number of signatures to have its proposal put to a national referendum accompanying the national elections. It was hoped that, even though formal unification or coalition of the two main left-wing parties remained for the time being unlikely, joint participation in such projects, as well as the regular work in the trade union and Cuban Solidarity movements, would promote a spirit of cooperation at the level of day-to-day political activity.[36]

The results for the major left parties in 1958 and the new coalitions in 1962 were as follows (the number of votes being followed in parentheses by their expression as a percentage of the total votes cast in the election):[37]

	1958	1962
Unión Cívica	37,625(3.7)	
Partido Demócrata Cristiano		35,703(3.0)
Communist Party	27,080(2.7)	
FIDEL		40,886(3.6)
Socialist Party	35, 478(3.5)	
Unión Popular		27,041(2.3)

The new Christian Democrat Party seemed unlikely to repeat the electoral successes of similar organisations in Europe or, closer to home, in Chile and Venezuela, although it would seem that most of the Unión Cívica's supporters had followed the new group. The barely papered-over dissentions involving the Unión Popular lost votes to the more viable FIDEL and perhaps, at the other end of the spectrum, to the more progressive factions of the major parties (whose returns are not given here). In fact, they even lost one of their candidates, who defected back to the Nationals at the last minute.[38] The result of all this was that, in 1962, the vote for the left as a whole actually fell slightly, while the Socialists lost all parliamentary representation.

The electoral performance of these first attempts to bring together the Uruguayan political left in thirty years inspired two influential analyses of the far from satisfactory results, the first by writer and Unión Popular supporter, Mario Benedetti,[39] the second by the sociologist and political scientist Aldo Solari, which, as its title implied ('Requiem for the Left'),[40] suggested that the election's message for the left was far from reassuring. Benedetti argued that, while FIDEL bought unity at the excessive cost of near total domination by the Communists, the 'atomization' of the Unión Popular was only too apparent, especially in the seemingly opportunistic pact beween the Socialist Party and a breakaway group from the National Party led by Senator Enrique Erro, which smacked of the unprincipled and hastily stitched up deals that had given the traditional parties such a bad name ('Postdata', 132–3), an observation also made by Solari ('Requiem', 145).[41]

Benedetti then urged the abandonment of the vicious sectarianism that only caused the groups on the left to squabble bitterly among themselves and advocated the burial of a past of petty disputes which kept the groups apart and prevented effective joint action in the present. However, he continued, there needed to be 'frank, sincere dialogue' about something 'realistic', a groping toward a 'possible advance' so that all groups trusted each other enough to participate in this 'frankness' ('Postdata', 133 and 145–6). Like Solari, who thought that talk about revolution in Uruguay sounded like deluded nonsense to most voters ('Réquiem', 153), Benedetti believed that the left had to learn the lesson of realism, but was also emphatic about the left's potential to become the only practicable way out for the crisis-ridden country. Hence the urgency of his appeal: since the traditional parties were likely to preside over the total bankruptcy of the state, the left must be ready to pick up the pieces when a confused middle class found their illusions destroyed and betrayed ('Postdata', 147–8). Solari was a lot less sure that the left could ever persuade a sufficient proportion of the middle classes to abandon their usual allegiances,[42] partly because the act of voting seemed separate from their normal daily concerns and partly because the parties, through their political clubs, supplemented the deficiencies of the state's social services. Because of this, Solari was pessimistic about the left's electoral fortunes simply because it was as hard in Uruguay as elsewhere to give a non-communist left a genuine radical feel without alienating voters. He was dryly eloquent about the way the left tended to delude itself about the real nature of those to whom it wanted to appeal, because it did not understand that the electorate understood perfectly well what was best for it. Rather than listen, however, the left preferred to substitute its idea of what the people ought to be ('Requiem', 145–152), a lesson the Uruguayan left could only learn completely twenty years later, after the dictatorship.

Solari concluded by wondering despairingly whether Uruguay might not end up committing suicide, and by throwing down the gauntlet to those responsible for thinking out the left's policies: 'those most totally defeated' [in the elections] were the left-wing intellectuals for having failed in 'the task of thinking about the country as it is, without the escapist nonsense to which we are so prone, without empty optimism' ('Requiem', 155), which repeats his attack on the intelligentsia to which I referred in Chapter One, but here clearly including himself in this self-criticism ('we'). However, where Benedetti thought the left should abandon the electoral option altogether because it had become irrelevant to the people's real needs ('Postdata', 131),[43] thus perhaps putting him among those Solari saw as ignoring the people's clear message to them, Solari himself urged on them the 'language of truth', since the language they were using won them no votes ('Requiem', 153).

While not a debate in the sense used in the exchanges analysed in Chapter 1, the juxtaposition of Benedetti's and Solari's responses to the 1962 national elections illustrate clearly the kind of options available to intellectuals on the left in the Uruguay of the time. On the one hand, there was the commitment to a kind of revolutionary politics which intellectuals and left-wing activists might see as appropriate and necessary, but which the electorate and every one else involved in the political mainstream considered irrelevant or ludicrous. On the other, the thankless task of trying to build genuinely new possibilities in a political system that seemed to make any such alternative all but unachievable. The efforts made to unite the left around a realistic program between the 1962 and 1971 elections amount to an attempt at retaining Benedetti's optimism while seeking to attach it to what Solari evidently believed to be impossible: a distinctly leftist political platform which eschewed enough of the stereotyped rhetoric of revolution to be of potentially general appeal but did not completely compromise some very basic positions for merely electoral purposes.[44] Eleuterio Fernández Huidobro summed up the sad 1962 experience many years afterwards: 'We were all partisans of unity [. . .] However, we all used rivers of ink to justify our own positions'.[45] Only a year later he would help to found the Tupamaros urban guerrilla organisation.

Frictions and Fractions (II): Towards the Congreso del Pueblo

The poor showing of the Unión Popular caused havoc in the Socialist Party. At a special congress in June 1963, it dumped the Unión, much to the glee of the Communists, who now – and as it turned out, erroneously – saw the chances of creating a united left much increased by the weakness of their main rivals.[46] The Socialist Party then split into two factions, neither taking the ultimate and no doubt suicidal step of forming a separate party. The more radical majority took the name Izquierda Nacional, which took for reality the dream of a Socialist-led leftwing coalition that was fast becoming a nightmare. The founder of the Party, the more moderate traditionalist Emilio Frugoni, who had already expressed considerable dissatisfaction with the manoeuvres that had produced the Unión Popular in the first place, led a minority under the title Movimiento Socialista. These events left the remaining groups floundering, some of them going over to FIDEL and others joining the progressive sections of the major parties (in particular, Zelmar Michelini's list 99 in the Colorado Party). The rest soldiered on under the now tattered banner of the Unión Popular, led by ex-deputy Enrique Erro's group, which had defected from the National Party in 1961 to form it.

Although the Sino-Soviet split caused the Communist Party to lose some adherents who formed the Maoist Movimiento de Izquierda Revolucionaria, the FIDEL coalition both stayed together and grew. Its first congress, also in June 1963, took advantage of the disarray in the socialist ranks to issue another call for unity, but under its control, of course. It advocated a coalition including the Socialists and the more progressive sectors of the major parties.[47] This strategy spoke from a position of strength, eschewing all ideological differences and emphasising, quite realistically, the wide variety of political opinion to be found even amongst unionised workers, let alone the others. Such words contrasted completely with the resolution on the same issue that emanated from the Socialists' congress, in which they rather patronisingly advocated a 'national revolution' to which only by their actions could other political forces 'prove' a right to adhere.[48] The Socialist Party refused to engage with other groups at the political level, probably fearing that, in its weakened state, it could lose all autonomy or control. The Communist Party went some way toward allowing for this, itself distinguishing between a party in which there might be supposed to be some ideological unity and one which would facilitate political unity by having everyone working towards a common program.[49] By September

1963, the Socialists had changed their tack, however, making a call 'free from sectarianism' aimed at harnessing the 'efficiency' of 'workers' and people's movements' to 'national and social liberation'.[50]

FIDEL's next attempt at forging the necessary links ended in farce. In mid-1965 they set up the 'Mesa por la Unidad de las Izquierdas', which comprised the Communists and groups close to them, breakaway fractions from both main parties, the catholic left and a number of more or less independent leftist journalists and writers, such as Carlos María Gutiérrez, Julio Castro and Mario Benedetti, gathered around Carlos Quijano at the printing presses of *Marcha*. When the majority of the Socialists joined the organisation, unity seemed assured.[51] The Mesa would seek unity around a common name that would allow the equal participation of all groups, each of which would keep its own title but donate its votes to the common [i.e. umbrella party's] list, an organising principle which anticipated that of the Frente Amplio in 1971. Unfortunately, as Castro reminded his readers, at the time Uruguayan electoral law only permitted this accumulation of votes if the main grouping had the name of a party that had actually gained parliamentary representation at a national level.[52] Luckily, one was to hand, the Democrat Party, the electoral name for the 'Agrupación Nacionalista Demócrata Social', created in 1928 by Carlos Quijano but not active since 1950, and therefore safe from accusations of bias in any direction. This was agreeable to all, provided, said the Socialists, that their party's minority, Frugoni's Movimiento Socialista, would join in. This Frugoni refused to do, leaving the Socialist majority little choice but to carry on disputing with him under the Socialist Party's banner. The *Marcha* independents suggested that this impasse could be solved if everyone were to vote under the Socialist Party's name, a proposal that was, predictably enough, rejected by FIDEL. Anticipating the tone of Fernández Huidobro's later remark on the 1962 mess, Julio Castro, who recorded this sad story, commented bitterly that the left said it wanted changes, but did not realise how much its refusal to change its old ways was responsible for the electorate's constant rejection of its appeals to vote for it.[53] He was pointing out the consequences of continued division and petty squabbling among themselves. The left was still unwilling to take on the challenge of Solari's comments on attracting votes in elections, and sympathetic intellectuals were as far as ever from finding anything like a viable answer to Juan Flo's question from 1952.

Castro was right. In 1963–4 the Partido Demócrata Cristiano moved steadily leftwards, alienating still more of the original Unión Cívica supporters, who joined those who had already left in 1961 to form the Movimiento Cívico Cristiano in 1965. The polling for left groups in the 1966 presidential elections was as follows (percentage of the total vote again being given in parentheses):

Partido Socialista	a) Izquierda Nacional	7,894 (0.7)
	b) Movimiento Socialista	3,646 (0.2)
Unión Popular		3,655 (0.2)
FIDEL		69,755 (5.7)
Partido Demócrata Cristiano		7,219 (3.0)

Clearly, the disunity within the Socialist Party had been disastrous; the Christian Democrat alternative did not look like proving as attractive to the electorate in Uruguay as it had been elsewhere, because a mildly reformist platform could not attract votes in sufficient numbers outside the main parties; and support for the left had, once again, barely increased over the previous poll. On the other hand, the FIDEL result implied that a genuinely progressive alternative put forward from a position of strength and unity had the potential to mobilise support, but would have to be far more broadly based if it was to break the stranglehold of the major parties on the traditional political allegiances of the populace at large.

It has been said that the 1966 elections substituted 'the apparently irrelevant issue of further constitutional reform' for the far more immediate question of the economic crisis.[54] While the finally approved conservative reform would assume considerable importance later by returning Uruguay to presidential rule after fourteen years of a collegiate system, giving added powers to the executive and providing for five-year terms of government instead of four, FIDEL was one of several organisations which had put up alternative proposals for constitutional reform, after having received no small help from the trade union movement in mobilising support for their offering.[55] In fact, it would be the unions that made the next crucial step towards the unification of the country's leftist forces.

They had much to contribute in this regard, their own path to unity having been long and tortuous, to say the least.[56] Since the late nineteenth century, unions had developed around different political or religious groups. By the 1950s, attempts to consolidate these separate organisations followed Cold War divisions: a largely Communist controlled Unión General de Trabajadores [UGT] and the Confederación Sindical Uruguaya [CSU], which affiliated to the international labour movement controlled by France, Great Britain and the USA. 1956 saw the first systematic attempts at unionising rural workers as well as the creation by the UGT, CSU, various autonomous groups and the students' union, of a coordinating commission to set up a single umbrella organisation. As the economic crisis worsened, such endeavours continued apace, although a leading trade unionist, Héctor Rodríguez, claimed that as late as 1958 there was still neither unity nor coordination in the union movement.[57] Eventually, a Congreso de Unificación

Sindical succeeded in September 1966 in turning the meaning of the acronym CNT into a genuinely unified Central Nacional de Trabajadores. This organisation would all but lead the resistance to authoritarianism in the ten years leading up to the 1973 coup.

The pitfalls and difficulties encountered along this complicated route have been variously charted. The main sticking points were the need to agree on common goals and methods; the devising of a program of solutions to the crisis; the difficulty of overriding already existing groups of unions; the conflict of interest between union and political party loyalties; and the decision whether to have full-time, paid officers and organisers.[58] Since the unions offered general proposals about the crisis as a whole and did not restrict themselves only to matters related to the work place, divisions in the union movement were as deep and as basic as those between the political groups and parties on the left. One of the principal aims of the Frente Amplio's structure would be, as we shall see in the following chapter, an attempt to halt the continuation of these debilitating internal wrangles by enabling union members and political militants to work side by side.

About a year before the final formation of the CNT, a document dated December 1965 and circulated in preparation for a National Trade Union Assembly tried to address these questions, advocating that the problems of individual member unions should not be allowed to compromise the effort to coordinate union activity generally, that a member union must have its tactics discussed by the central organisation, that there be a unified program to defend the short- and medium-term interests of the working class, that individual unions retain their autonomy in the immediate area of action while exchanging experiences and perspectives about the whole idea of unity to break down residual distrust, and that a questionnaire be circulated to all participating organisations.[59] Rodríguez, who had been involved in all the principal moves toward unity since the early 1940s, wrote in early 1965 that they had all failed because leaders had put their own, often ideologically blinkered agenda ahead of that of the workers they supposedly represented, and brought the sectarianism and doctrinal squabbling of their politics into the union arena, causing divisions which made working together practically impossible.[60] Clearly, the general problems raised by attempts to unify the union movement were analogous to those we have seen FIDEL, the Unión Popular and the 'Mesa por la Unidad de las Izquierdas' fail to solve.

Another obstacle that few probably even dared to broach openly was the divided attitudes of the union members themselves, particularly the frequently noted contradiction between workers' election of radical union leaders to seek the satisfaction of their immediate demands and their constant but perhaps realistic re-electing of the traditional parties into national government.[61] While Varela suggested that getting a job often depended on political favours granted to an individual, while maintaining wages and conditions once a worker had one required the collective pressure of unions and their members, Rama put it differently. Workers rejected both the option of a socialist revolution (even if their leaders did not) and a possible deal with the still weak industrial bourgeoisie to formulate a national development program, in favour of a struggle over wages, jobs and conditions, a choice which, in fact, strengthened the principles of the already existing forms of social democracy.[62] In short, unionists found themselves obliged to choose between a fully collectivist solution aimed at society as a whole and the defense of their own and others' individual rights as citizens and workers.

One way of dealing with this dilemma was to bring workers' organisations and the general population together, which was exactly what the 'People's Congress' ['Congreso del Pueblo'] in August 1965 attempted to do. This was the result of a call by the CNT twelve months earlier for a conference to discuss its Program of Solutions to the country's crisis.[63] The congress was to be open not only to unions but to students, pensioners, housewives, the unemployed, casual workers and intellectuals – in short, all marginalised sections of Uruguayan society collectively identified by the left as 'the people' – in an endeavour to construct 'a common national politics for everyone'. Notable omissions were political parties (an attempt to ward off accusations of specific allegiances) and, obviously, employer and government representatives; those in power were already assumed to be the enemy and were unlikely to see their interests as being served by the congress. They responded accordingly, dismissing the whole exercise as a communist plot.[64]

From the meetings held in April to prepare the ground for the congress, there issued a document that declared the severity of the crisis as so intense and immediate that separate group efforts had to be replaced by a united one, and extended an invitation to all interested on behalf of the whole union movement.[65] The same groups reemerged in the 'Call to the People of Uruguay', but now reformulated as a powerfully united first-person plural. Under the subheading 'Who We Are' appeared ten categories, shorn of their union and other affiliations, each introduced by the words 'We Are . . .' and followed by their professional or social role (such as teachers, office workers, pensioners, etc.). This substitution of more personalised terms for the more abstract titles of organisations only underlined the self-conceptualisation of the Congress as a living organism: 'All that lives, throbs [palpita], studies, thinks, works and produces is in our Congress', as if an impersonal life force found total bodily expression in the range of participants. Rallying around the Artigas battle cry of 'Unite, dear compatriots', the aim was to set off heroically 'to rescue a destiny that has been snatched from us'.[66]

The 'Program of Solutions to the Crisis', which emerged from the Congress' final plenary session that lasted an entire night and most of the following morning,[67] was, then, not only a radical response to Uruguay's political and economic woes, but a conscious and concerted beginning to the task of reversing the direction of the nation's entire history since independence, now conceived as one long despoliation of the people's patrimony by a privileged minority. It was the first time so grand a scheme had emerged from a union of workers' and citizens' groups, and was still considered valuable enough twenty years later for a new generation of trade unionists to think seriously of reviving it.[68] Indeed, the People's Congress has been seen as the most concerted attempt by Uruguayan intellectuals to permanently influence the country's life,[69] while another perspective describes it as something quite new in Uruguayan political history in that it amounted to a national program produced outside the major political parties.[70] Its influence on the Tupamaros and the Frente Amplio has been shown,[71] and everything suggests that the Congress resolutions were the most serious program of unified action put forward during this period by a left-wing assembly that included workers, union and political militants, politically aware citizens sympathetic to the left, and what amounted to organic, working-class cultural workers (represented especially by union leader Héctor Rodríguez). The final text was a collective document in that it had all been discussed in committee and debated and passed by the Congress as a whole.

The Program[72] began by self-consciously trying to ward off in advance its summary dismissal as the usual left-wing nonsense from the usual left-wing suspects: 'Crisis is not a word for propaganda; it is in everyday reality'. The root cause was identified as the unproductive and antiquated system of land ownership, and only secondarily the social, political, economic structures that supported it. Indeed, the entire system should be overhauled, but without exacting further sacrifices from those who had already made most of them, whose interests were now reclassified as those of the entire nation. The details of the Program are gathered unexceptionally under headings referring to different areas of political and social life (agriculture, industry, education and the like).[73] However, cutting across all these discrete categories are a number of themes that add up to a much more forthright political agenda.

The most pervasive of them is central planning, which the Program would apply to all areas of economic activity to eliminate those pockets of rural privilege that prolong the artificial conflict between city and interior. Centralisation is deemed a prerequisite for land redistribution, so that national interests and needs, now identified as those of the toiling masses, could prevail in all areas of industry, revenue collection, education and transport. While the Program did not envisage the nationalisation of the entire economy, the state should take over all monopoly enterprises, as well as any others essential for the nation's economy, and, especially, all finance and banking institutions, partly in order to abolish the concentration of economic power, but mostly because – and here the document betrays either a praiseworthy idealism or a depressing naïvety – financial services should be non-profit-making because they are not in themselves productive, a view that sounds quaintly old-fashioned now but fully understandable in a developing economy in which the financial sector had been recently shown to be riddled with corruption.

These often very costly measures were to be funded by the surpluses snatched from the coffers of the economic elite, which were presumed to be overflowing and, apparently, bottomless. Luxury imports were to be prohibited, non-productive expenditure reduced and new wealth taxes devised for the rich and infamous. Income and capital gains taxes were to replace the consumption tax, while the Program explicitly stated that high-income earners should finance the country's social services.

The corollary to this attack on privilege was a series of provisions to guarantee workers' rights and their emotional and physical health and well-being, services to be paid for by taxing the rich. All laws restricting unionisation and the right to strike were to be repealed, while the total democratisation of access to education at all levels from childcare centres to universities would erode one more bastion of privilege. In addition, a system of cooperatives would ensure full worker participation in all sectors of the economy.

Clearly, the political and economic elite were not likely to take this wholesale assault on their accustomed affluence lying down, but the Program seems to imagine they would be powerless[74] against a general population converted into a non-aligned mass pressure group, whose ultimate expression was the state itself: 'The people will drive [impulsará] and the State will activate the transcendent task of effecting the necessary changes for the benefit of society, changes to be carried out by the people duly organised'. In this circular and somewhat incoherent sentence, the Program apparently sought to bypass adherence to any existing political program (even to escape politics altogether) by leaving out any indication as to how decisions would be taken and exactly what forms organising the people might take. This lack of precision may well have been deliberate: there would be a need not to alienate groups or individuals suspicious of the established left, but also, perhaps, determination not to become bogged down in the left's already proven inability to line up in comradely fashion behind a common plan of action. Similarly, the Program avoided words such as 'revolution', 'socialism' and 'communism'. It is as if it looked merely to provide channels for the expression of the long fettered, collective will of an almost mystical entity called 'the people'.[75] As Rodríguez phrased it after the Congress, 'To put this movement in a front, a party or in any already existing category seems to me as difficult as keeping an elephant in a matchbox'.[76]

The limitations of this strategy were not long in making themselves apparent. Rodríguez had a much-publicised wrangle with Rodney Arismendi, the Communist Party General Secretary, over the Congress's refusal to allow its proposals to be subsumed into a conventional political platform.[77] In addition, Rodríguez himself freely admitted in 1984 that the Program was not put into practice and that the Congress's standing committees had ceased all effective activity by the end of 1966,[78] partly because of an ill-starred campaign against constitutional reform proposals put up by the major parties and well supported by the public.[79] As the crisis mounted in the mid to late 1960s, the state (the real one, that is, not the benign, provident version of it conjured up at the Congress) took a sharp and increasingly violent turn to the right. Yet the left remained stubbornly fragmented,[80] while the Congreso del Pueblo's determined effort to supersede conventional political representation was rapidly overtaken by events. Small wonder, then, that when the call came for the formation of what would eventually become the Frente Amplio, it came from outside those groups involved in the frustrated efforts at unification up to the 1960s, and that its first concern was with the pathetic impression this disarray was leaving in the minds of the left's potential electorate.

Onward Christian Soldiers: From Television to Political Vision

On 1 January 1965, Juan Pablo Terra, a Christian democrat attracted to a personal view of liberation theology,[81] brought his one-hundred-strong Movimiento Social Cristiano under the wing of the Partido Demócrata Cristiano [PDC]. In April of the same year, this left-leaning sector became a majority after internal elections, while by mid-1968 Terra had become the party's leader.[82] On June 23, ten days after the Pacheco government had inaugurated a virtual state of emergency to remain in force until beyond the 1971 elections (except for a three-month period in early 1969), and a fortnight before it decreed a wage and price freeze which would in practice only really affect the former, Terra read a statement on Montevideo television's Channel 12 which was then circulated among all the influential individuals and groups known to be opposed to the Pacheco administration. Importantly, it coincided with a series of articles in *Marcha* on the same topic, collectively entitled 'What To Do?' (Juan Flo's persistent question, once more),[83] and written by the militant but unaffiliated pen of centre-left journalist Oscar Bruschera,[84] who would have other parts to play in this story.

Terra began by putting forward a premise which represented a major advance over what we have seen to be the Congreso del Pueblo's virtual flight from politics and which was the tactical reversal of the usual equation that would make the Frente theoretically possible: 'we will not overcome the economic crisis if we do not overcome the political crisis'. Having accused the traditional parties of being treacherous, incoherent and undemocratic, he went on to ask an embarrassing question: what did the public see when it looked at those who claimed to offer alternatives from the left? It saw them 'atomised, pulverised, dispersed across different parties, paralysed by party discipline', anything but the 'real, different possibility' the country needed. The implication was that it was unforgivable for the more progressive sectors of the opposition to let the nation down, when there were common themes that ought to make dialogue feasible among the various groups, a dialogue impeded only by narrowly self-protective practices. Finally, under a banner of 'truth in politics' by which government supporters would actually really help it, while the rest would line up really to oppose it, Terra advocated persuading the executive to call fresh elections – a not eccentric proposal given that Pacheco, having inherited the presidency on the death of the previous incumbent, was enacting his legislation for austerity and repression without ever having to face the public at the ballot box.[85]

The idea of an opposition united around a common platform clearly attempted to head off the result of factionalism in the main parties: since they were twenty parties in one, they could 'gain power but could not govern'.[86] As Bruschera had put it about ten years earlier, the problem started with the double simultaneous vote,[87] which both kept parties together and encouraged the proliferation of factions within them by allowing the accumulation of votes for vastly different groups of candidates under the one party name. More briefly, it permitted conglomeration without insisting on unity, an invidious combination the Frente Amplio would strenuously try to avoid.

The system worked reasonably well in times of plenty when there was a large measure of agreement on essentials in each party. However, in times of scarcity and strife (such as the early 1930s and the post-1955 period), party consensus got destroyed as opinion diverged, resulting in wrangling, indecision and weak or ineffective government. For the electors, the system then often meant that a vote for a progressive ticket could end up getting a conservative president into office. For parliament, it frequently entailed the government factions becoming a minority which had to do deals with their like-minded counterparts on the other side of the house, with the opposition often trying to do the same in reverse with the governing party's dissenters. In mid-1968, in an atmosphere of increasing confrontation between police and student or trade union demonstrators, inflation running at over 100 per cent, an ongoing stand-off between the banks and the state over salary increases, followed by the state of emergency and the wage freeze, not to mention the beginnings of a guerrilla war, it is hardly surprising to find the executive tempted to bypass a parliament whose very structure all but paralysed it. Terra's wish to return politics to a position of primacy by creating a genuine and united opposition which would reform the way state and parliament functioned reflected a concern fully justified by events over the next five years: voters would see the deliberations of their elected representatives progressively marginalised, ignored, overruled and, finally, silenced.[88]

As the country's situation worsened, the PDC repeated its call in October, but now with greater precision and determination. They had concluded by then that the issue was not the party in power but a social class out to protect its privileges: 'the exploiters united can only be confronted by the people united', and the different sectors, whatever their provenance or field of activity, must retain their individual identities but unite around a shared set of aims and objectives. This is, in effect, a sketch of what the Frente Amplio would become until the coup in June 1973: a coalition of parties and groups, rather than a party characterised by internal coalitions between factions. Notable here, too, is the early stage of a double tactical and rhetorical move which would have serious consequences for the Frente Amplio in the future. The first step was to set up a confrontation between those over there who had a vested interest in maintaining the status quo and these others (including 'us') who wanted to change it; the second was to identify the latter group with 'the people' – a treacherous term which here means simply our supporters, whoever they were, but which could imperceptibly slide into indicating the people or nation as an undifferentiated, monolithic entity, on whose behalf and in whose name it then became possible to claim to be acting and speaking. Not unexpectedly, the document later likened the political situation to 'trench warfare' with 'the privileged classes' shooting it out with 'the masses', a battlefield imagery that would later become the norm and play into the hands of those who sought to govern without the checks and balances of democratic debate. Even so, we have in Juan Pablo Terra's pronouncements the first sign that it might be possible for a united left to speak the kind of realistic language we saw urged by Aldo Solari back in 1962. After four months of discussions with a range of groups and individuals in and out of parliament, the PDC was able to formulate more clearly the issues around which an alternative political organisation might coalesce. The direction was clear: to help those suffering most from inflation and unemployment.[89]

A joint approach on these people-oriented matters helped to coordinate opposition forces in parliament for the next two years and provided them with more support from outside through the Movement for the Defence of Civil Liberties and National Sovereignty.[90] This had been initiated by a broadly based gathering of political groups, trade union representatives, students and teachers, intellectuals and religious organisations in the wake of the first censorship laws and the deregulation of the Socialist Party in

December 1967. It held its first national meeting on 27–28 July 1968, followed by a general assembly on 1 November.[91]

However, a tactically determined coordinated perspective on certain selected issues was one thing; a unified political front was something else again, and even the PDC was forced to admit that Terra's original June 23 statement had not been received with universal acclaim, but rather with suspicion.[92] There were predictable worries about electoral difficulties, factions which would have to break away from the traditional parties and (even more predictably) the prospect of working with Communists bothered almost everyone.[93] In short, Terra and the PDC were willing to countenance breaking off all contact with those they blamed for the disarticulation of Uruguayan society at large, so as to enhance the possibility of communicating with an enlarged potential electorate through an alliance of those forces which had a real alternative to offer. The only problem was that at least some of the necessary participants in such a venture still doubted their ability to talk and negotiate fruitfully with one another.

Fortunately, Terra did not give up easily and persevered with his discussions until, in a much more confident interview in *Marcha* during December 1969, he was able to put forward for consideration nine points which had emerged from his conversations over the previous year, and which form the link between the Congreso del Pueblo's proposals and the eventual platform of the Frente Amplio. They were: the protection of civil rights and the reform of parliament and the constitution; a clear plan for structural transformation and dynamic development; the expulsion of foreign influence and private speculation from the financial sector; reform and modernisation of agriculture; nationalisation of main areas of foreign trade; restructuring of the nation's industries; expansion of the areas of health, education and housing; a major income redistribution; and the integration of Uruguay with other countries of the region to counter the limitations of its own small internal market and to resist foreign domination. He was also adamant that any coalition be as broadly based as possible, rejecting the suggestion of a bilateral agreement with the communists or FIDEL because the differences between them were too great, and because that kind of accord might create such a wrong impression that the whole process would get stuck there and go no further.[94]

Terra's efforts over two years can be seen as an attempt to bring forth a political party whose principles, structure and ways of working would be as coherent as his consultative approach was with the ideals of egalitarian humanism and democratic socialism espoused in his own party doctrine.[95] In the last few months before the official proclaiming of the Frente Amplio, the key problem was to persuade individuals and groups who had traditional ties to the main parties but were alienated from their party's dominant ways of thinking and acting, to honour that disaffection by breaking away. They could then aid in the task of building an organisation more in tune with their own convictions as individuals and participate in determining the direction of a collective, perhaps even a mass, of people with similar social and political objectives. The great advantage Terra had in his negotiations was that he came from the Christian Democrats, a political party not involved in the disputes between Communists and Socialists of 1962 and 1966, and one that was moving leftwards towards those he most wanted to convince while retaining credibility in a wider constituency. As the left recognised the need to reach out to a wider audience but simultaneously, through the pens of those like Solari, Benedetti, Gutiérrez and Bruschera, came to understand that the burden of its own past prevented it from doing so, Terra could be acknowledged as ideally suited to be the means whereby the creation of a party based on the very principle of dialogue both it and the country itself appeared to require might overcome this apparently insurmountable frustration.

3

Dialogue Engaged

The Frente Amplio as Coalition

You have something you must look after, which is precisely the chance to express your ideas; the chance to go forward through democratic channels as far as you can; the chance, in short, to create those conditions we all hope one day to see achieved throughout Latin America, so that we can all be as brothers, so that exploitation of one man by another will cease. This will not happen everywhere the same way, without bloodshed, without producing any of what happened in Cuba, where once you have the first shot, you don't know when the last will be.
Ernesto 'Che' Guevara in Montevideo (August, 1961)

While this chapter continues where the previous one left off, it does so by again relegating intellectuals themselves to the back seat, but only in order to focus all the more on the new political coalition to which those who signed the document published in *Marcha* on 26 November 1971 had publicly subscribed. My principal contention will be that the original Frente Amplio embodied a form of consensus that, although derived from the benevolent, paternalist notion of the State as provider and mediator between class interests practised under 'Batllismo' (see the Introduction), is achieved in the Frente through vigorous dialogue. As the opening to the previous chapter suggested, this made the new organisation very congenial to intellectuals because, however defined, they cannot thrive where critical analysis and the free exchange of ideas are impossible or not allowed. Potentially at least, then, its work and theirs had something very important in common. Consequently, I attempt to show here that dialogue between equals informed the moment of the Frente's formation, the ideas and personality of its first leader and president (Líber Seregni), as well as its structure and the content of its political platform. It is as though the Frente took literally this chapter's epigraph, Che Guevara's words at the University of the Republic in August 1961 to a huge audience that may well have contained many of those appearing in this book,[1] aiming to displace and counter the polarised, increasingly militarised view of society as a life-or-death battle between opposing armies.

On 7 October 1970, some 49 concerned citizens put their signatures to a brief statement that, in retrospect, appears as the overture to an orchestrated sequence of events leading to the official establishing of the Frente Amplio nearly five months later. It was important that this final initiative be seen to be taken by an apparently informal group of individuals in order to forestall the criticism, at least before it was formally constituted, that the Frente would be merely the plaything of one particular political movement. Among the names were several who feature elsewhere in this study: Oscar Bruschera, Héctor Rodríguez, Carlos Martínez Moreno, Carlos Quijano, Carlos Real de Azúa and Julio Castro. All these individuals were well known to be of the centre-left but with no particular party affiliations or (in some cases, as well as) to have been associated with the more progressive trends within one of the major parties. Included among the latter and heading the list (which does not seem to be in any particular order) was Arturo Baliñas, a distinguished retired general of impeccable Batllista provenance, who in this regard is a herald to Líber Seregni, who would be adopted early in 1971 as the Frente's leader and presidential candidate.

Referring first to the grave situation in which Uruguay found itself due to the Pacheco regime's policies, the signatories called on the leaders of all those forces that were 'democratic, progressive and anti-imperialist' and could be united 'without exclusions' in opposition to the 'current government's anti-popular and anti-national behaviour'. In these few lines, the document sketched the basic motivation for such an organisation, cast its net as widely as possible to catch any group at all that might be even vaguely to the left of centre, avoided any aspersions that might be associated with terms such as 'socialism' or 'revolution' and, most importantly, with the two words 'without exclusions', sought to establish a condition of entry that would hurdle the obstacles that had beset all previous attempts to unify the left since 1962.[2] The text also urged efficiency in the new movement's structure, expressed its unqualified support for the steps already taken (mostly, as we have seen, by the Christian Democrats [PDC]) towards the realisation of the signatories' aims and, anticipating a problem the Frente Amplio would not be able to solve before the military banned it, urgently demanded a reform of the electoral law, obviously so the new party could participate under its own name, whatever that might be.[3] In short, the document stressed the need for inclusiveness – with its implied request for tolerance of the diverse – and for communication and agreement on the basis of a minimum number of common grounds.

If the Frente was to become an effective third force in Uruguayan politics, it would have to attract to its ranks dissident factions from at least one, and preferably both, of the traditional parties. Such groups would require a formula whereby they could justify their change of allegiance to themselves, the party they were leaving and to the people who had voted for them. The lead was taken in this regard in the same month of October by the 'Movimiento por el Gobierno del Pueblo' [MGP] faction from the ruling Colorado party. As Terra admitted, this was something of a coup for the Frente at this stage since the faction had enjoyed not inconsiderable electoral success during the 1960s and its leader, Zelmar Michelini, was widely respected and liked. On October 3–4, the PDC's National Commission authorised the party's representatives to pursue formal negotiations with Michelini's group and, at a public meeting at the end of the month, the MGP's membership responded by voting to leave the Colorado party, a decision formalised in a document dated 5 December.[4]

It is in this text that the formula to be followed by later defectors is first tried out. The MGP claimed all its attempts to reform the Colorado party from within were rejected by the majority factions which had both supported the present government and, by so doing, had turned their back on the whole history and traditions of Batllismo. It points to the undemocratic nature of the party's decision-making processes, outlines in a highly accusatory tone the various ways the government had violated citizens' rights and reasonable expectations, and declares that the MGP's ideological direction was incompatible with the outlook and repressive nature of Pacheco's government. It then advocated the formation of a 'broad political front' and reaffirmed its commitment to the principles it put before voters in the previous election. The point was to capture the moral high ground by showing that the party the faction was leaving had betrayed both its principles and its electorate, whereas the faction itself had kept faith with both.[5]

The next move in this direction came from the National Party's ranks. The youth section of the 'Movimiento Blanco Popular y Progresista' [MBPP] issued a public request on 28 November 1970 that the faction officially resign from the National Party and take up the cause of the 'union' of 'progressive forces' around a 'nationalist programme'. Its wish was granted. At its national convention on December 7, the MBPP condemned the party's support of the current government, declared that its own ideological beliefs could not be realised within the National Party and, like the MGP in the Colorado Party, confirmed its adherence to the most valuable and radical trends in the Nationals' history. Other examples could be added (the Agrupación Herrerista and the Acción Popular Nacionalista[6] from the National Party, and the Agrupación Batllista 'Pregón' from the Colorados), but the basic pattern was now established.[7] The direction of such moves was underlined when, on 15 December 1970, the PDC, MBPP and the MGP combined forces in their desire to form, once again, a democratic, progressive 'broad front [. . .] without exclusions'.[8] There is nothing quite like leading by example. The three groups, none of them associated with the Communists or Socialists, illustrated the importance of negotiation, dialogue and compromise, shelving their differences (both with each other and as baggage brought from each individual group's past) in the interests of more urgent and shared goals of opposing the Pacheco administration and unifying the left.

Once the Christmas and New Year festivities were over, events proceeded apace. The citizens who had issued the October 7 statement had in the meantime been rallying support for the new movement both publicly and privately, and had constituted themselves into an Organización Nacional de Ciudadanos Independientes for the purpose. On 7 January 1971, their provisional executive (which included General Baliñas, Oscar Bruschera and Héctor Rodríguez, who had been instrumental during the 1960s in uniting the union movement) issued a report on the results of their activities to date. In their three months of consultations (which had included some 40 round table discussions and panels throughout the country), a number of priorities had emerged: the need for wide participation in the formulation of the Frente's program; the creation of rank and file organisations open to all; the need for a firmly democratic internal structure for the party; and the suggestion of a common electoral formula that might have wide appeal instead of a proliferation of lists that would only attract the already converted supporters of the groups that proposed them.[9]

One day later, the same concern with free, open democratic participation reappears in the text which formally constituted a 'Popular Front' [Frente del Pueblo] out of the PDC and the MGP, expressing a wish to create a 'workers' democracy, with advanced forms of social property and self-management'. This utopian socialist democracy extended to the internal organisation of the Frente del Pueblo since joining it did not imply the loss of any participating group's identity, ideology or program. The Frente del Pueblo seemed to be aware of its transient status by immediately calling for the formation of a 'Frente Amplio' [Broad Front] which would be a 'political front and not an electoral combination', a 'coalition' and not a 'fusion' of its affiliates, and whose minimum platform was an elaboration of the nine points of Terra's December 1969 proposal. This text's happy coincidence in time with the Independents' report is seemingly acknowledged as it closed with a flattering salute to that group's efforts.[10]

These actions by the PDC, MGP, MBPP and the Independents proved decisive. Less than a month later, on February 5, the Frente Amplio was formally established at 11.00 a.m. in a meeting room in the Senate and held its first plenary session that evening at the PDC's headquarters. Among those present were the leaders or representatives of what were now nine groups, including Bruschera and General Baliñas for the Independents, although eleven are named in the Frente's founding document dated the same day[11] and composed by Carlos Real de Azúa.[12] The document shows its signatories were well aware of the historical implications of their actions if they were successful:

> The political union of progressive currents culminating in the forming of the Broad Front – closing one cycle in the country's history, but simultaneously opening another of hope and faith in the future – was born out of the people's struggle against the fascist-like philosophy of force. This union, through its essence and origins, through having the people as protagonist, has allowed the fraternal grouping together of Colorados and Nationals, Christian democrats and Marxists, men and women with different ideologies, religions and philosophies, [. . .] all the representatives of labour and culture, the legitimate spokespeople of the very heart of our national feeling [la entraña misma de la nacionalidad]. (INDAL, *Frente Amplio*, 50)

The Frente would not break the traditional parties' monopoly on national government until 2004, but the founders were right in foreseeing that, once it did so, its arrival on the political scene would change the history of the nation. More important here, though, is the evident awareness in the document of the extent to which one of the Frente's main aims was to offer something both politically necessary and humane and heart-felt as an alternative to the 'us' versus 'them' mentality gaining ground all around them.

Perhaps taking its lead from the Congreso del Pueblo, the identification of the Frente with the 'people' and the very essence of the nation is now complete, as is the open-hearted gesture which will welcome all right-thinking and like-minded individuals and organisations into the fold. If I have not here dealt with the majority of groups which had already joined the coalition at this stage, it is not because they lagged behind: FIDEL was as quick to take up Terra's initiative as Michelini's MGP, for example.[13] Most of such groups were, however, able to bring their whole organisation with them; they did not have to face the political and psychological consequences of breaking off a dialogue and long-standing ties with one party in order to run the risks involved in opening them with another. What I have wanted to emphasise here is how, from the very outset, the formation of the Frente Amplio made that difficult double movement possible.

Nobody embodied this better than Senator Alba Roballo, who was a poet as well as being leader of the Agrupación Batllista 'Pregón', which defected from the Colorado Party on 5 March 1971. Accompanied by her son and other colleagues, she met with eight members of the Frente's executive, each of whom made a short speech of welcome. In her reply, Senator Roballo addressed several sentences to each of them by name, incidentally referring to Juan Pablo Terra as one 'who receives me in his home, home in two senses'. It is a formalised ritual of establishing new connections, a verbal equivalent of the physical shaking of hands that undoubtedly preceded it. She also spoke of the painful sense of separation that accompanied the decision but also felt that 'a piece of Batllismo' was coming with them.[14] In an interview a week or so earlier, after she had made up her own mind but before her faction had decided to follow her, she spoke even more personally about leaving a party she had served for forty years. At first she had felt as sad as when leaving a house she had lived in most of her life: 'But I have understood that I am not leaving home. I am taking it with me'.[15] The essential element is that even in its beginnings the Frente was trying to build up a sense of intimacy and belonging that would equal if not surpass the sense of traditional loyalty that had accrued for generations to the traditional parties.

Líber Seregni as the Good Father and the Frente Amplio as Home and Family

When, in 1989, the Frente's leader, Líber Seregni, reviewed the period of the coalition's gestation, it is the aspect of reasoned dialogue which stands out. In the six pages devoted to it in a book-length interview which ranges across his whole life, the word 'conversation' occurs twelve times, 'contact' six times and 'discussion' twice. He also spoke in very personal, even intimate terms of his relationship with many of the key political participants in the process. A few pages later, he generalised that for him 'the political factor' always meant 'separations, cultivating friendship, affection and hate, of a kind superior to that found in families, among friends, or even lovers',[16] turning politics into a surprisingly intimate process. Later still, Seregni would state categorically: 'I always liked collective leadership, talking things over with people'.[17] Clearly, close personal contact, a feel for other people as well as respect for their ideological positions, were part and parcel of what Seregni understood political activity to be. Not surprisingly, given how reluctant to engage in meaningful dialogue the Left had shown itself to be, there was no little scepticism on the chances of keeping the coalition together, even among its supporters.[18] For Seregni, however, this horizontal, egalitarian exchange of views made the Frente more 'a way of life' than a 'container for votes'[19] and led to the practice of what he called an 'unconventional open politics',[20] with the aim of setting by example a style and tone which would, if it worked, rekindle a politics dependent on a sense of community, and establish the Frente as something genuinely different in the Uruguayan politics of the time.

Like Arturo Baliñas, Líber Seregni was a retired general with no current party affiliation but who had in the past been associated with progressive sectors of the Colorado Party. He was seen as honest, law-abiding, austere and efficient,[21] all qualities designed to reassure an electorate at a time when its credulity with regard to politicians in general was being daily stretched to the limit. He was active but kept out of the spotlight during the months prior to the formal establishing of the Frente, but was officially proclaimed as its presidential candidate in mid-March 1971, and made his first public appearance as its leader at its inaugural mass rally on March 26. It is on his speeches at that and subsequent occasions up to the dissolution of parliament in June 1973 that I have based the following profile of Seregni's (for Uruguay, at least) unusual conception of leadership and the functioning of a political party.

Reviewing the Frente's first few months' existence in mid-June 1971, Seregni characterised the party as a 'privileged meeting place' where Uruguayans must 'dialogue among themselves, understand one another, revise their conception of history' (*Autoridad*, 42), not for the sake of debating with each other, but because there could be 'no effective mobilisation' without 'interaction' of the 'rank and file' among themselves and of 'the rank and file with their leaders'.[22] It was on this basis that Seregni elaborated to party workers in June 1971 on his own role in the Frente. He wanted to tell them his 'opinion' and 'experiences' so they could 'analyse' them and 'put them up against' theirs:

> My words will only have value to the extent they coincide with those of all. They will only have value to the extent they can hear the words and interpret the will of all, and to the extent we can all steer it efficiently towards practical objectives.
>
> I have everywhere repeated that I was not going to give lectures, that I was not coming with ready-made prescriptions, but rather that within the basic criteria determined by the bottom line of the program, I wanted to analyse concrete problems with the people involved. (*Autoridad*, 64)

There is here an explicit refusal to dictate terms on the grounds that his leadership was such only to the degree that he could speak for them all. He could only do that by confronting his experience with theirs, if necessary on a one-to-one basis, until all the lessons that could be learned were available to everybody. The leader figured in this process as consultant and facilitator, as creator and interpreter of a consensus arrived at among equals, always within the framework of the Frente's whole program, since that marked out the general parameters laid down by their group representatives for all of them, including him. He went on to say in the same speech that he wanted to know 'everyone's experience' so that each individual 'example' could be 'an example for all' (*Autoridad*, 71), the emphasis on experience once again underlining the idea that being in the Frente was an existential process, and not just a political commitment, but also that one's experience could be important politically as well as personally.

From such considerations there derived Seregni's double emphasis on unity and dialogue. In December 1971, during the Frente's period of self-assessment after the national elections, under the heading 'Toward a Unity in Dialogue', he said that unity was a 'difficult daily task' that could easily fail without 'discretion, a good touch [and] mutual understanding':

> Unity implies mutual confidence, mutual loyalty [...] The Frente is unity in dialogue, and in dialogue there is criticism [...] criticism implies certain disagreements [...] they must be disagreements among comrades, with the duty to loyalty and truth there is among comrades. (*Autoridad*, 22–3)

Barely concealed here was the plea not to let post-electoral blues push them back to the squabbles of yesteryear which so much effort had been put into overcoming. Six months earlier, he had stated that only if there were 'real communication at all levels' within the Frente, could it be a 'fruitful experience' for itself and Uruguay as a whole (*Autoridad*, 70). Moreover, this process should penetrate right into the heart of the electorate, so that what Seregni did in his relations with party delegates might be repeated by party workers with all the Frente's potential supporters and members. As he put it in May 1972, to 'insert' themselves among the people, they had to understand the real problems the people around them actually had (*Autoridad*, 66). This merely returned the Frente to its origins since it only existed because, during the Independents' preparatory work in 1970, they had known how to 'interpret' a 'demand', a 'feeling', an 'urgency' they sensed in the people they met (*Autoridad*, 20).[23]

It was this notion of dialogue as an 'an exchange of ideas' and a 'decanting of each individual's experience' (*Autoridad*, 69) that would ideally embrace the entire population, a technique that, in Seregni's view, set the Frente off sharply from the prevailing political climate:

> The president-candidate[24] offers us the guarantee that he will not allow any phrase that displeases him.[25] He offers us order: the order of silence. He offers us freedom: the freedom to shut our mouths. He offers us dialogue: the dialogue faced with repression and the gag. (*Autoridad*, 85)

For Seregni there could never be any excuse for censorship or state violence against the populace. Even in April 1972, at the height of the military campaign against the guerrillas, he noted a constant in all the many rebellions throughout Uruguay's history since independence: the powers that be 'have dialogued with the insurrection' (*Una línea*, 47). He then proposed the opening of discussions between the government and the Tupamaros, but not just talking for appearances' sake. Seregni had in mind a dialogue aimed at moving towards authentic pacification (that is, involving real social justice), not a phoney one 'on paper or in cemeteries' (*Una línea*, 49).

Similarly, in the crisis of February 1973, when the military announced their political agenda in a set of communiqués and when parliament, belatedly waking up to the dangers, weakly began attempts to head off the coup which looked ever more likely, the Frente demanded President Bordaberry's resignation because of his government's connivance in the by now all but overt transfer of civil powers to the military authorities. On February 9, Seregni said that his demise was necessary to re-establish a dialogue that would make viable a 'fertile interaction between people, government and Armed Forces' (*Una línea*, 107). According to an interview at the time, he even hoped to find in the vice-president who would replace Bordaberry 'an adversary who was also an interlocutor'.[26]

Such moves would be too little, too late, however. The military's course was set. When the people's elected representatives did finally dig their heels in, if only to protect themselves, by rejecting the armed forces' demand for the lifting of Senator Enrique Erro's parliamentary immunity, they gave the military the excuse they needed to dissolve parliament. It is, nonetheless, consistent with Seregni's desire to share his thoughts with the electorate at all times (and, of course, to justify the Frente's attitude toward the armed forces, which some found far too moderate) that, in another February 1973 speech at the outset of this final stage in the political crisis, he should say:

> I have spoken my thoughts up front, out loud, in public, as one should at difficult moments. Because it is precisely at difficult moments that all citizens have the right to know and participate in whatever is going on, as it is their destiny, above all, that is at stake. (*Una línea*, 112)

Seregni's view of the nation as a community of people joined together in productive dialogue informed his September 1971 description of the Frente's aims: Uruguay should be 'the setting for a harmonious living-together [convivencia harmónica]' (*Autoridad*, 28–9), recalling Seregni's Batllista origins.[27] This translated politically into one paramount imperative, which he voiced in 1972: 'Consult [consúltese]' (repeated four times) so that the people could participate and make their own decisions (*Una línea*, 96). But Seregni's whole conception of the Frente Amplio is perhaps best summed up in a remark made on 19 June 1973 (just one week before the final dissolution of parliament) to the effect that the Frente's rank and file committees (of which more below) should be 'home for the Frente Amplio family, a school for understanding and self-criticism' (*Una línea*, 147), while militants' own families responded by becoming important sites for transmitting the Frente's ideas.[28]

Participation, Cooperation, Equality: the Frente Amplio's Internal Structure and Political Platform

A good indicator of any institution's organisational framework is often the way it arranges its own finances. One glance at the Frente's plan for raising and distributing funds shows the complexity (and potential pitfalls) of establishing an organisation which was both an amalgamation around a coherent common program of well differentiated entities, as well as a mass political party which encouraged maximum participation by all individuals and groups.

An April 1971 statement indicated that initial funding was to be raised by the issue of vouchers in two separate series. In the first case, the money raised was to be shared between head office and the rank and file commit-tees. The second series was to be issued in the name of the coalition's political groups themselves, most of the money being retained by the groups involved.[29] It is immediately clear that the Frente's structure depended on maintaining an extremely delicate balance between two axes: one extending vertically from the national executive in Montevideo down to the smallest rank and file unit in some far-flung hamlet in the interior; the other linking horizontally the groups that made up the coalition. The task of this dual structure was to put Seregni's dialogic principles into practice.

The organisation's regulations, approved by 15 groups on 16 March 1971, established a three-tier structure within the party. The first was that of the rank and file committees [comités de base]; the second at an inter-mediate level for co-ordination; the third being that of the Executive and National Plenary Committee at party headquarters in Montevideo. The document devoted most space to the first and third of these, since they do the essential grassroots and top-level party organisation work, respectively; the second had the crucial but probably thankless, and potentially horren-dous, task of liaising between the other two, largely at provincial level.[30]

One later sympathetic commentator saw the 'comités de base' as a novel political method of involving hundreds of thousands of people, many of them too young to vote themselves, who carried away from the experience a lively sense of democracy at work.[31] Much later, Rosencof agrees, describing them as 'hotbeds of ideology and militancy',[32] which can be read positively in line with Seregni's view of these committees. As suggested in the quotation closing the previous section of this chapter, he wanted them to be the 'Frente's meeting place', where all militants could 'deliberate, participate, share their opinions, discuss and organise' (*Autoridad*, 70). Set up in the wake of the popular support aroused by the Frente from its incep-tion and gathered in 'neighbourhood committees', the rank and file committees were intended to be the total antithesis of the traditional parties' neighbourhood political clubs, of which by 1966 there were an estimated 8000 in Montevideo alone, and which many saw as having largely become little more than corrupt agencies for exchanging welfare for votes.[33] The Frente had nothing to offer in this regard, and set up its committees in a way more in keeping with the political club's original objectives. Its committees relayed the party's propaganda outwards to its supporters and workers, recruited new members and also made recommendations and suggestions to the central office in Montevideo. The danger, as left open by Rosencof's description, was that the rank and file committees might become sites of perpetual, unproductive ideological squabbling or, worse, intimidation.

If the rank and file committees, by way of the coordinating bodies, were organised along the Frente's vertical axis, the national Plenary and Executive committees followed the horizontal line in its overall structure. The Plenary was the Frente's most important body: it formulated and modified its policies and internal organisation, selected its candidates and decided on the inclusion or exclusion of groups within the coalition. It was constituted on the delegate system, each group's representation being determined according to the size of the membership (and, perhaps, electoral influence) it brought to the Frente. Such a distribution clearly prevented either the far left or the leadership from being able easily to dominate Plenary meetings, while ensuring that on most issues the committee's likely gravitation would be towards the centre rather than the left.

The aim of the Plenary's deliberations was consensus: all methods of securing 'unanimous agreement' having to be 'exhausted' on all but merely procedural matters,[34] unanimity being obligatory on policy issues, and a complicated process being laid down to achieve it. Everything was done to prevent the marginalisation of smaller groups and the automatic predominance of the more powerful ones, perhaps even at the expense of efficiency, while the Executive only served to implement the Plenary's decisions and oversee the Frente's accounts.[35]

The double axis of the Frente's organisation was mirrored in the theme of unity within diversity which permeates the 'Political Accord' signed by the then twenty member groups on 9 February 1972, virtually on the first anniversary of the coalition's constitutive assembly. Here unity first came expressed as the acceptance by all groups and their members of the Frente's constitution, program and internal structure. However, the document then devoted most space to the need to base the party's political activities on the 'reciprocal solidarity' among the forces that made up the Frente.[36]

In sum, the Frente's internal organisation reflected what Seregni, in his recollections many years afterwards, called the Frente's 'so much discussed double character' of being both a coalition of political groups and a mass movement.[37] Its status as a unified party was symbolised in its offering of a single, unanimously agreed national election ticket for president and vice-president,[38] as well as single candidates for mayor in Montevideo and major provincial centres. Only in the Senate and Chamber of Deputies at the national level and for lesser positions elsewhere could the Frente's various groups put up their own preferred candidates.[39] In this sense, despite being an alliance which bent over backwards to ensure representation of its member organisations at all levels, the Frente could advertise a greater degree of unity than pertained elsewhere.[40]

In the other direction, as Castro went on to explain, the Frente sought to establish 'dialogue, direct communication, exchange of ideas and public discussion' – almost recalling Nardone's open rural councils – as the line of contact between potential supporters or electorate and militants and party leaders.[41] And, as made clear in the final paragraph of the Frente's first thirty government measures, agreed on 25 August 1971, it was this open, democratic structure which was to guarantee the content and implementation of the party's policies: the rank and file committees should ensure fulfilment of the program and exercise control over those responsible for implementing it.[42]

Oscar Bruschera recalled that one of the Frente's aims was consistency between the democratic nature of its internal structures and that of its political platform.[43] Indeed, the party's programme,[44] passed on 17 February 1971, translated Seregni's commitment to the principle of free dialogue between equals into giving pride of place in its first two sections to the liberty of the country's citizens and to Uruguay's ability to act as a genuinely independent agent in its foreign affairs. It opened by guaranteeing the rights of individuals, trade unions and political parties and groups, the autonomy of all educational institutions, and the complete independence of the judiciary, and goes on to call for an amnesty to reintegrate into society all those barred from it for political reasons.

This free association of individuals and organisations within the nation's boundaries was then mirrored in the program's view of Uruguay's dealings with other countries. Attaching the principles of self-determination and non-intervention to its notion of national sovereignty, the program calls for a completely independent foreign policy that would promote Latin American integration and solidarity with all peoples, especially within Latin America, engaged in national liberation struggles. Like the Congreso del Pueblo, the Frente sought an independent and nationalist foreign economic policy not at the beck and call of overseas financiers or the International Monetary Fund, and advocated the nationalisation of the banking sector.

The thrust of the idea of unity obtained through the maximum participation of many diverse contributors, already noted as the principal feature of the Frente's internal organisation, was underlined in its intended social, economic and political reforms. So, as in the earlier Congreso del Pueblo proposals, the Frente envisioned planning the economy in the national interest and carefully overseeing even those sectors not brought under total state control. It called for representation from unions, producers, technicians, government and the University on the body overseeing the process. Similarly, it would seek worker and popular participation in the management of all state agencies, as well as in the whole process of industrial reform and the formation of a wages and prices policy, and would give teachers a major role in the democratisation of all levels of education. In fact, the document made a special point of promoting cooperativism in all spheres of the economy and promises to set up mechanisms to ensure the defence of the progressive nature of the system.[45]

For the individual, the program promises a reform of the tax system similar to the one advanced in the Congreso del Pueblo document, moving taxes from services and consumer goods to high incomes, accumulated wealth, unproductive capital and property, and to what were primly termed 'social vices'. The aim behind the wages policy would be equal pay for equal work with cost of living adjustments, while the social welfare provisions (now adding the Congreso's provisions to the PDC's principles) would be designed to guarantee individuals the 'well-being and security [tranquilidad]' necessary for their full development as human beings, taking in their whole life cycle 'from conception to death',[46] again reviving the Batllista idea of the state as permanent nurturer and home. When five months later the Frente published what it promised as its first thirty measures once in government, it felt obliged to add to a summary of its program an objective not touched on before: measures designed to redistribute income and generally improve conditions for the 'dispossessed' and unemployed were an effective way to 'pacify' the country by attacking the 'socio-economic causes of violence'.[47] This provision clearly reflected increasing social and political tensions as the elections got nearer and implied that the Frente had the answers to them, but can also be read as an attempt by the Frente to distance itself from the armed struggle option represented by the Tupamaros, with whom government propaganda insistently tried to associate it.

On the political front, the program reaffirmed the Frente's commitment to a pluralist democracy, foreshadowing reforms to the electoral law and the regulations governing political parties to make both more responsive to electors' wishes, and promising wider popular participation through greater use of plebiscites and referendums. It advocated the strengthening and democratising of local and municipal government bodies and the implementation of controls to ensure that no public office could be used for furthering its incumbent's private interests, a provision repeated in the regulations governing its own organisation. Unlike the Congreso del Pueblo's resolutions, to acknowledge the change in the tenor of the times since 1965, the Frente's program ended with some essential if brief references to the role of the armed forces. It proposed to enhance the military's nationalism by invigorating the continuity with the tradition established by Artigas.[48] This reference is crucial, since the left in general and the Frente in particular actively promoted an image of the national hero as a supporter of regional integration, a defender of popular democracy and the leader of a people's army, as the numerous mentions of his name and quotations from his writings in Seregni's speeches confirm. One should remember here that the Frente adopted the Artigas banner as its own and celebrated its first public rally on the 26 March 1971, the anniversary of the day in 1811 when that flag was first raised in Montevideo. Indeed, some effort was made to posit Seregni himself as the bearer of the Artigas myth.[49] Since all political parties called on aspects of the national hero, the aim here was to assert the Frente as an equal player in the electoral stakes, as well as to mark out a different position by laying claim to a more radical side of his legacy.

Although there was no official trade union representation as such in the Frente's structure (as distinct from the role played by trade unionists as individuals or followers of member left-wing political organisations), its political platform, as we have seen, borrowed heavily from the final statement issued by the 1965 Congreso del Pueblo, to which the unions had made a decisive contribution. One major feature it inherited was its rejection of such marked terms as 'revolution' and 'socialism', just as the coalition's name – Broad Front – studiously avoided any overt association with words such as 'left' or 'popular'. While this reflected the attempt to widen the electoral appeal from the traditional left to the liberal, democratic centre, it left open how radically or mildly reformist the program actually was.[50]

Time seems to have clarified this issue. Bruschera, explaining that the program was not radically left-wing or socialist because of opposition from more than a few of the Frente's members,[51] he went on to describe it as salvaging the most progressive aspects of Batllismo and the anti-imperialism of the conservative 1950s National Party leader Herrera, and adding them on to the thinking of a de-utopianised, non-olympian left.[52] Germán Rama, noting the absence of the rhetoric of class struggle and its substitution by a humane sense of solidarity, concluded likewise that the program was not radically new but defended past social advances then projected into the future, a view repeated by Trigo.[53] More recently still, Garcé and Yaffé have drawn attention to its strong emphasis on decentralisation and participation.[54] It also contained elements of the democratic socialism and Latin American integration that Carlos Quijano had been advocating for decades in his *Marcha* editorials.

This assessment of the program as looking to the future while, Janus-like, having its eyes firmly fixed on the past is not unjustified. Its essential thrust was redistributive, economically and politically. The Frente sought both greater access by the people to the benefits derived from exploiting the country's resources as well as greater popular participation in making the decisions about what was to be produced, how and by whom. In other words, it looked to strengthen and broaden the influence and relevance of existing institutions, not to overthrow them and start afresh with others, becoming a fitting if elusive legitimiser of the system.[55] While obviously hoping to appeal to the electoral middle ground, this fundamental characteristic of the Frente's platform may owe its existence not only to the Congreso del Pueblo's resolutions and to Juan Pablo Terra's nine points for discussion from 1969, but to an authoritative source which may lie behind them all, but which is certainly not frequently associated with the Frente's proposals.

In 1960, the National Party government founded the Comisión de Inversiones y Desarrollo Económico [CIDE], which over the next few years produced two major reports whose recommendations seem to have been largely ignored by succceeding administrations during the decade. The first appeared in 1963 and was a multi-volume exercise in data gathering about the Uruguayan economy. Two years later, building on their preliminary fact-finding effort, CIDE published the results of what its title reveals as a much more ambitious and forward-looking venture: *Plan nacional de desarrollo económico y social*. Shortly afterwards, the director of the CIDE team, the prominent young economist Enrique Iglesias, put out as a separate volume the summary of the second report he had written originally as a guide to it.[56]

Iglesias listed the rights he felt all Uruguayans should have and which the Plan looked to secure: the right to a job; to work their own land; to have access to decent housing, education, health care and to a full social security system; to participate in the management of the country's economy; and for all inhabitants to have equal access to all resources and opportunities – all of which adds up to a near résumé of the Frente's platform. Iglesias wanted the Plan to be a vehicle for change that would clearly reveal the contradictions of the current structures and the benefits to be derived from renewing them. Singled out as requiring immediate attention were problems in the areas of natural resources, public savings, the administration of state enterprises, the funding of social services, the management of overseas trade, housing, productivity, and the participation of labour and management in running the country's economy.[57]

Iglesias both anticipated and even exceeded Seregni's faith in dialogue and consensus as the means to achieve the Plan's aims, appealing implicitly to exactly the notion of dialogue within the nation and the threats to it that have formed the backbone of this thesis. Pointing out that Uruguay's situation in the mid-1960s presented a special challenge to the community's leaders, Iglesias went on to urge them to exploit the nation's 'great powers of communication' to get it out of the doldrums. Iglesias advocated a 'Social

Accord' to be worked out with equal representation by all players involved in any sphere of economic activity, so that any sacrifices could be shared around, since failure to do this would jeopardise the entire Plan. The Plan was, therefore, perhaps more trusting than the Frente's platform, which, while retaining a state-regulated private sector, proposed wholesale nation-alisations to ensure public control of the economy, as did the Congreso del Pueblo statement. However, Iglesias's Plan contained a crucial proviso: no violence was to be done to the average Uruguayan's sense of well-being and need for security. Here, the conservatism of the average Uruguayan was accepted and affirmed, with a strong resulting sense that the aim of the proposals was to recover gains made earlier but now lost or under threat, rather than to dismantle the entire social edifice and replace it with one less vulnerable to the vicissitudes that had plunged this one into violence, poverty and chaos.[58]

To some extent, then, all three projects for social reform (the Iglesias Plan, the Congreso del Pueblo statement and the Frente Amplio program) can be seen to display what might be called a nostalgia for the future, a product of what one writer has seen as the dominant characteristic of the Uruguayan populace at the time: 'a peculiar mixture of utopian expectation and conservative conformity'.[59] It is now time to see how the most recent of those proposals, complete with its endeavour to re-establish dialogue within the body politic, was received by those whom it sought to address.

The Right of Reply: Responses to the Frente Amplio

The 1971 national elections were a sad blend of farce and fraud. They were farcical (as far as most reasonable definitions of democracy are concerned, that is) in that they took place while a state of emergency and press censor-ship were in force; while right-wing terrorist attacks on workers, candidates and premises of the Frente or its member organisations were carried out almost with impunity, including one assassination attempt against Seregni himself;[60] and while the electoral laws prevented the Frente using its own name on the voting papers, forcing them to adopt the 'permanent' title of one of the parties making up the coalition, the PDC (rather than the other possibilities, all tainted by their long association with the traditional left).[61]

Accusations of fraud were rife during the two and a half months it took the electoral commission to release the results. They have multiplied since and it is now all but taken for granted that the government manipulated the ballot.[62] And not without reason. Franco gives instances where it is clear that the electoral rolls had not been vetted to take out the names of those who had died (or, I would add, migrated)[63] and points to elementary arithmetical inconsistencies in the published figures which show that in some electoral divisions the number of votes cast exceeded the number of people eligible to vote, while in others the sum of the votes allotted to candidates differed from the total number of votes recorded as valid, and so on.[64] Other sources would indicate several cases of tampering with sealed ballot boxes and potentially numerous instances of the double counting of votes,[65] while Moreira has noted a further anomaly: for the only time in Uruguayan electoral history, the party which won most of the municipal elections (in 1971, the Nationals) failed to win the presidency.[66]

None of the serious complaints were answered and there has been no subsequent official comment on the figures, so everyone was stuck with the final result as published. This gave victory to the incumbent Colorado Party over the Nationals by a margin of just under 13,000 votes out of a national total of nearly 1,665,000, or less than one percent. The governing faction of the Colorados retained power but under the fall-back formula headed by Bordaberry, since the constitutional change required to allow Pacheco to be re-elected was not passed. However, by far the most solidly supported of the presidential candidates was the National Party's reformist candidate Wilson Ferreira.

The Frente Amplio's performance in its first national poll was, at best, promising. It received just over 18 percent of the vote country-wide, but managed 29 percent in the capital where its candidate for the position of mayor was the most favoured by the electorate but the accumulation of votes within each party allowed the Colorado candidate to beat him into second place. In the 30-seat Senate the Frente had five candidates elected,[67] while in the lower house of 99 members, the Frente had 18 deputies,[68] of whom four were from FIDEL (which included the Communists), seven from the PDC, five from the Unión Popular, while the Socialists and Independents provided one each.[69] However, only five of them were elected in the interior, the remainder all coming from Montevideo.[70]

This hints at one of the Frente's major difficulties in the election: its message had not got through to the electorate out in the rural areas. In some ways, this is hardly surprising, since political allegiances in the countryside are traditionally often intimately bound up with personal and family ties and with the relationship between employer and worker. However, according to some of the delegates at the congress of the Frente's rank and file committees a few weeks after the election, country folk were not necessarily resistant to the Frente's policies. Rather, there had been a lack of experienced party workers who knew how to talk to them in their own way, and of propaganda material they could understand.[71]

The problem of the interior was only one of several points listed by Arismendi in his analysis of the Frente's performance for the Communist Party Central Committee,[72] but it is closely linked to another: the fact that the Frente had only existed for nine months. This is, indeed, a very short time in which to get a new party up and running smoothly and to fight a hard election campaign in adverse circumstances, and especially so when its policies were more radically reformist than any the electorate was used to hearing and when the party's structure was something of an experiment. While the Frente could use the networks already created by some of its member groups and their ties through the trade unions, this was not going to help break the stranglehold the major parties had had for about a century on the rest of the population in a country where political loyalties were something one was born with.[73]

The Frente's limited success in accomplishing this latter task may have been advanced rather than hindered by what Arismendi identified as another problem: the acts of repression mounted against organisations, publications and individuals on the left generally, and the vicious, hysterical propaganda from the State and most of the mass media which accompanied them. However, others have argued that the targeting of the Frente by the repressive forces actually enhanced its legitimacy and authority in the eyes of the public, giving its supporters and workers the chance to be seen as heroes leading the fight against the government's dirty war tactics.[74] It must remain a moot point, however, whether this would have compensated for the practical difficulties created by the constant attacks on the Frente's property and personnel.

The other major problem mentioned by Arismendi, and referred to by others since, was the presence in the National Party of the reformist faction led by Ferreira Aldunate. His influence almost certainly prevented a mass defection of more progressive National Party voters (as happened in the Colorado Party, whose share of the vote dropped by nearly 10 percent compared to the 1966 results, whereas the Nationals retained theirs). On the other hand, any potential Frente voter, alarmed by government claims that the coalition was Communist-controlled, had available an apparently reform-minded alternative which might have an even better chance of winning because it was under the umbrella of one of the traditional parties. The existence of both options certainly seems to have split the forces opposed to the Pacheco regime. For, if the results for the Frente, Ferreira and the anti-government factions within the Colorado party were added together, the total was an impressive 63 percent of the electorate.[75] Arismendi even suggested that many of those who took part in the Frente's demonstrations and rallies ended up voting for Ferreira,[76] thereby repeating a phenomenon noted earlier in our discussion of trade unions: centre-left sympathisers were prepared to go with a more radical alternative on particular issues but stepped back from this position when asked to translate it into a vote for dramatic change at a more general social and political level.

Arismendi's last point bears on one of the decisive miscalculations made by many of the Frente's supporters during the campaign. First noted by

Castro within days of the poll,[77] Seregni incorporated it into his own assessment of the Frente's election showing in the middle of the following year, admitting that most of the Frente's voters were also activists, whereas the traditional parties had a large passive following.[78] Indeed, Rama's later breakdown of those who voted for the Frente as being of the salaried and professional middle class, the traditional leftist sectors of the urban working class or some of those who supported the progressive wings of the major parties, and as being politically active, among the better educated, predominantly young and living in Montevideo,[79] reads suspiciously like a profile of party workers or of the up to 200,000 people they could bring out on to the streets.[80] This confusion between 'mobilising capacity' and 'electoral capacity' led both supporters and opponents to think that the Frente had at a stroke solved all the problems mentioned by Arismendi and was likely to sweep the board.[81]

They were wrong. The new organisation had not worked quite that well. The rank and file committees, it was argued, became more like centres for debating political arguments than agencies for attracting the unconverted,[82] an opinion not uniformly held, however. Some delegates to the special congress of these committees held three weeks after the poll had hoped for more political discussion than actually took place. Others blamed the overly intellectual content of the Frente's election material, the failure of the central office to publicise the program widely enough or to provide enough campaign orientation, while a few still had the ghost of sectarianism hovering over their committees and threatening their unity.[83] Seregni himself saw 'double militancy', any individual's loyalties divided between the Frente and the party of origin, as the Frente's major internal problem.[84] There was more agreement on another issue: that the communication channels between rank and file and the Montevideo office had not functioned as they were supposed to, resulting in a lack of direction and feelings of being ignored.[85] Bruschera was to feel later that both the juggling between member groups and the composition of the committees had hampered the Frente's ability reach the quick decisions events often required.[86]

There is considerable uniformity among the overall judgments on the Frente's early days. In March 1971, Bruschera had begun his summary of the party's platform with a thumbnail sketch of the interpretation of Uruguayan society that underpinned it: 'The choice is clear: either the oligarchy liquidates the Uruguayan people, or the Uruguayan people liquidate the oligarchy',[87] a view maintained by Seregni at least up to February 1973.[88] Panizza has since shown to what extent the 'us' versus 'them' mentality permeated the rhetoric of all the major political players of the time.[89] Varela argues that one view of the Frente's 19 percent rating in the election is that 81 percent of the population disagreed that their enemy was the oligarchy,[90] but it may simply be that they were too cowed by the violent turn of events to think past their usual loyalty to what was familiar. Having had more than enough time to think about the matter, Bruschera later recognised his and the Frente's error, quoting Carlos Quijano in an October 1972 editorial to the effect that it was wrong to see only one real confrontation: that between people and oligarchy. As important as that was, the immediate issue was to ensure that 'military authority did not take over from civil authority'.[91] In other words, the Frente was attempting to reform the politics of a society at a time when the real danger was that any or all of the country's political arrangements might be stood aside. It was, as it were, attempting to revive a much more urgent version of *tercerismo*, the controversial 'Third Way' alternative to the Cold War dualism we saw debated in the previous chapter, in a context that would rapidly make it redundant.[92]

In a process that accelerated once the elections were over, the Frente – and gradually all opposition political forces and, eventually, even the crudely elected government itself – were left stranded, first between two military solutions (the Tupamaros and the Armed Forces),[93] and then by the second as it translated its military victory into a progressive militarisation of the state, a stage set as early as 1968 when Pacheco had first called in the army to break strikes in the finance and public sectors. This increasing polarisation allowed the Frente's program to be perceived as dangerously revolutionary by conservatives and as a signal for change by its supporters, and gave the reactionary press the chance to project the elections as a choice between 'a new Cuba' and 'a regressive authoritarianism', as any middle ground disappeared between two extremes.[94] As Quijano had already seen in 1972, the class struggle or the confrontation between people and oligarchy had been replaced in importance by the rupture between civil and political society. Few appreciated the danger in time, and armed polarisation led to a total dissociation between the state (identified after June 1973 with the military in a process that began well before then) and society,[95] or to what Rama terms a separation between state and nation.[96] As a more recent writer has it: 'Caught between insurgent and counter-insurgent violence, the Uruguayan state and society were tested to their limits', both straddled between the possibility of radical change and 'the barrier of tradition which validated the rhetoric about an idealised past and happy future'. She continues: 'These two utopias – the tomorrow-as-yesterday and the yesterday-as-tomorrow – did not generate a new one capable of mobilising the citizenry for change'.[97] There seems little reason to disagree with any of these commentators.

Such a scenario does, however, show Seregni's (and the Frente's) emphasis on new forms of dialogue and participation in a special light, as they can now be seen as a means whereby the Frente could have become the vehicle to bring about the reintegration of a society whose fabric was coming apart. In this sense, the Frente was, I would argue, the culmination of all the attempts by intellectuals to address the issue of the nation as a problem and of their search for an answer to Juan Flo's 1952 question about what it was thinking young people were to do in and about Uruguay, and to Solari's later despair about the Uruguayan left ever being able to come up with a realistic alternative it could offer the population at large. Had the project been fully realised, one consequence could well have been the prevention of the social and political breakdown underlined by Rama and Varela. Obviously, the program enjoyed – perhaps could only have enjoyed – limited success. Nonetheless, it is easy to see its attraction for intellectuals long concerned about the state of the nation, and Bruschera is right to count their support among the Frente's achievements,[98] since it provided a bridge for them to rejoin the political mainstream for the first time in nearly forty years.

The parlous, fragile nature of the Frente's endeavour and its ambiguous relation to the forces that in the end overwhelmed it are illustrated by the position of one left intellectual, Mario Benedetti. As mentioned in the opening to the previous chapter, he had been one of the nearly 170 writers, journalists and other cultural workers who had signed the statement published in *Marcha* a day or two before the 1971 elections urging people to vote for the Frente. At the same time, however, Benedetti had been since early in the same year one of the leaders of the 'Movimiento de Independientes 26 de Marzo', a radical left movement which had joined the Frente Amplio but was, in fact, the legal political face of the Tupamaros guerrillas. Although they declared a truce for the length of the election campaign, they diluted their tepid welcome to the Frente with a statement that emphasised their conviction that electoral democracy could no longer bring the transformation of Uruguayan society they advocated.[99]

For the Tupamaros, the opposition between two forces was not rhetorical but literally a war they were prepared to fight: 'the people/oligarchy contradiction' was the local expression of the struggle between 'imperialism and the underdeveloped countries'.[100] In July 1971, the Movimiento 26 de Marzo turned this into two 'sides': 'the oligarchy and the bankers', united with the landowners under 'Pacheco's dictatorship', who have stolen 'our' Uruguay which must now be 'rescued' by 'the combatant people united' in the Frente Amplio, the 'trench' where the people must 'fight' to 'take our nation back form the oligarchy and landowners'.[101] While Benedetti was undoubtedly involved in writing such statements, nearly identical examples appear concurrently in his own political essays: 'the confrontation is not between two barely distinguishable emblems [ie. the National and Colorado parties] but plainly and simply between the people and the oligarchy',[102] and 'the oligarchy's enemy is now and always was the people'.[103] Benedetti's propagandist writing advocated a violent confrontation that threatened to make all intellectual work impossible or irrelevant, while the Frente Amplio found itself including under its unifying umbrella groups whose relationship with democratic politics was as ambiguous as Benedetti's own. The contradictions in Benedetti's position as an intellectual on the left and the strains and difficulties evident in the Frente's attempt to install the notion of dialogue in the centre of its practice and political program illustrate the debilitating effects of the polarised situation to be exploited by the security forces and the military between the elections of November 1971 and the coup in June 1973.

The conditions that brought the Frente Amplio forth could hardly have been more adverse, yet its methods of responding to them, which must include not only its political platform but also the profoundly democratic procedures embodied in its structure, clearly differentiated it, at least potentially, from the two traditional parties. These were seen by the intelligentsia, if not in the end by the public at large, as hopelessly implicated in the crisis enveloping the country. What is more, the Frente seemed to offer intellectuals a specific role: the principle of dialogue exemplified in its political vision and way of working exactly mirrored the relationship a dissident intelligentsia had been trying to have with its public for years. Unfortunately, this opportunity came too late: the space required by the Frente's and the intellectuals' need for dialogue with their public disappeared, itself implicated in an increased militarisation of society that had escaped any party's political control.

There was one thing, however, that nobody at the time had any doubts about. Neither the Benedetti who signed the statement of support for the Frente nor the Benedetti who led the Movimiento 26 de Marzo and compiled his weekly propaganda missive to accompany it, neither Carlos Real de Azúa, Angel Rama, Carlos Martínez Moreno and others who wrote their academically respectable analyses of Uruguay in the hope of influencing the populace in the early 1970s, nor any of those who had written about the fate of the left over the previous decade or had had even a minute input into the Congreso del Pueblo's final resolutions, nor any of the authors of the often high quality imaginative literature of the period – no-one anywhere among the Uruguayan intelligentsia of the time seems to have entertained even the vaguest suspicion that what they did might not matter, might not influence someone, might – in short – be useless. Underpinning all involvement in the Uruguayan left project and all the writing that in any form accompanied it, was the unspoken modernist assumption that intellectual and artistic work, however defined and practised, made a difference, counted for something important. What nobody foresaw was that, when they emerged after the dictatorship in 1985, intellectuals would have to begin learning how to work in an environment where that long-held, unquestioned foundation could no longer be taken for granted.

INTERLUDE

The Armed Forces and Failure

. . . intransigently dogmatic, blind and immutable convictions affirmed in the faith of the enlightened who believe they hold in their hands all reason and truth and who automatically ignore and deny everyone else.

Uruguayan Armed Forces General Command (1976)

When the Uruguayan military dissolved parliament on 27 June 1973, they put the finishing touch to a process begun well before that date.[1] Among the first measures instituted by President Jorge Pacheco when he assumed office in December 1967 were the de-legalisation of some left-wing groups and the closure of some radical press outlets. He went on to govern increasingly by executive decree in an all but permanent and constantly renewed state of emergency (thus bypassing an increasingly wary but ineffective parliament), oversaw the 'militarisation' of service sectors such as banking which were deemed essential, and in September 1971 – just two months before the crucial national elections – asked the military to take charge of internal security matters. One possible measure of Pacheco's presidency, Myers informs us ruefully, was that, when he took office, administration of the nation's prison system was in the hands of the Ministry of Education and Culture, but when he left in March 1972, it was under the Ministry of Defence.[2]

From that time, the presidency of Juan Bordaberry, whose complicity with the armed forces was underlined by his becoming after June 1973 the first non-military nominal head of what was for most of its twelve years formally a combined civilian and military regime, witnessed the increasing persecution of all forces associated with the left, especially the Tupamaros until their military defeat by September 1972, but also the union movement, the more radical parties within the Frente Amplio and, eventually, all political parties and their members or representatives who did not make clear their allegiance to the military's aims. The armed forces would turn out to distrust democracy Uruguayan-style and the political elite quite as much as the guerrillas they claimed to be fighting. Their communiqués of February 1973, optimistically seen as progressive in some quarters, were the first public demonstration of their clear determination to override any civilian authority that stood in their way, intentions graphically illustrated by the tanks surrounding the legislature on 27 June.

After an initial period of establishing itself (characterised by the brutal shutdown of all opposition, actual or potential, accompanied where necessary by the substitution of military personnel or civilian supporters,[3] exemplarily at all levels of education), the dictatorship set about consolidating itself around an account of what the Armed Forces salvaged as essential from Uruguayan history and tradition, reorganised to place themselves prominently as its guardians. This project would fail for three successive, powerful reasons, the cumulative weight of which would drive the military, after much internal debate, to begin discussions with the political parties that issued in a negotiated transition back to formal democracy. There would be national elections in October 1984, with the first post-authoritarian civilian government taking office on 1 March 1985.

Chronologically the first of the events that eventually defeated the armed forces was the withdrawal of military aid by the United States in 1978. While important in itself, this also signaled the success of the campaign against human rights abuses in Uruguay waged in international peace and justice tribunals and United Nations organisations largely by those whom the economic crisis had obliged to migrate or the military had forced into exile,[4] and the corresponding total failure of the military's propaganda aimed at countering it. The second major setback for the armed forces was the clear defeat in the 1980 plebiscite of their attempt to cement themselves into Uruguay's constitutional arrangements. Not only did this mean that the military had badly overreached themselves and misjudged the electorate. It also suggested that unexpressed subterranean opposition circulated freely at levels the military's system of censorship and repression was ill equipped to penetrate and which the massively biased 'yes' campaign failed to reach or convince.[5] This word-of-mouth resistance, the only one possible under total censorship, manifested itself again in the traditional party internal elections permitted in 1982, and would go on to generate the participatory sense that became the social movements[6] that helped to both stem the tide of neoliberalism under the Colorado and National party governments in the 1990s and transform the way the post-authoritarian left reviewed its approach to institutional democracy. Such expressions of civilian discontent were exacerbated by a serious economic downturn in 1981–3, which suggested that the intermittent economic successes of the previous decade were not stable,[7] although the military's market-driven economics, however inconsistently applied by them, would be the model even more rigorously followed by the first post-dictatorship administrations.

These three reverses meant that across the years around 1980 the military lost considerable ground and credibility as national political and economic managers, and as honourable members of the international community. This combination allowed the defeat of the hardliners within the armed forces, enabling the more constitutionally mindful among them at least to begin negotiations about the return to democracy largely on the military's own terms, a factor that would influence the kind of democracy Uruguay recovered, especially as regards such sensitive matters as impunity for human rights violations.

It may seem at best uncharitable to refer to this twelve-year period as merely an 'interlude' when it undoubtedly was nothing of the kind for all those who were imprisoned, tortured, banished or, of course, killed, or for the majority who suffered only the everyday indignities and deprivations of dismissal from work, impoverishment, constant intrusion and surveillance, and petty self-righteous officiousness. Yet, I agree with Achugar that, in the end, the dictatorship was a 'parenthesis' in that it only delayed the transformation of Uruguay's political and cultural life already clearly begun in the late 1960s, but which would have to be restarted in 1985,[8] which also explains how De Armas and Garcé could write a whole study of the links between the critique of the state of Uruguay and its institutions in the 1950s and '60s and that mounted more recently since the 1980s without mentioning the dictatorship once.[9] During this 'interlude', having suppressed or suspended just about all manifestations of intellectual and artistic life that were not frivolous or acquiescent (at least up to about 1981), the military effectively became their own organic intellectuals. It was as such that they produced a gargantuan two-volume account of their motives and actions in the unremittingly dense, monochromatic prose of a battlefield report,[10] modeled on the doctrine of national security promoted in United States military training centres and widely practiced throughout the Southern Cone.[11]

It began with a guiding metaphor, the nation as living organism, and posited the Uruguay of the time as the near-perfect body politic, an idealisation of Batllista principles: 'a homogeneous, peaceful free society', with deep-rooted republican ideals and practices but without racial tension or major class differences, in which all levels of education and health care, an almost too generous social welfare system, and all individual freedoms were provided by the state and guaranteed by the constitution. The danger was that these 'pure [limpias] traditions' might be 'stained' by the 'epidemic' of anti-Western, anti-Catholic Marxism being unleashed on the world from the alien East, which would then become 'the Uruguayan nation's sickness'.[12] Consequently, the 'gravest threat against the body of the Nation' was the 'foreign ideologies' out to ensure 'the total destruction of what currently exists'. These alien germs or microbes (or self-reproducing cancerous cells, perhaps) were the 'tiny groups of angry, resentful delinquents' and 'fanatical mercenaries' who, driven by 'homicidal coldness', 'fear, hatred and evil', were responsible for the externally inspired 'seditious aggression' whose aim was to wound fatally the healthy organism that was the Uruguayan people. Only the 'labour of sacrifice', 'duty' and 'spilled blood' of the security forces could protect and save it.[13]

The results can be seen for anyone engaged in cultural or intellectual activities such as teaching in the following articles from 'The Uruguayan Educator: a Declaration of Faith':

3) I believe in the essential values of Mediterranean, Graeco-Latin-Christian culture and in Education framed by that culture and those principles.

5) I believe that to de-Christianise is to de-nationalise and, in the last analysis, to enslave.

6) I believe in the teacher as a forger of the spirit, a sower of Wisdom and a trainer of the Platonic charioteer; and in teaching as a sounding of the veins of youth.

10) I believe that education which rejects or omits the Nation's culture turns the native into 'Helmatlos' [stateless], a cosmopolitan, mechanised, passive and submissive subject of a future world Super-government.

13) I believe in the clear nobility and decorousness of intellectual and manual work, and in the indignity and vileness of wastrels and parasites.

14) I believe that any education system or organisation that is a machine-like producer of depersonalised, numbered, massified human beings, of 'socialist' rather than social animals, is to be repudiated.

15) I believe in the radical priority of the father over the teacher, of the Family over the State, of the Home over the School.

19) I believe that the best antibody for marxist poison is a proper education.

20) I believe that the best guarantee of liberty is order and discipline.

21) I believe that primary form of liberty is the Liberty of the Nation, and that Education should be at the service of the Liberty.[14]

In one important sense, such a text defies reasoned commentary: its self-generating, self-sufficient, self-justifying circularity means it can only be accepted or rejected en bloc. Some factors can be noted, however: the neo-fascist appeals to the supposed ideals of education in Ancient Greece; the paranoid, utterly hypocritical and contradictory trumpeting of individual freedom in a document that demands its exact opposite; and the 'I believe' not as an expression of one person's beliefs but as subservience to a collective pseudo-religious 'Credo' imposed from above. All this indicates not merely the total abolition of independent critical thinking and its expres-

sion, but also of its replacement by a system designed to be a radical nega-
tion of it. It is in this sense that the military were quite literally their own
authors and consequently had no need of any others.

However, perhaps the most frightening aspect of such documents is that
the hermetically sealed, opaque nature of the resulting intellectual and
moral construct totally cuts its creators off from the world outside, and
therefore completely impervious to any sceptical or critical gaze, and indeed
to any form of self-analysis or self-awareness. Thus, the epigraph to this
chapter is taken from the military's assessment of the Tupamaros reports
and statements they had perused,[15] but might also be read as a possible
description of the portentous myth-making in which the armed forces
themselves engaged. Such self-reflection, ironic or not, is simply not
possible for a monolithic authority utterly convinced of its own correctness.

Against this the left and its intellectual and cultural followers could do
little within Uruguay until the 1980 plebiscite began a slight relaxation of
censorship and oppression,[16] which increased to become a real opening after
the party internal elections in 1982. Despite some rather self-congratulatory
accounts,[17] during the 1970s there seems in fact to have been very little real
resistance to the dictatorship that was not clandestine or ineffectual, quite
simply because rigorous if arbitrary censorship, as well as ruthlessly
enforced prohibition of all forms of political and trade union opposition,
made it all but impossible.[18] For example, once the general strike called on
the day of the coup was lifted fifteen days later,[19] no further strike of that
kind was possible until 18 January 1984.[20] In this climate, such resistance as
was possible became passive, private and mostly unorganised,[21] a distancing
of the self from its surroundings that sociologist Rafael Bayce likened to a
kind of autism.[22]

Poet and Frente Amplio supporter Roberto Appratto has written a brief,
lyrical evocation of life in this kind of heavy atmosphere in which the mere
act of breathing is almost an act of resistance. Throughout the dictatorship,
he had the sensation of inhabiting another planet, so removed did he feel
from even the most loved elements in the world around him. It was as
though the air itself assumed such viscosity that – rather like Roquentin in
Sartre's *Nausea* – the very 'thing-ness' of objects became numbing, the most
everyday acts serving only to remind him how strange the familiar had
become in an alien world. He avoided the Left and its rhetoric since he experienced any continuation of pre-dictatorship political language as
acquiescence in the regime as a legitimate mode of normality, an almost
personal act of betrayal in that it seemed to imply that what was abnormal
was not his surroundings but him.[23]

Appratto was one of many who, not militant enough to require banish-
ment or jail, were, however, considered too dubious to be left in positions
of influence (Appratto had taught literature at a teacher training institute)

and so had to find work for which they were unsuited, untrained and unqualified. One outlet for the more academically inclined and qualified of those similarly dismissed by the military were privately funded research institutes. In part a product of more liberal economic policies beginning in the 1960s, these organisations, funded through foundations in North America and Europe, sheltered and employed a number of otherwise vulnerable people,[24] and allowed them to extend their research through contacts with people and developments overseas, giving them access to materials, theories and methods that would be crucial in the years following 1985.[25] Indeed, unless written abroad, it is difficult to find a major work in the Uruguayan social sciences published in the mid- to late-1980s, especially those that begin the necessarily delayed task of evaluating aspects of the period beginning around 1965, that does not acknowledge financial or logistical aid from at least one such institution. The blanket condemnation of these organisations as sites in Latin America where formerly pro-revolutionary Marxist intellectuals were induced to sell out to the imperialist enemy[25] was simply not true for Uruguay.

Many of those on the Uruguayan left, intellectuals or not, inevitably found themselves in exile. Since expatriate writers and intellectuals became a continental phenomenon in the 1970s and '80s, Uruguayan examples have been studied in that context, while major figures such as Onetti, Benedetti, Galeano, Martínez Moreno and Quijano are examined in their own right. Moreover, the focus of this book is on the left intelligentsia in Uruguay – another sense in which this section on the dictatorship is an 'interlude' – so I shall restrict myself here to a few comments on two aspects about the left in exile which are relevant to the discussion to follow.

First, the dismembering of the Frente Amplio (exemplified by the continued incarceration in Uruguay of its leader, Líber Seregni) meant that the left abroad was not only geographically dispersed, but also lost its central rallying point, making it difficult to establish a united anti-dictatorship front overseas. The result was that, despite the cumulative effect of its campaign to alert world opinion about human rights abuses under the military, the expatriate Uruguayan left tended to repeat the divisions that had beleaguered it during the 1960s. The Frente's determination to retain its unity delayed decisions dependent on directives from Montevideo, while initiatives made by the coalition's more radical groups (such as the Unión Popular's Enrique Erro, whose ideas were close to the Tupamaros') were distrusted by more moderate members, and few on the centre-left were prepared to support wholeheartedly the laudable efforts of the exiled leader of the Nationals' most progressive faction, Wilson Ferreira Aldunate, who had been the Frente's most able competitor in the 1971 elections.[27] Moreover, the Nationals could use Ferreira Aldunate's sterling work abroad to build up his anti-dictatorship credentials at home, a situation that threatened to upstage the exemplary and heroic stoicism of an imprisoned Seregni. This would be the Nationals and Ferreira's undoing, however. In the post-1982 preparations for transition, the military recognised Seregni's importance in ensuring the left and union movement's acceptance of any agreement and increasingly included him in the negotiations. The Nationals, on the other hand, eventually excluded themselves because the armed forces refused to allow Ferreira to return home and, when he in effect called their bluff by coming back in early 1984, they imprisoned him. Although Seregni's participation was not universally applauded within the Frente Amplio, there is little doubt that it helped the centre-left to reposition itself on the post-authoritarian political scene. While this spectacular finale only underlined the failure by the progressive forces in exile to present a unified anti-dictatorship front, the enforced dialogue with human rights ethics and the primacy of others' suffering over their own quarrels would colour everybody's, even the revolutionary left's, re-introduction to the values and practices of democracy in 1984.[28]

The second factor, still unresolved at the time of writing, is the need by the Uruguayan left as a whole fully to come to terms with its own role in the defeat during the 1970s of the ideals that had sustained it since the Cuban revolution of 1959. This raises several major issues. The intensely personal nature of the convictions, decisions and actions involved may make the process of individual self-analysis difficult, even traumatic, as well as politically sensitive.[29] The second problem is that such exercises in self-criticism might threaten the unity on the left that has been so hard achieved. Although the public demonstration of internal differences of opinion helps keep alive the origin of the Frente as a gathering together of disparate, independent left groups around a shared program, the open discussion of such thorny matters as the armed struggle and the declaring or lifting of major strikes runs the risk of reinvigorating in the present old disputes about past responsibilities.[30] In addition, such a debate could not but issue in probably bitter disagreement about the equally vexed, related matter of the far from full commitment by many groups and parties on the left to parliamentary democracy.[31] As Carmen Perelli put it in an interview, even her generation was guilty (she was in her teens and twenties during the dictatorship) because of its tacit complicity with the guerrillas' viewpoint.[32] Some such collective public admission by the left would play into the hands of the Frente's current political adversaries, and would also oblige some groups within the Frente to admit to having contributed substantially to the warfare mentality that helped erode belief in Uruguay's political institutions, thus assuming responsibility for preparing the ground for the battle that cost the entire left so dearly after 1968.[33]

Writing about what he saw as Uruguay's preference for casting the recent past into oblivion, novelist and Tupamaros sympathiser Híber Conteris commented that his country had passed from pre-modernity to post-modernity without fully absorbing the period in between.[34] While perhaps overstated, this remark powerfully conveyed the sensation that, if the dictatorship felt like living on an alien planet, the transition to a restored democracy only underlined that the world to which Uruguayans awoke on 1 March 1985 was anything but a continuation of the one they had been forced to leave on 27 June 1973. Oreggioni's *Diccionario de literatura uruguaya* referred to above provides a small but clear illustration of the gap. The project was begun by major intellectual and academic figures before 1973 but censorship and exile had meant that it had to be redone with different staff from 1979 on.[35] Its eventual joint publication by a major publishing house that had survived the dictatorship and a new local credit card provider of a kind unimaginable in 1973 was a small-scale herald of what would be a totally new relationship between culture, commodity and a new economic order. The authoritarian period in Uruguay was a hiatus in a process that continued after it, while at the same time it completed the destruction of the myth of Uruguay as the model republic which was arguably holding the country's development back, ironically destroying in the process the very cultural elitism that had in part made possible the Uruguay they were defending.[36] Alvaro Rico, whose politics had been close to the Communist party, eloquently expressed the shock administered by this situation in both form and content of a piece which reversed accepted logic by seeing the dictatorship as less the consequence of previous democratic breakdown than the first stage of the democracy that followed it, so that the silences imposed by the military become the traumatic absences and tacitly accepted omissions of the restoration. This very confronting argument was underlined by the anti-historiographic text that conveyed it: a series of disjointed fragments, notes and quotations typeset in the manner of a poem in prose by the likes of Benedetti or Bukovski.[37]

The dictatorship may have been an interlude, but the military intervention had so precipitated the processes begun in the 1960s that the acts following it were less connected to what preceded it than it first appeared. It would take the Uruguayan left and the progressive intelligentsia about twenty years to adjust fully to the new way of things.

PART
TWO

Political Unity; Intellectual Dispersal

4

The Revenge of the Foreign

Uruguay on the Eve of De(con)struction

*'But shitty people pigeonhole me, don't listen to me, immediately pin a label on
me. It's all shit'. [Rosalía] sighed deeply and leaned her head on Martín's
shoulder. 'How hard it is being on the left these days', she said sadly.*

Gabriel Sosa (2004)

In March 1985, Jorge Zabalza, one of the long-time members of the
Tupamaros held in prison at the malicious insistence of the military until
the Colorado government elected the previous November actually took
office, was out walking with his daughter, Laura, shortly after his release. His
biographer reconstructed the scene confronting him in a square of the
working-class Montevideo suburb of Villa Biarritz:

> Through 'mate', joints, long hair and booze, the smell of patchouli flooded
> the whole square crowded with young people in colourful clothes.[1] The
> outlandish attire stretched from fluorescent to threadbare black, while these
> youngsters with hair scraped up in crests openly passed bottles of wine from
> hand to hand at midday. They were punks, anarchists, Laura told him. Jorge
> was amazed at this paradise of 1980s-style impulses which, to the rhythm of
> rock groups with curious names like the Idiots, the Stomachs and the
> Traitors, related to nothing local and wanted to break with everything. It was
> hard to take in so much raucousness, so many weird new hair styles, but
> Jorge liked it because it revived a nostalgia for his days as a long haired, anar-
> chist bohemian, his hippie sympathies and liking for the Beatles and the
> Stones.[2]

The contrast with the world of Montevideo youth Zabalza had left behind
in the early 1970s could not be more stark: no obvious political allegiances
or commitment; no nationalism (unless the 'mate' is evidence of anything

other than habit) but an invasion of alien, foreign tastes; a complete break with and rejection of the past; a cult of idleness and an ostentatious but anti-chic, self-destructive hedonism. But also Zabalza's attempt to tame its disruptive newness by relating it to his own 1960s individualist rebelious-ness, a personal manifestation of a general trend in post-dictatorship Uruguay of wishing to see the return to democracy as a continuation of life before the authoritarianism of the late 1960s, the dictatorship itself being relegated to a brief interruption of life and business as they should naturally be.[3] Those on the left who thought that way were in for a series of rude awak-enings over the next twenty years, beginning immediately.

Gerardo Caetano, an intellectual close to the Frente Amplio, was more aware than many of his politically committed colleagues of the temptations of anti-politics and the extent of disenchantment with politics and distrust of politicians among the intellectual and artistic community.[4] However, what Caetano lamented could be celebrated by others. Thus, Rafael Bayce (to whom I refer in more detail below), a professional sociologist person-ally involved with and committed to much of the thought and feeling in the post-dictatorship youth movement, praised its opposition to all existing political models and their consequences for the way people actually related to one another on a day-to-day basis.[5] Similarly, what follows is part of a summary appreciation of the activities of the young generation of artists and intellectuals who matured during the military dictatorship or in the first period of the transition to democracy that succeeded it in 1985. In other words, it could be an interpretation of the spectacle witnessed by Zabalza:

> An anarchic and rabble-rousing anti-politics by people who think not about Revolution but about revolutionising, not about implementing a policy limited to the area of state institutions, but about activating the political as a mobile, nomadic and ubiquitous dimension for constructing and confronting social identities that emerges in every social sphere: an anti-politics-of-disillusion-with-politics-as-it-is, interstitial slippages, ludic practices, a politics of the edge which de-ritualises the imaginary of the Model Republic, theatricalisation of the theatre of the institutions of democ-racy, that high point of the nation's patrimony and first prize in the New Year's Eve lottery.[6]

Not merely an interpretation of the anti-politics of a generation, this diatribe, with its ironic play on revolution, the sarcastic capitalisation of 'Model Republic' to show the redundancy of the myth of the Batllista state, and its scornful dismissal of current political institutions in the final phrases, energetically endorses those who engage in the playful questioning not only of all conventional politics, whatever its ideological hue, but of the very idea of Uruguay itself. With its ponderous syntax and terms borrowed from foreign thinkers such as Derrida, Castoriadis and Deleuze and Guatari, the sentence enacts within its form the very movements and gestures it praises.

In the epigraph to this chapter, Rosalía expresses effectively a similar mood. In the story to which her sentence ('How Hard It Is Being On the Left These Days') gives the title (which is also the name of the whole volume),[7] she lives what could probably be termed an unproductive if attractively bohemian existence. She comes from a well-off but often absent family, wears extravagant clothes, tries to write what she describes as poetry, does occasional stunts for a publicity agency, and seems to be involved with preparing what looks like something between a performance and a sixties-style 'happening'. Rosalía and her boyfriend Martín's relationship is alternately hilarious, grotesque and sad, but is also allegorical. He is from a lower-middle class family and works for a pittance in a rock-music store, which is where they meet over a shared taste in music. He has reason to be a left-wing activist but is not; although she does not need to be one, she would like to be a rebel, but is not sure how. In this chapter I use Rosalía and Martín as emblems of those Uruguayan intellectuals who felt estranged from the established left and had to find other outlets for their opposition to the status quo.

Mario Benedetti as Problem

The principal directions in post-dictatorship Uruguayan culture began to become clear in the late 1980s, two or three years after the return to formal democracy. Perhaps the best way to get a feel for the way things were moving is through the polemic that erupted in 1987 around the figure of Mario Benedetti. First, though, a brief account of what he had done since the coup in 1973. By the early 1980s he had abandoned the revolutionary stance that had brought him to lead the legal, public front for the Tupamaros (see Chapter Three above). Indeed, in a sense the 1982 novel *Primavera con una esquina rota* reverses the narrative and ideological thrust of the narrative poem *El cumpleaños de Juan Angel* [1971], dedicated to Tupamaros founder, Raúl Sendic. The latter tells the story of a bank clerk[8] in his mid-thirties, Osvaldo Puente (his surname suggesting he is a 'bridge', a man of transition), a young husband and father, who elliptically reviews his birthdays from childhood onwards to record the progressive distancing from his lower middle class background to his recent clandestine joining the Tupamaros guerrillas (Juan Angel is his *nom de guerre*). *Primavera*, on the other hand, tells what awaits Santiago, about to be released after five years of interrogation and torture in the jails of the Uruguayan military for having been caught in action as another Juan Angel. Meanwhile, his wife, Graciela, in exile with their young daughter in what appears to be an unidentified

Mexico City, has fallen in love with one of Santiago's best friends and former comrades in arms, Roberto, released and deported earlier. The novels ends with Santiago not totally sure what to expect as he goes forward to greet the three of them (plus his widowed father, who has just got a Mexican girlfriend) at the beginning of his own damaged spring season (hence the novel's title) as a refugee. None of these characters (including Santiago while in jail) makes any reference at all to continuing political work in exile; all are wholly preoccupied with reconstructing their maimed private, emotional lives as spouse, partner, lover and parent. In short, between *Cumpleaños* and *Primavera*, Benedetti had simply inverted the relative weight given to the personal and the political.

A pivotal moment in this process is the collection of essays and lectures *El recurso del supremo patriarca* [originally 1978], the earlier pieces of which were composed in Havana, where Benedetti's own enforced exile had taken him after being hounded out of Buenos Aires and deported from Peru, and retain much of the utopian thrust and revolutionary rhetoric of, say, *El escritor latinoamericano y la revolución posible* [1974], the last of Benedetti's essays wholly inflected by his Cuba-inspired activism in the early 1970s. As *El recurso* progresses, however, the markers of revolutionary fervour become fewer and more formulaic,[9] until by the time of *El desexilio y otras conjeturas* [1984], consisting of articles written for the Madrid daily *El País* from 1982, they have disappeared altogether.

It is, then, in one sense ironic, and in another, inevitable that he should become the centre of what was at times an acrimonious debate. It is ironic because, since returning from exile in 1985, Benedetti had renounced direct involvement in politics, and held no position from which he could exercise any control over literary or cultural matters. He seems to have devoted himself entirely to writing, but it is precisely that which is key to the inevitability of the whole affair. Benedetti had published (including anthologies) roughly a book a year since 1945, the year which names the generation of which he has become since the 1980s the most publicly recognised and admired member. Moreover, in addition to his well-known militancy before the coup, he was recognised for his resistance to the dictatorship abroad while in exile. For, even if he no longer adhered to revolutionary positions, all his published work written abroad, fiction and non-fiction, lucidly and often poignantly illuminated the experience of exile, denounced the abuses of the military throughout the Southern Cone and had worked and written independently but consistently against the dictatorship while in exile,[10] loudly denouncing the initial support of the military regimes by United States administrations and international financial institutions. In other words, Benedetti had by no means become a conservative; he had merely reverted to being an independent left-wing intellectual.

In addition, exile had made him famous internationally. First through the Editorial Nueva Imagen founded in the late 1970s in Mexico, then Alianza in Madrid, as well as regularly syndicated essays originally written for Spanish publications, all of Benedetti's new and old work, banned in its entirety by the military in Uruguay, reached an international public for the first time. By the time he returned from exile in March 1985, Benedetti was effectively identified as *the* Uruguayan writer, one closely associated with the left-wing values of the 1960s, and one of the very few Uruguayan writers who could afford to live just off his writing (he could even afford to maintain an apartment in Mallorca, where he would spend part of every year). Benedetti, in other words, simply took up too much space: although largely out of touch with changes that had occurred inside the country during the twelve-year dictatorship, afterwards he walked back into an immediate position of pre-eminence. In other words, as Hugo Achugar admitted,[11] Benedetti was a problem.

And Achugar should know since he was present in March 1986 at a conference on Uruguayan culture in the period of transition from dictatorship to democracy where Benedetti became the focus of an exchange which suggested that the meeting of the two waters of Uruguayan culture (one produced under oppression at home and the other in exile abroad), as Achugar himself anticipated in his own contribution,[12] was going to be anything but smooth. In a discussion period, Leo Maslíah, writer but principally author of some of the most subversively humorous songs of the 'canto popular' movement from the late 1970s, suggested that the censorship of Benedetti's works by the military had since become a publicity tool for promoting his and others' books, making it difficult for younger, home grown writers who had had to cope from the inside to get heard. He then suggested that this was only one example of how the whole 1945 generation had effectively 'stifled' more experimental creative writing, a process begun in the late 1960s which the dictatorship only extended and exacerbated.[13] Maslíah then added insult to injury by mocking a poem by another member of the '45 generation, Amanda Berenguer, dedicated to those who had suffered under torture and read at the conference by the author.[14] He renamed it 'Description of Torture Undergone by a Latin American in 1860 Remembered by a Spaniard in 1920', as though consigning their whole approach to language and history, form and content, to a museum of dead letters.[15] Achugar, trying to relieve some of the ensuing tension, inadvertently summarised the whole set of difficulties by being undecided whether it was a case of many Uruguays or one Uruguay divided into many communities.[16]

So it might have come as no surprise when some injudicious remarks by Benedetti in an interview caused a furore. Of the two comments that caused offence, the first said that 'formalist, structuralist and deconstructionist criticism and all the recent -isms' were not for the common reader. Now, since this was what younger Uruguayan literary intellectuals had been reading, such opinions made Benedetti look old-fashioned, irrelevant and arrogant. He then compounded this error by patronisingly suggesting that it was only young writers, critics and intellectuals who had any problem with him,[17] whereas he got on well with young people in general.[18]

It was not long before those summarily dismissed made their displeasure felt. In a letter signed wth the pointed pseudonym 'Today' (later identified as one Gustavo Escanlar Patrone, a poet and journalist of the 80s genera-tion)[19] the writer explained that, along with many other university-educated people born in the '60s, he had once been an assiduous reader and admirer of Benedetti. Now, however, 'Benedetti-style arguments' seemed irrelevant, and they were 'bored with bar and committee discussions, with a cultural framework imposed and dictatorially marked out by the 1945 generation'. They could no longer talk to their 'cultural parents', but being orphans left them free.[20] The tone is sarcastic and aggressive, while the use of words such as 'dictatorial' and 'omnipotent' only two years after the end of the dicta-torship and applied by association to someone famous for resisting it is the equivalent of an accusing finger: you are lording it over us now just as the military did before, but now we can say 'no'.

'Today' was soon joined by others. For Tomás Linn, the new generation wanted to 'wake up the population's dozing capacity to be astonished' through means unfamiliar to it (the 'isms' Benedetti did not like, perhaps), and that 'Today' was one of a generation for whom nothing was fixed and for whom 'there were no utopias', a reference to the presumed irrelevance of the revolutionary dreams of the past. More restrained than 'Today', Linn thought Benedetti and his like should 'share the available space' in the newly reclaimed democracy,[21] but tacitly acknowledged a gap not only between two generations but also between those who spent the twelve years of dicta-torship abroad and those who struggled silently at home.

However, what best exemplifies the extent of the disagreement is the exchange between Jorge Castro Vega and Omar Prego, a novelist and critic only seven years younger than Benedetti. Essentially, Castro Vega argued that, with very few exceptions, those in control of cultural and political power were living in the past, but that now, in an act close to secular sacri-lege, the 'imprudent' young were on the attack against those 'whose exile or imprisonment imposed on us if not a heated, emotional and irrational defence of those not here, then at the very least the moral obligation to hold our tongue'. These 'untouchable popes', 'a bit older, more prudent [unlike the young, that is], a bit tired, but with their laurels and verbal pyrotechnics intact', 'ruled once more'. This was insulting and intended to be so, effec-tively accusing the pre-dictatorship progressive intellectuals of having joined the ranks of the enemy, singling Benedetti out and criticising him for repeating himself to less and less effect. Castro Vega worried that, because of their influence, the end result might be that the nation's culture would go in for 'restoration instead of creation, rebuilding instead of building anew', the implication being that the combined weight of the 'popes' would prevent others from building for the future.[22] Unfair and grotesquely overstated it may be, but this essay could not state more eloquently the frustration and powerlessness felt by a generation of intellectuals who earlier were prevented by repression and censorship from realising their full potential and were still helpless when democracy finally brought them the freedom they needed.

In the same journal 'Today' restated his position that the younger generation only wanted some space in which to be effective, to fulfill a need to communicate in an environment that threatened to turn them into 'little autistic monsters'. However, he reserved his biggest salvo for Benedetti in a defence of his use of a pseudonym:

> By signing as 'Today', I connote, which I don't do if I sign as Gustavo. 'Today' is today, the now, the 'come on, get on with it'. Today is opposed to the yesterday when I was not yet born and the tomorrow when I'll be dead. I am born and die each second, each now. I never knew Pakistan, but I am getting to know it. To live now, already, as it comes. Without hypocritical yesterdays [yesterdays de cola de paja]. Without tomorrow's imaginary revolutions. Yesterday and tomorrow: a meaningful title that separates and unites us with Don Mario.[23]

Here was a fierce assertion of a desire to live independently in the present, distant from the radical left stance inherited by some from the 1960s. As 'Today' implied, post-authoritarian Uruguay was a foreign country he was only just getting to know.

Prego's riposte did not help much, being nearly as hysterical in defence of Benedetti and his generation as Castro Vega had been in impugning them, its author virtually becoming the out-of-date, snobbish caricature Castro Vega and 'Today' had invented. Accusing the young of 'imperiously' demanding all cultural power for themselves, Prego sneered that they had probably not even read the authors they condemned and asked how they could be expected to understand complex literature, surrounded as they were by rock music, television and semi-literate illustrated novelettes [historietas].[24]

Benedetti himself continued in this vein a year later, accusing the '80s intellectuals of being defeatists spoiled with opportunities to publish and be noticed compared with what his generation had in the 1950s, of valuing the likes of Charles Bukowski because they had not read Henry Miller ('who did it better'), and of producing only faded copies of dadaism but nothing valid enough to back up their 'parricidal' aggression. His position can be summed up in the 'desolate' impression made on him by *Mum Was a Punk*, a 1988 TV documentary about the movement that interviewed the sort of people Zabalza saw in Villa Biarritz in 1985: 'swearing at everything does not get you very far', opined Benedetti.[25] An 'excellent documentary', one sypathiser thought.[26] It depended on whether scorn was seen as evidence of quietist, cynical desperation or of negative but nervously creative energy.

The supercilious attempts to disqualify Benedetti's detractors certainly merited Achugar's comment on the paternalist tone of his defenders,[27] and served only to reinforce the truth of 'Today's' feeling of having become a cultural orphan. Achugar's further statement in the same note that the polemic had no larger implications, however, severely understated the importance of the dispute in revealing to what extent and with what difficulty Uruguayan culture generally had in coming to terms with the radically changed society the dictatorship left behind it.

Indeed, so important was it that its echoes could still be heard over a decade later, on the occasion of Benedetti's eightieth birthday. Writing about a homage to him organised in Paso de los Toros, the town where he was born, one commentator worried that he was less read but more valued in terms of second-hand ideological clichés. He then went on to compare Benedetti and most of his generation to decadents who could not bring themselves to question their experience of the world they saw.[28] Once again, the argument was that Benedetti was less read because he was irrelevant to the post-dictatorship world with its revised neoliberal agenda. However, Benedetti may have abandoned his revolutionary politics, as I showed earlier, but he consistently spoke out against the ravages of neoliberalism, even if persistently in a vocabulary acquired much earlier.[29]

Benedetti may have had a somewhat unfortunate last word in a book that went on sale on his eighty-fourth birthday (13 September 2004). Addressed apparently to 'the young in general' with whom he got on well according to the Campodónio interview cited above which started off the whole dispute in 1987, it is subtitled 'message to young people'. It is a hardback, glossy, large-print book of ninety-one pages, ten of which are blank, thirty-one are photographs, with several others taken up with poems lifted from earlier books. In other words, Benedetti's 'message' was short, but got celebrity treatment: 'What can an eighty year old poet say to young people that has not already been said? Not much'. At this point, many readers might have wished Benedetti had taken himself at his own word and stopped. Regrettably, he did not: 'Only tell them how happy and good I feel that, in my eighties, an entire life time's values are still alive and present, that I've never been tempted to renege on them and I still adhere to them'. It was precisely this self-satisfied feeling that nothing about him needed changing that some of his younger readers had held against him in 1987–88.

Readers were then treated to a predictable lecture on the dangers of leaving home, drugs, hypocrisy, rock music, on the usefulness of sport, the joys and woes of sex and love. The young were abjured to speak out against power but not become its allies as they matured, because 'the reins of power are always in the hands of veterans', it never apparently occurring to Benedetti that this might be applied to himself.[30] Benedetti had apparently become what some already thought he was over ten years before: a somewhat sanctimonious and utterly humourless grandfather relying on his own experience to tell people sixty or even seventy years younger how to live their lives.

All Shook Up – The Libertarian Breakout

Some years after the original debate, one of the participants in the intellectual and cultural movement created by those who had become disenchanted was to say that they had reason to thank Benedetti, for had it not been for his words in the 1987 interview, they would not have received the publicity they got.[31] What this loose-knit group of artists and intellectuals mostly in their twenties were doing in the mid to late 1980s would eventually be christened 'La Movida', with its double implication of being in constant movement it (always impermanent and provisional, a process that never coagulates into becoming a definition) and of wanting to shake the world around it into movement. Within the movement were two main trends. The first involved throwing off the shackles (personal, social, aesthetic and intellectual) that had held them down during the dictatorship, and celebrating the resulting sense of freedom. Hence, rock journalist, playwright and novelist Gabriel Peveroni could invoke their determination to live 'against the current of what older people insisted on calling "the democratic spring"'.[32] The use of 'dionisiac' to describe the movement[33] catches the impulse to live for pleasure in the moment, there being nothing in the past deemed worth emulating or living up to, and nothing in the future worth sacrificing anything for. As Barros-Lémez (born in 1945, so hardly one of them himself) had put it in Maryland in March 1986, in a paper subtitled 'Can One Go Back Home?': 'Uruguay is still not fertile ground for its own children'.[34] Hidden here is La Movida's most lasting intuition: that the dictatorship, far from interrupting an otherwise secure historical development to which it was now possible to return, had accelerated changes so irrevocable that going back to the way things were was impossible since all continuity with that past had disappeared. They were indeed a Generation that was 'Absent' (oppressed and repressed) and 'Solitary' (orphaned because cut off from both the safety of a comforting past and the promise of a worthwhile future – and from those who still believed in both), *GAS* being the name of one the most influential of the usually short-lived, cheap but adventurous little or underground magazines they founded.[35]

The second comprised their realisation that the myths that had sustained pre-dictatorship Uruguay's idea of itself had been definitively destroyed: the state was not benign and nurturing; Uruguay's democracy was not sacrosanct and stable; Uruguay was not a civilised outpost of Europe in the Southern Cone, but a country that had been 'latinamericanised' late by the dictatorship; Uruguayans could not be relied on to automatically respect each other and the rule of law.[36] Interviewed in 1989 after the release of his book on Uruguayan political culture, Bayce saw the country wallowing in masochistic nostalgia, summing up the Uruguay of post-authoritarian transition as 'uncultured, incredibly rude [deseducado], mean, fatalistic, tango-like in its resignation [tanguero], pour[ing] water on any change, murderous toward its young people, [and] profoundly conservative'.[37] There was no need to take Bayce at his word (after all, he was promoting his own book) to appreciate the depth of feeling that inspired both his book and the attitudes he shared with La Movida. In a more restrained manner, Raúl Zibechi, another social scientist sympathetic to Uruguayan youth movements of the 1980s and 90s, could similarly contrast them with the 1960s, emphasising the former's de-ideologised, anti-organisational, vertically unstructured nature, with its loose, fluid, sometimes chaotic but never more than provisional groupings and its emphasis on spontaneous, local and insurrectionist kinds of militancy.[38] As Zabalza could see in March 1985, nothing could be further from the crude realities that had led to his imprisonment in the early 1970s, but, as we shall see in the following chapter, the mainstream left and its intellectuals would not remain immune to the contagious attractions of the libertarian, anarchic mood of post-dictatorship youth. Indeed, the mixed political fortunes of La Movida are entirely due to its inchoate character: it could only betray itself by coalescing into anything like the sort of political party it despised and distrusted, but not doing so meant that any specific weight it might have would be diffused by its own preferred lack of structure. Thus, while there seems little doubt that one of the reasons for its slow disintegration was the impact of the Frente Amplio's election win in Montevideo in 1989 and the increasingly decisive role within it of the now legalised, 'de-revolutionised' MLN (thus offering La Movida adherents more attractively radical mainstream political options), La Movida's emphasis on informal, grassroots, neighbourhood campaigns fed into the Frente's own organisational methods.[39]

To all of this was added a sharp and growing disillusion about Uruguay's mainstream political and intellectual culture's ability to come up with anything new to address the situation.[40] As already noted, the left in general, including its parties' youth sections, was seen as old fashioned, out of touch, still in thrall to the politics of pre-authoritarian Uruguay, quite simply already old and only too ready to follow the military's example and stamp on all signs of real rebellion and social change.[41] Those behind La Movida were identified by Bayce as mostly the young 'dionisiacs' or 'counterculturals' who had engaged in underground cultural activities as adolescents during the dictatorship, with some young 'marrones', named after the fake Jewish converts of sixteenth century Spain who maintained their own faith but appeared on the surface to conform to Catholicism, but here denoting young people who kept alive their rebellious attitudes while apparently conforming to authoritarianism.[42] Bayce offered the first substantial account and assessment of La Movida, joining the theory and methodology of a practising academic sociologist to the passion of a cultural activist to advance a psycho-sociological interpretation of the movement, correctly anticipating its future relevance.[43]

Retrospectively, Espinosa evoked a Proustian task of setting off 'in search of their lost identity' so as to 'compose an image of Uruguay and its people', a claim I take up below in Chapter Six. This in turn entailed a major change in direction in Uruguayan culture as a whole: '"The culture of resistance" and "canto popular"[44] are going to find their heroes in a ruined slum'.[45] The new cultural models were to be found not among heroes enshrined in literary classics but among those omitted from conventional definitions of Uruguayan culture: blacks, lumpen, the very poor and other similar sectors, whether ethnic, religious, or sexual. Those, that is, that had been marginalised or silenced, first, by the suffocating uniformity of the homogenous Uruguayan nation's construction of itself, and then by the military's aggressive defence of its own conservative version of it.

These foreigners from within, together with those invited in, literally and figuratively, from outside (of whom returning exiles were only the most visible and – mostly – welcome examples), headed by a mob of youngsters who identified themselves primarily through precisely what they saw as the most unacknowledged facet of themselves (their youth, that is), would transform Uruguay in ways utterly unforeseeable as late as 1980. First to go, the traditional strong emphasis on middle-class, middle-brow literary culture (the mid-century Uruguayan version of Rama's *Lettered City*)[46] was about to be called into question. Poet and performance artist Héctor Bardanca, perhaps inadvertently, caught La Movida's uneasy relationship with even the best of Uruguay's modern literature at the end of an article in late 1986: 'If behind there are one gaucho, two gauchos, thirty-three gauchos, . . . ahead of us there may be one traitor, two idiots and three stomachs'.[47] The first half of the sentence quotes the ironic summing up several decades earlier of Uruguay's excuse for a tradition by the country's best known novelist, Juan Carlos Onetti, in his debut 1939 novel *El pozo* [*The Well*], whereas the future is left to three local 1980s punk-influenced rock groups, precisely the same ones listed years later in the quotation about Jorge Zabalza in this chapter's first paragraph.

The poet and essayist Eduardo Milán shared La Movida's view of the traditional left as paralysed and urged others to do what it should but could not: welcome plurality, open up an emancipatory dialogue for all. Uruguayan culture was haunted by the ghost of postmodernism, he argued, which it could not face because of its distorted experience of modernity. He then warned: 'A culture contrives its own failure and shuts itself inside the prison of thought when it denies difference: of ideology, sexuality, behaviour, any kind'.[48] Twelve years of authoritarianism had dragged Uruguay though the remains of modernity and into a whole new global order, while simultaneously prohibiting all cultural expression of the tensions and anxieties aroused by such change. It was now essential to catch up with the rest of the continent.[49] Similarly, Linn observed that it was also time to depend on the 'underground currents' running through the 'frustrated, ignored' younger generation.[50] Not only was it no longer possible to go back to some non-existent golden age, Uruguay needed to open out and let in recent foreign intellectual developments that were influencing, even dominating, contemporary thinking throughout the western world. Uruguayans must make the required 'inner change', as Linn's title puts it, so as to face a future which the dictatorship had ushered in but for which it had ill prepared them.

In a short but provocatively titled essay, Carlos Muñoz and Gustavo Escanlar (the 'Today' of the Benedetti polemic), two of the principal adherents of La Movida, list the elements that comprised it: local rock music, graffiti from the dictatorship and the transition to democracy, underground magazines of many types, alternative theatre, film, radio and the discovery of the potential of video.[51] The reference to the growth of Uruguayan rock music is crucial here since it continues a trend begun during the authoritarian period. Censorship of the printed word, the prohibition of all kinds of dissident political activity and the exile or imprisonment of all of the country's best literary and intellectual figures, had meant that from 1973 to the end of 1984 music carried the burden of becoming one of the most important means of keeping alive something resembling a national culture, however fragmented and clandestine it had to be. As already indicated, this was coupled with the rediscovery of local folkloric and Afro-Uruguayan music and the continuation of the 'Canto popular' as a kind of underground resistance to the military state's terror.

With the restoration of democracy, and running parallel to the influx of the theoretical 'isms' Benedetti had declared to be unreadable, these national musical styles combined almost syncretically with rock music largely from the United States and England, but now not the protest and hippie counter-cultural music of the 1960s and early 1970s, but the punk and post-punk trends of the late 1970s and 1980s. Sometimes via post-punk imitations from the fledgling democratic culture in Spain, The Sex Pistols' 'Anarchy in the UK' and 'God Save the Queen', Syd Vicious's merciless send-up of Sinatra's 'My Way', The Clash's alternative left politics, and, among many possibilities, Joy Division's angry and poignant record of the experience of those forgotten by the Thatcherite mainstream, would all find counterparts in Uruguayan rock's sarcastic parodies of the national anthem and Discépolo's tangos, and its evocation of the grinding, grey poverty of much of post-dictatorship Montevideo and its rural surrounds.[52] The centrality of rock music in La Movida makes a couple of anecdotes about live performances clear illustrations of the movement's fraught relationship with traditional radical left politics. In December 1985, The Traitors were performing some of their fiercely satirical punk-influenced numbers about Uruguay when they were interrupted by a group of thirty-somethings (the immediately preceding generation, that is) singing from memory songs by Silvio Rodríguez, the leading representative of post-revolutionary Cuba's 'Nueva Trova' [New Song] movement that had inspired a whole generation of political singer/songwriters throughout Latin America, precisely the kind of politics *and* music post-dictatorship Uruguayan youth was seen by many as having 'betrayed'.[53] In the opposite political direction, late in 1996, whenever the group Asphyxia (an eloquent name for the emotions of youth mugged by authoritarianism) performed Carlos Puebla's 'Hasta Siempre' [Until Always] about the legacy of Che Guevara, the bass player remembered feeling 'his hair stand on end'.[54]

So prominent did Uruguayan rock become in the cultural scene of the 1980s that even traditionally middle- to high-brow publications such as *Brecha, Cuadernos de Marcha* and the more conservative *El País Cultural* could not afford to ignore it, although they still favoured the established categories of literature, visual arts and cinema. But no matter how La Movida was viewed, even in its version of little magazines – modelled, as they were, more on the comic strip and the commercial art of advertising than on the prized experimental literature journal so important all over the western world for the dissemination of high modernism in the early twentieth century – the movement was in effect heralding the dethronement of literacy and the written word as the apex of Uruguayan culture (and as the source of at least some of the myths about Uruguayan uniqueness unmasked by Rial), and replacing them by forms and genres marked by being ephemeral, aleatory, provisional – and foreign.

In the same piece, in a move whose apparent weakness perhaps disguised an anxiety, Muñoz and Escanlar asked rhetorically whether it had occurred to anybody that younger people might be questioning their entire social, cultural and political legacy not because they were all nihilists but because they had a 'different perception of life, hope, and therefore, also (and why not?) of the revolution itself'.[55] The important point here is that not only were the authors hinting at a form of rebellion beyond the merely political, but also broadening the concept of culture to include the trivial stuff of daily life. They were suggesting that La Movida worked to promote nothing less than a transformation of the Uruguayan way of being in the world. Small wonder, then, that although promising a special article on literature for the following issue, they came up with an account of La Movida's most important and memorable cultural event,[56] which Muñoz and Escanlar organised, with help from the poet Rosario González.

'Arte en la lona' (which took place 14–25 April 1988 at Montevideo's Palermo Boxing Club, [hence the idea of 'Art on Canvas'], an anti-art venue if ever there was one) was timed to be an independent, counter-cultural alternative to the much more formal and mainstream Muestra Internacional de Teatro, and was also, according to Zibechi,[57] the first time disparate, informal groups united for a common purpose. They wanted a space for 'multidisciplinary creativeness' where nobody criticised anyone else or made any aesthetic judgement on what they did or made, a whole environment loosely gathered together, that is, rather than a hierarchically structured organisation dedicated to the perpetuation of established aesthetic values. The whole event was done on a shoestring, partly to show that large resources were not essential for original artistic enterprises. All the organisers did was provide a space that, although a boxing ring, could also be a setting for punk rock, theatre, performance art, hindu music, yoga, mime, a drumming group, inside a gym 'decorated by visual artists'.[58] There was not only a bizarre combination of different arts and crafts, of elite and mass art, but a deliberate juxtaposition of the artistic with the non-artistic, again underlining the intention of changing a whole manner of living, of promoting what we have already seen Linn call 'inner change'.[59] The article closed with a number of unanswered questions about culture and power, and the nature and status of the work of art in the (post)modern world, the repeated use of the rhetorical question in this and the preceding piece indicating that the project was ongoing, that there could as yet be no conclusions, only pressing questions that were not merely political but radically existential.[60]

A selection from Eduardo Roland's influential book of 1980s graffiti captures the feel of La Movida: 'the people work for it but it does not work for the people' ['it' being parliament]; 'country for sale, with three million idiots'; 'Everybody makes promises; nobody keeps them. Vote for nobody'; 'if only Groucho had written *Capital* . . . '; 'better once with Snow White than once with every dwarf'.[61] Some of the participants and initiators of La Movida confirmed this essential mood in July 1997, when they had a chance to review what they had been up to a decade earlier.[62] While they repeated the essential characteristics of the movement outlined above, accepting

Bayce's 1989 assessment, they added one or two points of substance. They remembered particularly the scandal caused by their deliberate individualism, their self-conscious determination to be just themselves and not to try to represent anyone or anything, while Bayce himself argued against the traditionalists that the impact of the movement far outlived its brief existence: 'Cultural criticism in Uruguay changed totally after the 1980s La Movida', an opinion more acceptable when taken in conjunction with another of his to the tune that it was important to deconstruct the old Uruguay, 'laying bare its foundations; deconstructing in the Derrida sense'.[63] For the fact is that, three years before 'Arte en la lona', five months before even the Sosnowski seminar on the problems of Uruguayan culture during the transition, a group of invited foreigners much quieter and much more polite than British punk bands, were introducing into the heart of Montevideo a discourse of dissent that, when joined to the impact of La Movida, would indeed change the course of Uruguayan thought in the arts and social sciences.

Deconstruction and After

Partly funded by the French Embassy and the Fulbright Commission, the Uruguayan Association for Semiotic Studies invited Jacques Derrida, two of Yale University's deconstructionist literary critics (Geoffrey Hartman and Harold Bloom), the Brazilian Haroldo de Campos and (most importantly from the local viewpoint) Emir Rodríguez Monegal, the Uruguayan literary critic, then also at Yale, who had left the country for Paris in the 1960s and had never been back since, to give a series of seminars on deconstruction between October and December 1985. In her introduction to the proceedings, critic and linguist Lisa Block de Behar showed she was perfectly aware of the event's implications, seeing it as the introduction to Uruguay and Latin America of a way of thinking in which 'iterablity becomes alterity, iteration is alteration, and repetition can only be identical when it differs' in order to reveal how cultural what appears natural is, that what is unknown is what is most taken for granted and unwittingly agreed to, underlining in her presentation of Derrida the 'foreign'-ness of such notions.[64] Block de Behar underlined, in other words, deconstruction's lesson that no discourse could be free from ideology, precisely because there was no secure ground outside language on which to found any neutral, eternally valid bases for authority and legitimacy from which absolutely and permanently true statements could then be made. Given that Derrida's two lengthy contributions complicated and questioned, first, nationalism and nationality, then the place(s) of self and other in language,[65] the contrast with a security regime that had emphasised the need to keep the nation's body politic immaculately free of contamination by the alien and foreign could hardly have been more pointed.[66]

For the Montevideo intelligentsia, however, it was probably the mere presence of Emir Rodríguez Monegal that threw these matters into sharpest relief. He was the only really important Uruguayan literary intelectual of the 1945 generation not to have been convinced by the example of the Cuban revolution, and his literary criticism, which he practiced in *Marcha* as contributor and literary editor in the 1950s as well as in numerous books, was heavily indebted to the anglophilic, cosmopolitan modernism of the Buenos Aires journal *Sur*. Rodríguez Monegal rejected the post-1959 move leftwards, putting him at odds with many of his Uruguayan colleagues,[67] so when the chance came to go to Paris to edit a new literary magazine, *Mundo Nuevo*, largely a showcase for the Latin American 'Boom' novelists of the 1960s that were becoming the centre of Rodríguez Monegal's literary critical interests,[68] he seized it enthusiastically. However, when it was later discovered that *Mundo Nuevo* was a CIA-financed front in the cultural Cold War, its aim being to neutralise the effect of the Havana-based *Casa de las Américas*,[69] its erstwhile editor took up a post at Yale University, thus making it easy for his carefully cultivated professional objectivity to look, in the ideologically overwrought atmosphere of the time, suspiciously like implicit opposition to the Cuban revolution and, later, tacit complicity with the military dictatorship in Uruguay. When invited to give the paper in Montevideo, Rodríguez Monegal had sensibly made the demise of the military regime a condition of his attendance, but during the same period that allowed this requirement to be fulfilled, he himself had been diagnosed with terminal cancer (he was to die only weeks later back in the United States). The sight of a frail, wheelchair-bound Rodríguez Monegal dutifully honouring a commitment to the country of his rise to literary-critical maturity, to which he was returning for a long-delayed and now final visit, where his reputation was, to say the least, not whole-heartedly positive, must have brought a whole range of conflicting emotions to the surface for all concerned. Rodríguez Monegal was not, in any strict sense, a foreigner, but to many he must have appeared more alien than those who were.

Some of these issues surfaced in his contribution to the deconstruction seminar. Introduced by Alsina Thevenet – a film critic and participant in *Marcha* during Rodríguez Monegal's time – in a manner that emphasised his atypical way of being Uruguayan, Rodríguez Monegal was preceded by a one-page welcome sent by an also very ill Jorge Luis Borges, in what would be one of his last communications from Buenos Aires.[70] In it, Borges – himself so unconventionally Argentinian as to irk his more committed nationalist compatriots – claimed never to have read the intellectual biography of him written by his 'friend' Emir[71] because he did not want to confront himself as imagined by another.[72] The main title of Rodríguez

Monegal's four-page communication says it all: 'Borges/De Man/Derrida/Bloom',[73] an Argentine with English ancestry as read by a Belgian American, a Frenchman born in Algeria and a Jewish American, all filtered through the perspective of a Uruguayan expatriate intellectual. The seminar's few pages by and about Rodríguez Monegal and Borges exemplify the whole event's symbolic impact within the national situation: the authoritarian period had dragged Uruguay willy-nilly into the world of late twentieth century globalised capitalism (including its intellectual manifestations), and now the way Uruguayans saw themselves and interpreted their relations with others was going to have to catch up.

The effect of French poststructuralism cannot be separated entirely from that of the other currents that had come in with specialists and technicians used by or with the acquiescence of the military or from the many other trends in modern thinking to which returning exiles had been exposed while abroad. Although in Uruguay, as elsewhere, it transformed much of the activity in the humanities and social sciences generally, here I will just point to some of the dangers the uncritical adoption of oversimplified versions of it could present to a dazzled left intelligentsia. One major trap was to take desire for reality by imagining that the exposure of the ideological and mythical underpinnings of a particular worldview was tantamount to at least beginning the demolition of the real institutions and structures built up with the aid of such models. This seems at least in part to happen because of the widely shared, but mistaken, conviction that Derrida was responsible for a sentence that said, in effect, that there was nothing outside the text, as Block de Behar, for example, had reported in 1986,[74] resulting from a paraphrase of a misreading of the French original of Derrida's *Of Grammatology* [1967], where he wrote that there is 'no outside-the-text'. This error turns the proposition that what cannot be or is not textualised (that is, turned into discursive form) is not representable into a confusion of reality with representations of it.

In Sosnowski's seminar on Uruguayan culture and redemocratisation, the paper by social anthropologist and fiction writer Teresa Porzecanski on the narrative of anarchic excess that first appeared in the late 1960s and acquired oppositional status during the dictatorship when cultural manisfestations were effectively called on to replace the prohibited formal political opposition, showed the early signs of this dangerously seductive slippage between real and textual worlds. Porzecanski emphasised that 'the insistence on turning toward the very materiality of language, in the sense that rhetorical style serves as the depository of all ideology, is what put these writers more in the role of subversive interpreters' because 'only fantasy could rescue the essence [of the real]', fiction being 'a resistance value in itself, a sign of convulsion within a culture of confinement', its excesses countering the limitations of official discourse.[75] It is the double move here of seeing language as 'material' and what is written using it as potentially 'subversive' that allows an attack on one to be only too explicably conflated with the overturning of the other, resulting in acting as though the mere existence of desire was sufficient in itself to produce the desired result. In this context, it may be far from coincidental that Porzecanski's references are to Michel Foucault, whose historical work is very much concerned with the discursive construction of social reality in the West, and to Julia Kristeva, some of whose principal themes were desire, revolution and language, all of which must have come as a breath of inviting, fresh air to those forced to labour under an authoritarian blanket.

Another experiment in seeing oneself as other involving recent French thought all but eliminated Uruguay altogether. In a speech in December 2002, novelist and essayist Amir Hamed argued that Uruguay was a 'misunderstanding' in three syllables, and that even to assume the country existed was to 'problematise the non-existent'[76] instead of screwing it up in a paper ball and talking about something else.[77] This is exactly what Hamed achieved in his *Retroescritura*,[78] a collection of essays form the early to mid 1990s. Combining Derrida with Baudrillard's simulacra and Deleuze and Guatari's schizoid analysis, Hamed manages an eclectic mix of often very perceptive observations on myth taken from Plato and other classics of the ancient world (complete with occasional quotations in Latin), recent Hollywood horror and science fiction movies (notably the *Alien, Back to the Future* and *Terminator* sequences, *The Silence of the Lambs* and later films featuring that cannibal who reads, Hannibal Lecter) and examples from the history of literary high modernism from Baudelaire to Eliot, all not infrequently peppered with untranslated phrases or sentences in English. The only reference to Uruguay is some paragraphs absorbing clauses in bold type from Javier de Viana. Here is a not untypical paragraph, part of a meditation on late capitalism as spectacle portrayed in the 1993 film *Delicatessen*:

> Nothing in this construction is surprising; rather, it is only too familiar. Approximately neo-gothic with a modern setting. As appropriate, on top of the building is a non-transcendental antenna [a lack of transcendence to which our time is not resigned], the medium between some nearby source and a television as black and white as any Cyclops eye. (The mediated ray gives energy to Frankenstein's monster. It gives it life)[79]

If all this were simply a late twentieth-century version of a previous *fin de siecle* preciosity as arrogant as it was decadent, it would not matter very much. But it is not. As his name suggests, Hamed (like Porzecanski, a Jewish woman of migrant family background) is a member of one of the many minorities routinely excluded by any discussion of Uruguay that assumes its homogeneity as nation and society. What Hamed does in *Retroescritura* is to question the complacent, backward-looking and thereby irrelevant view of themselves projected as the epitome of Uruguayan-ness by those Uruguayans who controlled the dominant culture, by doing to it what it did to him and other 'aliens': he ruthlessly excludes them. As in the paragraph above, the hotchpotch of foreign references and the taste for abstraction and categorical affirmation (the reader has no sense of being invited to debate the issue) incorporate inside the writing itself a set of alienating procedures. By simply expunging 'Uruguayan' as a useful interpretative or explicatory tool, Hamed enacts revenge by the foreign or alienated 'Other' by suggesting that, in effect, any self as peripheral as the Uruguayan is an alien monster penetrated (defined, even) by ideological currents centred elsewhere or nowhere but definitely not here.

However, if one risk encouraged by the adoption of a too ingenuously optimistic version of deconstruction was the elision of desire and actuality (as I suggested in regard to Porzecanski), Hamed suggests another: that of finding oneself condemned to write what is in effect an interminable commentary on one's own powerlessness, with prose fiction the only possible escape. This potential inability to get a permanent toe hold on reality and its attendant frustrations emerge clearly in a work by one of Hamed's closest friends and collaborators, Sandino Núñez. In his *Disneywar*, Hamed's horror films have become a mightmarish reality. For Núñez, the capitalism of 'circulation and consumption' has succesfully absorbed and neutralised everything from orgy to the kind of radical, horizontal freedoms advocated by La Movida. Its insatiable need and desire to melt down opposites produces ever new demands and addictions. In his paranoid vision, what Núñez wrote of AIDS could be extended to all of 'Disney capitalism': 'organic mechanics and conspiratorial hypothesis replace the processes of social critique. Contagion, epidemic, poisoning. Magic versus process once more. No commitment, no responsibility'. Even though Núñez can see that 'a culture that substitutes interpretation for respect is obscene', and that 'the intellectual who defends it' refuses to see his or her own place within it, he cannot offer any alternative because even a 'counter-police' culture turns out to be complicit with its opposite: 'There is no residue that does not begin further circulation, does not inaugurate another parasitical market, another peak in the inexhaustible polyhedron of diversity'. While not exactly quietist, and certainly not celebratory, Núñez's view of capitalism is fatalistic, that of a system so totally without fissures that 'hyperconsumist capitalism' may itself be 'the only really horizontal democratic game' since it can finally abolish all forms of representation, state and politics.[80] Here, the liberatory potential of deconstruction's articulation of difference has been swallowed up by a combination of Adorno's pessimistic version of popular culture and Foucault's view of power as ubiquitous and ineluctable to produce a situation in which any alternative to late capitalism is not only currently impractical but permanently unimaginable. The inherent pessimism to which this approach could succumb was not far away: 'the referents for an intellectual *traditio* do not exist; they lie dispersed in video memory, dusty archives or in libraries, real museums in the university'.[81] The use of the Latin word is revealing: nostalgia for past cultural forms that now look to have been made redundant turns into, or becomes an excuse for, the conviction that nothing can be done in the present.

A representative example of the frustrations attendant on this position might be university philosopher and semiotician Ruben Tani, a La Movida fellow traveller who when interviewed in 1988 had never been a political militant and looked like a forty-year old punk (having been born in 1946). Tani saw the traditional left as dogmatic, parochial, blinkered and uncreative, while the dictatorship allowed those like him to break free from having to think politically. Not that he was under any illusions about what it left behind: he felt like Mersault,[82] stranded in a grey concrete desert.[83]

Later, Tani could look back at his time as co-editor of *La República de Platón* [Plato's Republic][84] (where he collaborated with Sandino Núñez) as a moment when a more theoretically self-aware deconstructionist essay writing continued the thrust initiated by La Movida. The magazine set out to differentiate itself from mainstream Uruguayan cultural journalism by adopting a deliberately 'mannerist' style, as a self-reflexive deconstructive experiment dedicated to challenging what Tani saw as the 'classical', linear tradition of the naïve and empty commonplaces in the prevailing middle-class culture he abhorred.[85] This amounted to an attempt to tie advanced first-world philosophy and literary theory to a specifically Uruguayan mood which began as subterranean opposition to the dictatorship and continued as an alternative to the main cultural trends re-established during the period of transition to democracy. It is, indeed, difficult to imagine Mario Benedetti reading *La República de Platón* with much pleasure or understanding, but Núñez and Tani are not clear-cut examples of the benefits of cutting experimental intellectual work off from the local and the political.

It would be Rafael Bayce, the sociologist who was both a professional observer of La Movida as well as an older sympathiser with its aims and intentions, who would follow through that movement's creative energy to produce a set of genuinely political proposals that ostentatiously absorbed a large number of foreign contributions but applied them to creating a blueprint for progressive government in Uruguay. He had already indicated the need for such a project in 1989 with his accusation that, despite there having being more changes in Uruguay between 1970 and 1985 than in the previous six decades, the political elites insisted on trying to fit the new situation into old patterns rather than devise new ones while simultaneously criticising the twenty-year-old protagonists of La Movida for not coming up with any really new and creative alternatives.[86] In the first years of the new millenium,

Bayce accepted the implied consequences of his attack, using Uruguay as an example to advance his own set of five Herculean tasks to address what he identified as the three fundamental difficulties facing any government in the twenty-first century: 'governability, legitimacy and confidence [of citizens]'.[87] To accomplish this Bayce set out to 'found a new utopian imaginary' (119) for the left in 'modern, capitalist, consumerist and hedonist societies with uneven wealth distribution' in which there was wide distrust of all the utopias, socialist or social democratic, east or west (7).

Bayce emphasises the role played by foreign mentors and masters in his undertaking, not in continual referencing as in academic writing, but in lists. So we find in just two pages mention of relevant contributions by Habermas, Baudrillard, Mauss, Malinowski, Marx, Parsons, Weber, Herbert Spencer, Evans-Pritchard, Murray Edelman, Ricoeur, Girard, Lévi-Strauss and Veblen (26–7), to whom he adds Claus Offe, Albert Hirschman, Tibor Scitovsky, Morris Janovitz, Gilles Lipovetsky and Simmel (39, note), while a subheading names Aristotle, Kant, Weber, Parsons, Habermas, Bourdieu, Luhmann, and the Frankfurt and Chicago sociology schools as Bayce's 'comrades' in his project (63). The implication is that Uruguay, peripheral though it may be, is as relevant as any metropolitan community to the terms of analysis of these European and North American luminaries of philosophical, social and anthropological analysis. This is underlined by the constant penetration of Bayce's Spanish by terminology and syntax borrowed from such sources. The overall effect in Spanish is to foreground the unfamiliarity of the abstract and professional vocabulary in Uruguayan written Spanish, stressing not its irrelevance (which might be a conservative or complacent inference) but rather Bayce's conviction of Uruguay's need to open itself to the kind of self-analysis such verbal tools make possible.

However, the place where Bayce most visibly highlights the impact of the foreign and alien is in the title of his fourth labour of Hercules, which is in many ways the centre of his project as well as (by two pages) the longest chapter of the book: '*Empowerment* of Civil Society' (63), the first word being in italics *and* in English in the original, despite the existence of a Spanish equivalent ('empoderamiento', a literal translation) to which Bayce refers (8, note) while maintaining the English when he most needs to define the term as the lynchpin of his program (64). The defamiliarising effect of the English word underlines the necessity Bayce sees of rebuilding society from the civil society outwards and upwards rather than from its political structures, which is easier because it is what has usually been done, civil society being relatively underdeveloped in Uruguay (64, 69–73, 94–5). It is the ensuing emphasis on self-management and autonomy that shows most clearly the influence on Bayce of the participatory democracy favoured by the activists of La Movida twenty years earlier.

Bayce's first two Herculean labours are dedicated to how a progressive government can prevent itself from being a fetish later dumped as scapegoat as the wildly extravagant hopes which attracted ideologically uncommitted electors are inevitably dashed and the floating vote deserts it. Echoing Rial's account of the dominant myths that govern the way Uruguayans tend to think, Bayce fears that that the relatively new phenomenon (in Uruguay) of the swinging voter will be imprisoned in a 'lumpen tango ethic', a deeply conservative longing for a 'retro neo-Statism', a political 'simile' for the 'night of nostalgia' (14–15). To prevent the slide into a populist neo-Batllista resurrection, Bayce advocates a third labour of Hercules: a total renewal of the notions of supply and demand that emphasises finding out what consumers really want instead of the left imposing what it thinks the people should want, taking into account the crucial place of the ephemeral and non-durable in consumerist desire (31–62), the more widely applicable notion of citizen 'empowerment' then first appearing in this context. The book closes with the fifth task of building a communications policy that has citizen-generated information at a local level replace the lies, misinformation and rumour too easily disseminated by all media controlled from a centre, wherever and whatever it is (again closely following the practices of those involved in the 1980s Movida).

Bayce's 1989 book was an emblem of its time: a perfect exercise in playing catch-up that could not have been published in Uruguay before 1985. The vindication of a cultural movement of defiance that modelled many of its postures on icons of English and European punk rock, *Cultura política uruguaya* used North American sociology and the 1960s countercultural philosophy of Marcuse and Reich to cast a jaundiced eye over the fear and loathing left behind as the detritus of authoritarianism's distortions of Batllismo's legacy. Bayce acknowledged the emancipatory impact of Derridean poststructuralism as a tool to open up deeply internalised mythologies,[88] but, as I have briefly suggested, deconstruction would prove too volatile and ambiguous to be a reliable ally for the left. Leaning on the libertarian potential of the local La Movida and post-1968 French theory, Bayce's *5 tareas* remained faithful to the author's sociological roots by diverging from traditional left political programmes in two important repects. First, it pragmatically dealt with the realities of late capitalism as Bayce found them in Uruguay; second, it correspondingly omitted any utopianism based on some future socialist or post-capitalist alternative. It thereby confirmed what the irruption of the foreign in post-dictatorship Uruguay was trying to tell those who could bring themselves to listen: there was no going back.

The intellectual left in Uruguay were going to have to do what their confederates all over Latin America were doing in the wake of the collapse of the revolutionary dreams of the 1960s: re-evaluate the actual and potential strengths of electoral democracy, and work out, if they could, how to marry a politics forged in a still revered past of insurrection and opposition with the realities of governing a nation state in the globalised, postmodern present.

5

Dialogue Resumed

Democracy, Intellectuals and the Frente Amplio in Post-Dictatorship Uruguay

The abandoning of revolutionary utopia as a horizon for thought is in one way entry into the kingdom of death, since it supposes a resigned embrace of wretchedness, that is to say, of the wretched dimension of day-by-day reality as it is.

Alberto Moreiras (1993)

The Latin American Left Gropes toward the Ballot Box

In the national elections on 31 October 2004, the Frente Amplio[1] won the presidency of Uruguay as well as an absolute majority in both houses of parliament. While this victory had already been anticipated by centre-left forces elsewhere in the Southern Cone (notably Battellet in Chile, Kirschner in Argentina and Lula in Brazil), the Frente Amplio's triumph had a clear Uruguayan significance. When he assumed power on 1 March 2005, Tabaré Vázquez became the first Uruguayan president not to be a product of the national political elite – he was born, lived and worked as a doctor in the working-class Montevideo suburb of La Teja. In addition, his administration was the first since the country's independence not to come from either of the two traditional Uruguayan political parties, the Colorados or the Nationals. The arrival of this new centre-left government can justifiably be seen as a pivotal event in Uruguayan political history, making the 2004 elections as important a marker of change as those of 1958.

The focus of this chapter will not be on the history of the Frente's climb to electoral success, although inevitably frequent reference will need to be made to it. Rather, it will concentrate on the changing role of intellectuals in the formation of political alternatives to neoliberal orthodoxy, and on the counterweight of the declining influence of the intelligentsia in determining the direction of government policy. Indeed, I will begin by recalling Zygmunt Bauman's distinction mentioned above between intellectuals as legislators and interpreters and restated more forcefully as 'an emphatic rejection of the earlier claim to the "legislative" role of philosophers, and of the supracommunal, extraterritorial intellectuals in general, in questions of truth, judgement and taste':

> Modernity is reconstructed ex-post-facto as an era possessing the self-same features the present time feels most poignantly as missing, namely the universal criteria of truth, judgement and taste seemingly controlled and operated by the intellectuals.[2]

Although useful as a framework, we shall see that it requires at least some modification if applied to Latin America in general, and Uruguay in particular.

The influence of this view in Latin America is, however, undeniable. For example, Burity, taking Bauman as his principal theoretical point of departure, writes revealingly:

> We, as intellectuals, should be coherent about the interpretative nature of our position/activity, through the awareness of its contingency, non-totalization, and entanglement in regimes of truth which have strong political tones. We should ironize our seriousness, laugh at the circumspection of our gatherings and at a certain heroic view of the intellectual's mission.[3]

That first person plural is relevant to some extremely personal comments by Nicolás Casullo, who says in an interview: 'The Sartrean intellectual, the intellectual who transforms his life into a kind of engagement through which he must speak and discuss the whole social enterprise, disappeared, or is about to disappear', and goes on more contentiously to pronounce the demise of all utopian or messianic discourses.[4]

However extreme and over-pessimistic such views might be, there is no doubt that intellectuals throughout Latin America are currently less confident and more modest than their immediate forebears in their dealings with the politics of a post-dictatorial era. Thus Norbert Lechner, the Chilean political scientist with a very strong background in current European theory, could open a book on politics and the state in Latin America in 1981 by stating that political theory, while potentially helping to think through solutions, is itself part of the problem, and that consequently, when it turns to democracy, it can only do so honourably if it refuses the temptation to offer solutions and restricts itself willingly to participating in a debate. If revolution was the burning question of the 1960s, the turn to democracy in the 1980s, following the collapse of both left and right versions of the totalitarian state, must, for Lechner, be accompanied by the acceptance of intellectual debate as 'an itinerary without a script' and of the search for the truth not as an operation of logic but a moment in a 'historical practice', because utopia must be reduced now to simply working out 'what to do'.[5] Here we can see why the post-authoritarian intellectual left puts such an emphasis on rethinking democracy as the rebuilding of a sense of community after its devastation by the armed state and a virtually unrestricted market economy,[6] a preoccupation incorporated into the role of participatory democracy in non-state and non-party grassroots organizations collectively known as social movements.[7]

Juan Flo could expect someone in 1952 to know the answer to his question about Uruguay, 'What do we do, then?',[8] but some thirty years later Lechner had to humbly see in it only the first move in a debate. Benjamín Arditi, another ten years on, could only manage a much more tentative but nonetheless important question: 'what does it mean to be a socialist in our *fin de siècle*?', a necessary preamble to Flo's direct query. Arditi then divided the post-authoritarian Latin American left into two. On one side were the 'apocalyptic' militants who want ethical purity and work within a closed self-justifying system in order to destroy their class enemies rather than negotiate with them. On the other side are the 'integrated' ones who have abandoned the old and failed revolutionary models, accept that the changes following redemocratisation are irreversible, and see that only a revitalised and re-energised democracy can solve the 'great problems of solidarity, equality and participation'.

Like the Uruguayan Aldo Solari in the 1960s,[9] Arditi insisted on the need for political realism and efficiency, and suggested that intellectuals have enormous opportunities by working outside the influence of the state and articulating for the public 'demands, themes, proposals or critiques' for use by organizations, parties, even the state itself.[10] Similarly, Lechner also made an 'appeal for realism' to the left intelligentsia so they could establish politics as a place of negotiation by separating legitimacy from a sense of final, incontrovertible truth.[11] Such 'modest proposals' have found favour among a large number of Latin American progressive intellectuals, including Uruguayans struggling to find a role in a post-dictatorial scene. Long gone are the heady days of revolutionary change that had appeared to guarantee them the position of harbingers of a new and imminent utopia.

For example, Hopenhayn examines (even laments) the passing of revolutionary utopianism,[12] but also advocates a revaluation of democracy and the revalorization of civil society in order to work through and articulate alternatives to the new neoliberal fundamentalism frequently promoted by the state throughout much of Latin America.[13] Brunner also offered intellectuals only much reduced roles,[14] while Sarlo, echoing Walter Benjamin, reminded everyone that unfulfilled tasks and uncorrected injustices made them as responsible for the past as for the future, the problem being to find new ways of responding to the old challenges.[15]

But it is again Lechner who by the mid-1980s saw the leftist intellectual's main difficulty most clearly: how to work out whether or how socialism could be connected to available forms of democracy.[16] The issues are clear: What is the role of the intellectual in the redemocratised societies transfigured by the neoliberal economic hegemony? What is the relationship between the left and a civil society often left stranded by the terms of this new economic and political order? In reply, there seems some general agreement at least on a basic perspective:

> For a significant part of the Left, the struggle against the authoritarian states unfolded into a struggle against all forms of authoritarianism and reinforced the refusal of orthodox and rigid conceptual categories for political analysis . . . An emphasis on pluralism, diversity and flexibility inspired not only the appropriation of Gramsci's thought but also its blending with several other Marxist and non-Marxist authors. From Foucault to Cornelius Castoriadis and Agnes Heller, from Claude Lefort to Jurgen Habermas, Norberto Bobbio, Tocqueville, and Hannah Arendt, the renovation of the Left opened itself to an antiauthoritarian eclecticism that makes it difficult to single out particular influences.[17]

As one recent commentator summarised the whole matter: it's no longer a question of an alternative to democracy, but of an alternative form of it.[18]

There do remain, however, more than a few unreconstructed adherents of the 'apocalyptic' left, among the best known being Petras and Morley, who in effect accuse the majority of Latin American intellectuals of betraying Marxism and the revolution by selling out to their imperialist enemies.[19] This sort of critique seeks to disqualify those it attacks rather than meeting their ideas on their own terms. It resembles the tactics we saw Carlos Rama use much earlier in Uruguay to impugn Aldo Solari because he had, in Rama's estimation, betrayed the cause.[20] Old habits die hard.

This kind of diatribe can be easily shrugged off perhaps, but it is more difficult simply to dismiss the work of Neil Larsen. Significantly, he praises Morley and Petras while criticising the likes of Arditi, Brunner and Lechner, but the main focus for his attack is Ernesto Laclau and Chantal Mouffe.[21] The backbone of his critique is contained in the following paragraph:

> The fact that the 'third path' calls itself 'radical democracy', draping itself in the 'ethics' if not the epistemology of Enlightenment, the fact that it outwardly resists the 'fixity' of any one privileged subject, makes it, in a sense, the more perfect 'radical' argument for a capitalist politics of pure

irrationalist spontaneity. And we know who wins on the battlefield of the spontaneous. While the oppressed are fed the myths of their own 'hegemony' (and why not, for 'on the threshold of postmodernity', humanity is 'for the first time the creator of its own history'?) those already in a position to 'articulate' the myths for us only strengthen their hold on power.[22]

Larsen can be as sarcastic as Morley and Petras, even if his position is more densely argued, but that does not excuse his apparent inability to distinguish between a resolutely post-Marxist argument and an anti-Marxist one, which Laclau and Mouffe's is not. Although Larsen complains that Marxist organisations have not undertaken the right kind (if any) of self-criticism, the same may be said of himself as well as Morley and Petras. All of them are writing and thinking (notice especially Larsen's very conventional Marxist vocabulary) as though nothing had changed, as though the global economic and political environment is as it was in the 1960s, and that consequently there is no real need for them to rethink their views either. What none of them explain is how they or anyone else is going to be able to turn the clock back, or how an alternative to capitalism (as opposed to variously modified or regulated versions of it) can be put into practice in an all but totally globalised planet.

All these large issues are nicely summed up in the combination of the worry that, although 'the left has dressed up as democracy, it is not clear that democracy wants to dress up as the left',[23] and the reminder that 'modern constitutional democracies owe as much to Locke and Montesquieu as to the *levellers* and *sansculottes*'.[24] The question will be how the Uruguayan left and its intellectuals can negotiate the tensions between a constituency's rights and the lingering suspicion that democracy itself was the problem. However, as Alberto Couriel – to whom we shall return, since he is a writer, university teacher and a prominent Frente Amplio senator – reminds us: conditions in the 1990s might be conducive to one, but 'there is neither revolution nor anyone advocating the possibility of starting one'.[25]

Revolution or Election? The Uruguayan Intellectual Left Faces Reality

The remainder of this chapter looks at those intellectuals who are closely aligned to, or even form part of, the political process that led to the electoral success of the centre-left in the November 2004 presidential elections. They occupy an uneasy position somewhere between Bauman's categories of 'legislators' and 'interpreters', but fit more neatly into Arditi's idea of being 'integrated' in that they are heavily committed to the revaluation and strengthening both of democratic procedures and of the notion of a civil society that exists separately from the state. Also, in being close to the political mainstream, they follow in the tracks of those leftist intellectuals deeply involved in the processes that led to the foundation of the Frente Amplio in 1971. They either participate in or bear witness to the two major dilemmas facing the Uruguayan left-wing intelligentsia in the post-authoritarian period: what to do about socialism, whether, as for the Socialist and Communist parties, it harks back to Marxism and the Russian Revolution, or is associated with the more recent anti-imperialist nationalism inspired by the Cuban revolution of 1959; and secondly, how to continue or transform the Frente's own tradition of being in legal opposition to the conservative and increasingly repressive governments up to the 1973 coup, or subsequently in clandestine or indirect opposition within Uruguay, and openly and noisily if in exile abroad.

When it emerged from the dictatorship, the Frente was faced with an entirely different context from that in which it was hatched. In 1971 the Cuban revolution and its influence, together with a local guerrilla war and a population sympathetic at least to the initial aims of the Tupamaros, had encouraged the hopes of a determined reformist Left. In 1985 the Uruguayan left confronted a very changed world: transition to democracy, a process that not only rejoined the best traditions of Uruguayan politics but also latched on to the general trend in the Southern Cone; a dictatorship that had ushered in neoliberal economics with its rounds of privatization and deregulation, a trend continued in succeeding civil administrations. 'Politics and politicians are no longer what they were', wrote one commentator, and neither were the citizens: the state had been rolled back leaving them to fend for themselves, with the result that individualism ruled, deflecting everyone's energies away from what promoted solidarity or a sense of community and toward their own needs and desires.[26] Of the many pressing problems besetting post-authoritarian Uruguay, two would prove decisive for the left: the collapse of 'real existing socialism', leaving the left (in Uruguay as elsewhere) without an international model to which it could reliably appeal; and an appalling economic crisis, growing since 1999 but at its worst in 2002, precipitated mostly by the recession in Argentina.[27]

Between 1971 and 2004 the Frente Amplio evolved from a 'coalition of parties' into a 'unified party of coalition'.[28] As such, over the last twenty years it has successfully attracted support from two sectors traditionally bound to the Colorados or Nationals: the very poor and marginalised, and workers and middle class voters in the interior. It has done so despite (or perhaps because of) the very public wrangling that has occurred within its own ranks. Because of its make-up, the Frente has had no alternative but to make public any internal arguments, a necessity that has over the years become a virtue, if only because the other two parties have tried to keep theirs secret. For the Frente, open dialogue and debate have been at the forefront of its appeal, because they have seemed a guarantee of its honesty. Numerous daily and periodical publications,[29] radio and television interviews and features, as well as books of the sort to be discussed below, keep the presence of individual members and different groups within the Frente before the public eye. While parliamentary representation and municipal and (since March 2005) national government have demanded a public record of disciplined and unified efficiency, the Frente's origins as a coalition of disparate ideological forces has meant that there is greater, though not unlimited, public tolerance for internal disagreement and debate. Given the Frente's electoral success over the last twenty years, there seems little doubt that this display of frequently substantial difference of opinion within the party has not been taken as evidence of incapacitating disunity. To the contrary, it may have contributed not only to the Frente's own credibility but also to rekindling the electorate's more general trust in civil society as a site for reasoned intellectual and political debate. Along the way, as we shall see more specifically below, all who want to can participate as 'organic' intellectuals for their sector.

During the transition after the dictatorship, the Frente had very little time to gather its forces together before the elections of November 1984. Moreover, one element the military exacted for leaving power was that neither Wilson Ferreira Aldunate of the Nationals nor the Frente's Liber Seregni would be permitted to stand as presidential candidates of their respective parties. This almost certainly lost Ferreira Aldunate the presidency for a second time, and also required that Seregni's place be occupied by a token substitute, the honourable but rather uncharismatic Juan Crottogini.[30] Under the circumstances, that its 1984 electoral showing just about matched that of 1971 was a positive outcome for the Frente.

Since those early moments of redemocratisation the key years for the Frente Amplio have been 1989 and 1994. The earlier of the two saw the first major split in the Frente's ranks since its foundation in 1971. The Christian Democrats (crucial in 1971) and the Movimiento por el Gobierno del Pueblo [MGP] but renamed the Partido por el Gobierno del Pueblo [PGP], now under the leadership of Hugo Batalla (who had replaced the assassinated Zelmar Michelini), broke away to form the Nuevo Espacio. This later split into two, with Hugo Batalla taking his more conservative section back into the Colorado party (from where Michelini had originally brought them in 1971), with the remainder, now following Zelmar's son Rafael, returning to the Frente's fold under the title Nueva Mayoría.

The reasons for the split seem to be twofold. First is what appear to be Batalla's personal ambitions. He was rejected as the Frente's presidential candidate for the 1989 elections and after his defection would later join forces with ex-President Sanguinetti's moderate Foro Batllista faction of the Colorados and become their vice-presidential candidate in the 1990s.

Secondly, these moves were made possible because the centrist groups in the Frente felt in danger of being displaced by what was happening on their left.

One of the most divisive issues was the admission into the Frente of the now legalised MLN-Tupamaros, a move that the old leadership had been planning since their days in prison.[31] Later re-titled with the more electorally focussed Movimiento por la Participación del Pueblo [MPP], it gathered under its wing various other small more radical sectors of the Frente as well as some independents and renegades from the other two main parties, and would prove essential in the decade to come in ensuring that the Frente could retain its left-wing credentials while moderating its program and its rhetoric. José 'Pepe' Mujica in many ways epitomised the internal changes undergone by the MLN, being one of its founders and a guerrilla fighter in the 1960s, a political prisoner for the whole of the dictatorship, and then, unpredictably, a senator from 1994, a minister from 2005, and potential presidential candidate in 2009! His attractive, deliberately rustic style made him the most recognised and popular figure on the Frente's left, as well as one of its most interviewed and humourously articulate spokesmen.[32] However, the internal controversy originally caused by their application to join in April 1986 can be measured by the fact that it took the Frente three years to persuade itself to accept them.

Their doing so coincided with one of the wide ranging discussions frequent in the post-dictatorship Frente Amplio as the groups within it began to negotiate the fallout when events in the socialist bloc during the late 1980s forced a confrontation with the realities of Soviet-style communism, and then with its demise. A representative debate took place between Manuel Laguarda of the Socialist Party's executive and Hebert Gatto, a political scientist and at the time also an official from Batalla's PGP, then in the throes of divorcing itself from the coalition. Gatto had predicted some two years earlier that eventually there would have to be a debate between those who wanted to reform and modernise the program and structure of the Frente and those who merely sought a reinvigorated mobilisation to implement the original platform.[33] Although the first salvo came from Laguarda in 1989, it is far from clear that he intended to set off a full-scale quarrel. The kernel of his brief one-page essay is captured in two quotations: 'we have to choose: with the nation or with imperialism; with the bourgeoisie or with the workers', thus reinstating the stark alternatives that appeared to be the only option in the 1960s, and the assertion that the reformists 'confused renovation, which is critique and going beyond, and thereby taking on socialist thought, with abandoning it'.[34] The conventional terminology, the bland assumption that everyone was agreed on what socialist thinking was, and the either/or mentality suggest a backward-looking stance that assumed little had changed from the emotionally charged political climate of the years preceding the military coup.

Gatto was not slow to jump on what for him were the obvious drawbacks in Laguarda's views. He began rudely, accusing Laguarda of writing one more example of unreconstructed 'classical' left ideology, and of being a prisoner of a Marxist-Leninist rhetoric that had not changed in nearly a hundred years. History had made Marx and Lenin's forecasts obsolete, while neo-Stalinism wiped out personal liberties, showing that violent revolution proved incompatible with democracy. It was essential to stop being 'conservatives in radical clothing', Gatto concluded.[35]

Laguarda's retort reaffirmed analysis based on class and accused Gatto of advocating a society of undifferentiated and unconnected individuals that ignored the collective and communal.[36] In a continuation,[37] Laguarda advocated a self-managed socialism with most decision-making centred on workplace or organization and an emphasis on the development of civil society over and above the official power of the State. In other words, Laguarda was calling for a highly participatory democracy that combined, as it were, the functions of an ideal rank-and-file or neighbourhood committee with the sort of social mobilisation we saw Bayce recommending in the previous chapter or that was demanded by the use of plebiscites and referenda (see below).

This relatively minor debate was one of many public events that highlighted major differences of opinion within the Frente Amplio between the late 1980s and the mid 1990s. The occasions and the titles may be different but the problem being addressed was essentially the same: in what ways would the Frente's political programme, internal structures and overall strategy need to be changed to adapt to the new circumstances, including a necessary commitment to the compromises of electoral competition, while still offering a genuinely leftist alternative to the traditional parties. The form and content of Harnecker's examination of the Frente at the time is exemplary, displaying clearly the problems besetting the Frente but also illustrating its commitment to open dialogue as the means of resolving them.[38] Using roundtable discussion, one-on-one interviews and (but only when absolutely necessary) written responses to set questions, Harnecker transcribes the often conflicting opinions elicited from leaders and representatives from the full range of the Frente's groups and currents between April 1990 and May 1991. The result is a cross-section of perspectives within the party on the Frente's history, structure and political platform, and on how it should go forward. Enrique Rubio, who spoke at the end for all those who participated in the project, said they all realised they were 'exposed, out in the open [a la intemperie]', that only a 'culture of debate and dissent within unity' could 'produce something solid', thanking the editor for her determination to make a book that was 'intelligible and useful for the left in Uruguay and Latin America'.[39] Since the Uruguayan left was so aware of the local and international importance of the process they were undergoing, it is no surprise that it was one of a number of similar enterprises.

In June 1990, a seminar on the impact of the collapse of 'real socialism' on the Uruguayan left featured participants from positions across the Frente as well as journalists, political scientists and historians,[40] while two years later the weekly *Brecha* could publish a special edition promoted as 'the debate the Uruguayan left had to have' on the same topic, with a similar array of participants (some of them, indeed, the same individuals).[41] Two years later still, coinciding with national elections and the process leading to the creation of moderate Encuentro Progresista within the Frente (see below), came a book of short conversations with thirty members of the Frente (mostly from 1992) followed by relevant extracts from previously published articles and interviews, all on the theme of exactly what it meant to be on the left in the 1990s. The painful question of whether moderation of pre-dictatorship views constituted betrayal, whether of oneself or (worse) of others who had suffered or even died for the original model, often hovered over the whole inquiry.[42] Two close observers at the time saw that the idea of a party as vanguard was giving way to an alternative in which democracy gradually replaced socialism as the principal focus, and the whole notion of 'the people' was redefined in a context of open debate among equals.[43] The continuing relevance of these polemics is shown in a recent attack on the Frente for abandoning its original 'national and demo-cratic, anti-imperialist and anti-oligarchy program for the people', as well as the whole idea of revolution.[44]

The year 1989 was not only important for polemics. The accelerating implosion of the Soviet bloc would erode the influence within the Frente of the Communist Party (despite its rechristening as Democracia Avanzada), its proud history suddenly converted into a dead weight when compared to the younger, fresher and more participatory style of the MPP, which would become the Frente's most voted sector by 2004. Equally significant in the long term was the Frente's first electoral victory: it captured the municipal council of Montevideo under the candidacy of Tabaré Vázquez, whose support base was the Socialist Party. The Frente's policy in Montevideo emphasised renewal of infrastructure in the poorer, frequently ignored areas of the city, a general clean-up of the centre, an attempt to roll back the all-pervasive practice of clientelism[45] and a deliberate if only partially successful campaign to decentralise the bureaucracy and involve residents in making important decisions that affected them directly, as well as holding back wherever possible the worst effects of the aggressive neoliberal economic policies of the National and Colorado national administrations. It was also, of course, the Frente's first chance to exercise political power. Its performance has been efficient enough to guarantee its hold on Montevideo's town hall until today.[46]

Also in 1989, the internal structure of the Frente changed, which would have very significant consequences. One was the creation of a new sector, the reformist Vertiente Artiguista under the leadership of Mariano Arana, who in 1994 succeeded Vázquez as Mayor of Montevideo. That allowed Vázquez an early shot at the presidency as leader of the Frente on Seregni's retirement in 1996. The importance of the Vertiente Artiguista is underlined by the fact that its line-up included two people who had been instrumental in getting the Frente Amplio together in 1971: Héctor Rodríguez and Oscar Bruschera. Having helped to found it, they were now ready to aid in renewing it.[47]

The turning point in this process was 1994. The economist Danilo Astori created the Asamblea Uruguay in May, anticipating the national elections in November. This sector's eloquent leader was a strong rival to Vázquez until he made the mistake of supporting Seregni in 1996, which fatally weakened his challenge for the presidential candidacy in 1999,[48] and facilitated the ascendency of the MPP. More important was the appearance of the Encuentro Progresista (EP), which seems to have been the personal creation of Tabaré Vázquez, and arguably would become the lynchpin of the Frente's electoral fortunes in 1999 and 2004.[49] The EP was principally made up of progressive Christian Democrats, who returned after leaving in 1989, and a group called Alianza Progresista, fugitives from the National Party headed by Rodolfo Nin Novoa, ex-mayor of Cerro Largo, who became Vázquez's running mate in 2004. Combined with Vázquez's Socialist Party affiliations, the EP became a potent reformist force within the Frente, and enabled Vázquez to see off Astori's challenge to be the Frente's presidential candidate in 1999. Astori was rewarded in 2004, being named as Minister of Finance in any future centre left government well before the elections, a gesture designed to reassure commercial and banking circles, where he is held in high esteem.

Several other historical matters need to be briefly examined before passing on to the role of intellectuals in and around the Frente. The most important of these were the constitutional changes of 1996. While some elements of the Frente in opposition supported them, they do seem to have been constructed by the Colorados and Nationals to prevent the left from winning power, a strategy that worked in 1999. The essential 1996 provisions divided municipal from national elections; imposed a single presidential candidate for each party (which the Frente had always done since 1971), a mechanism that stopped national elections doubling as 'primaries' determining the ranking of sectors within each party; and, most significantly, instituted a second round if no party got more than 50 percent in the first.[50] This latter measure meant that although the Frente was the most voted party on the first round in 1999 (it achieved just over 40 percent of the national vote), it was forced to run off against the Colorados' candidate (who had come second) and who arranged an alliance with the Nationals, whose supporters for the first time in Uruguayan history were obliged to vote for their traditional arch enemy. The strategy worked in the short term (Vázquez lost to Jorge Batlle), but set a dangerous precedent: it taught traditional party followers that they could vote outside their normal party lines, thus encouraging the creation of a relative novelty in Uruguayan electoral politics, the swinging voter. What is more, the Frente's activists learnt they needed to win on the first round, a goal that suddenly seemed reachable: the Frente had doubled its vote since 1989, and had got over 30 percent in the interior, where their support had been historically low. As the National and Colorado administrations moved further to the right, especially in their implementation of neoliberal economic policies, the Frente was picking up votes from the vacated centre and the marginalised poor without having to move to the right itself, a process sealed by the financial debâcle of 2001–2. The left did not so much move to the centre; the right vacated it and the left expanded to include it.[51]

Two further points can be more briefly outlined. The first is that the Frente's current political platform is a pared back moderation of its original program.[52] Gone are the once almost obligatory references to 'anti-oligarchy' and 'anti-imperialism' (the tone towards the United States is more conciliatory though still critical, and the need for dialogue with local business and political elites is recognised). Also expunged is the idea of nationalising financial institutions and implementing complete control over foreign trade. Retained, however, are the desire to redistribute income, a commitment to those in most need, the determination that the State will mitigate the worst effects of the application of globalised market forces, and a reinvigorated plan for regional integration through Mercosur and other alliances. Similarly, although the process has been streamlined somewhat so that more decisions can be taken by majority than by consensus, the emphasis of the Frente's decision-making procedures is still on dialogue, consultation and open debate.[53]

The second point is what has come to be called ironically the 'traditionalization' of the Frente Amplio. It is ironic because the Frente is becoming more like the two 'traditional' parties in that its own history or 'tradition' is becoming a more essential element in its identity, while association with globalised, non-national kinds of modernisation has increasingly 'de-traditionalised' the Colorados and Nationals.[54] The Frente's history is one of sacrifice and courage dating from the days of its resistance to Pacheco's authoritarianism in the 1960s and to the twelve years of military dictatorship. This has produced a 'tradition' by successfully passing loyalty to it from one generation to the next, and moreover 'stealing' the children of 'traditionally' Colorado or National families.[55] The Frente's standing and the loyalty it inspired were enhanced throughout almost the entire post-dictatorship period by its role in organising plebiscites or referenda to oppose proposals varying from the one guaranteeing immunity to the military for human rights violations in 1989 to those attacking privatisation legislation a decade later. These exercises honed the party's mobilisation skills and built up a legion of activists and supporters by associating it with popular opposition to both Colorado and National governments, even when the projects themselves failed to win the approval of a majority of the electorate.[56]

The whole general situation before the 2004 elections has been eloquently summed up as follows:

> the social State became a trading post, the State as businessman went over to services and the State as regulator increasingly accepted the free play of the market. Even so, this State is far from the privatised and minimalist State embraced by so many in the region.[57]

When the Frente Amplio won with 50.45 percent of the vote, it might seem on paper a slim majority. It was not: since 1954 no party has received more than 50 percent of valid votes; not since 1950 has any party received more than 50 per cent of all votes cast, valid or not, both occasions well before the advent of the Frente Amplio or any other party that could challenge the traditional parties' hegemony. As Yaffé has justifiably reminded everyone,[58] Solari in the 1960s was wrong to write off the left so soon, but he was not wrong in insisting that, if the left could not take power through revolution, it would only have any chance of doing so if it embraced wholeheartedly the route via the ballot box, and would only convince voters if it offered alternatives that looked practicable rather than utopian.[59] Since taking office in March 2005, the centre-left government has had a mixed record in its response to its historic challenge.[60]

The first two years of the Frente Amplio national government have seen most success in two areas: first, it has not only continued the post-2002 economic recovery but has exploited it to improve the plight of the very poor, the unemployed and generally most disadvantaged. Second, it has honoured its pledge to circumvent the laws giving the military immunity from prosecution for human rights abuses during the dictatorship by investigating cases of the 'disappeared' and putting on trial not only high-ranking officers but also one ex-president, although its attempt to legislate a 'Never Again' reconciliation day has predictably caused huge controversy both within and outside government ranks. Reforms in such areas as welfare, health, education and income tax, however, seem to have stalled or remain unfinished. The government's pragmatic (and not always conspicuously competent) foreign affairs policies have dismayed some, especially on the left: Vázquez has worked with Venezuela's Hugo Chávez[61] but has also given

George Bush the ceremonial keys to the capital. However, Uruguay's conflict with Argentina over the use of the River Uruguay and its quest to reform Mercosur structures are unresolved. Internally, the attempt to marry the need to represent Frente's different groups at government level with the equally imperative need for efficiency, initiative and skill has not always been successful, while some have felt that executive decision-making practices have made redundant much of the lively internal debate. Such wrangling has not yet caused disunity but has rather resulted in better policy, anticipating or neutralising parliamentary opposition from Colorados and Nationals still unaccustomed to their new less prominent role.

Politicians as 'Organic' Intellectuals

In addition to the 'traditionalization' and the gradual restructuring of its original 'coalition' form, the Frente has gone through a process of professionalisation. While in part resulting from the experience of governing Montevideo, this has also come about through the background and careers of some of its leading personnel. Some of the Frente's 'organic' intellectuals therefore come from within the party. As we have seen, Mujica is university educated, while Vázquez himself is a surgeon, Mariano Arana an architect and town planner, Astori and Alberto Couriel are both economists and Vertiente Artiguista Senator Rodrigo Arocena a scientist, while the signatures of historians and political scientists such as José Rilla, Alvaro Rico and Gerardo Caetano appear on internal Frente documents, and the latter two plus the revered historian José Pedro Barrán were appointed by Vázquez to write a new report on the 'disappeared'.[62] What is more, all of these except Mujica are or have been teachers and researchers at tertiary institutions at home or abroad.

Enrique Rubio is a prime candidate to represent one current among the Frente's 'organic' intellectuals. A university-trained history teacher, a trade union activist imprisoned by the military, a senator and one of the leaders of the reformist Vertiente Artiguista sector, Rubio's abilities were recognised in his appointment by Vázquez to head the Budget and Planning Office in the presidency. He also illustrates what can happen to socialist thinking when it takes on board the sort of questioning of its own status that we earlier saw so preoccupying the likes of Norbert Lechner. In a jointly authored volume that suggested the post-authoritarian period could not be adequately addressed with theories and methods derived from the 1960s and earlier, Rubio already indicated that the left would need to 'revolutionise' its whole approach to political theory.[63] However, it is in his work from the 1990s onwards that the full extent of the crisis is analysed.

Rubio sees all his books as growing one from the other: the second is co-written with one of the two co-authors of the first and is dedicated to the other (as well as to 1960s unionist Héctor Rodríguez).[64] The third book (Rubio's first as single author) attempts to bring the second up to date and supersede the 1985 volume,[65] while the most recent to date[66] offers an accelerated, abbreviated and more urgent summary of both the 1999 book and a detailed analysis of the new knowledge industries.[67] Moreover, running through them all is a growing sense of doubt and tentativeness that characterises not so much their content but the tone and manner of the writing. If in 1994 he could speak of theory on the left as a 'tower of Babel' as different voices competed to tell it which way to go when its 'classical centres' did not hold (*UE*, 6), by 1999 the theories he previously hoped would remedy the situation had become part of the problem (*IF*, 17–19). Seven years later, there were 'no predetermined outcomes and no pre-selected methods. No ends to justify means and no means to determine any end' (*ID*, 69), as the need to de-totalise left thinking (*IF*, 27) became the task of 'complicating' ['complejizar'] logic to avoid 'totalitarian' thinking (*ID*, 53), an endeavour summed up in the title of chapter three of *Izquierdas y derechas*: 'Revise Marx or Drag Rawls to the Left?' The most noticeable effect on Rubio's method of presenting his arguments is the increasing frequency and ubiquity of phrases like 'in my opinion' (the opening words of chapter one of *Izquierdas*), 'in my judgment' and 'I believe that', often coupled in his recommendations with expressions of weak obligation such as 'it is necessary' or 'we must' that guarantee no outcomes and suggest no particular strategies. There is no lack of passion and commitment on Rubio's part; just the painful and laborious recognition that there are no longer any grounds for presumption.

Rubio's socialism is founded in both the mature and the currently more popular younger Marx, though here in conjunction with Gramsci (a long time companion of the Latin American left) and the 'post-Marxism' of Foucault on power, Laclau and Mouffe on strategy, as well as the likes of Rawls and other philosophers of more individualist notions of liberty. This eclectic combination is the product of what he sees as the left's need to revisit basic principals (*IF*, 90–1). For Rubio the view of capitalism as forever stranded between permanent crisis and definitive victory is unproductive (*UE*, 84) and he also believes that 'post-capitalism presupposes societies of abundance not yet in sight' (*ID*, 70). In the 1994 and 1999 books, he advocates working toward a 'utopia of democracy' because socialism depends on a kind of post-work freedom as yet unavailable (*UE*, 159 and *IF*, 245). Consequently, he would not abandon socialism, but rather sort out its confusions to democratise and internationalise it (*ID*, 54–5 and 70), although there is little doubt he would arouse the traditional left's suspicions by using 'left' and 'progressive' as synonyms. He wants a republican sense of citizenship that is on 'the left of the rights of man' (*ID*, 64), the key to human rights being the decentralisation and dispersal of power and the revision of the concept of private property (*IF*, 211 and 140–1). Although Rubio accepts that nationalisms are going to be around for the foreseeable future (*ID*, 126), the underlying theme of both the 1999 and 2007 books is the need to find international and democratic alternatives to neoliberal economics, for which he reserves the word 'globalisation', against which he opposes a democratic and progressive 'planetisation' (*IF*, 44 and *ID*, 12, 18, 24–5, 103 and 128).[68]

The passage from Rubio to Alberto Couriel illustrates not only similarities and differences among the Frente's intellectuals but also, more generally, its inclusion of varying perspectives under the one umbrella. Couriel is a university economist with a lengthy bibliography on national and regional issues and a long career as an academic in national and Latin American universities. He has been consultant with international organisations on labour relations and economic matters, has been since 1995 a senator for the non-MLN independents in the MPP, and was in the lower house for five years before that. The book considered here, published in the lead-up to the 2004 national elections and explicitly about the left and Uruguay's future,[69] mixes conference papers and articles with two long parliamentary speeches on the economy and specific proposals for implementation by the Frente in government.

Couriel comes from the same background of doubt and uncertainty as Rubio but his attitude to it is down-to-earth and decisive. In the move from 'radicalisation' to 'moderation', the certainties of the 1960s have gone, along with the temptations of 'authoritarian extremism' and all assumptions about who the real subjects of history are. Although he personally favours a 'socialist solution', he cannot put one forward, partly because it was never part of the Frente's program, but mostly because the collapse of 'existing socialism' has made unviable all current theories on the transition from a free market to a planned economy and from privately to socially owned property. So, despite his wish to promote the continuation of a 'totalising' vision (which Rubio saw as a danger), Couriel no longer urges a 'confrontation with the enemy' in the form of an anti-oligarchy and anti-imperialism struggle, but accepts that social and class conflicts must be resolved through dialogue, negotiation, accords, pacts and agreements, because the democratic ethics of equity and equality demand that no class defeat another and nobody's property be confiscated or forcibly nationalised.[70] Vindicating Aldo Solari's questioning of the Uruguayan left's capacity for political realism and commitment to the formalities of electoral democracy in 1962,[71] Couriel put forward what amounts to a suggested immediate plan for government whose two touchstones are democratisation and redistribution, with quite specific recommendations in the areas of the economy, international relations, taxation and reform of the state, a proposal he considered important enough to be published separately in English.[72] Coming to grips with the current situation as it is and getting into a position to do something about it is Couriel's way of dealing with the theoretical vacuum that worries Rubio much more. Couriel would no doubt agree with Mujica, his sector's leader, that the MPP had moved towards 'reality' and 'common sense'.[73] At least some of Solari's doubts concerning the left's capacity to be realistic about the electorate's needs and potential would seem finally to have been answered, but, contrary to the axioms of the diehards of the traditional 1960s left, this no longer means giving in to the right. When asked by an *Economist* reporter in early 2007 whether Uruguay could be 'the next Chile', political scientist and historian Adolfo Garcé replied that they would like a capitalism as 'dynamic' as Chile's but 'with more emphasis on equality', to which the reporter commented that 'Uruguay may have to choose between dynamism and egalitarianism'.[74] As the likes of Rubio and Couriel make clear, along with the Frente Amplio's policies in government, this right-wing political logic is precisely what the Uruguayan centre-left refuses to acknowledge, and it does not need a theory of socialism to do it.

It cannot be said, however, that either Jorge Zabalza or Jorge Torres lacked such a theory, coming as they did from the ranks of the Tupamaros. Zabalza was not only an early recruit but, after being released from prison in 1985 as one of the dictatorship's last nine 'hostages', played a key role in the MLN's transformation into the legal MPP. Although he resigned from the MLN itself in 1995, he was elected as a Montevideo councillor as a radical independent. Torres was a founder of the MLN but since returning from exile in 1985 preferred writing (poetry, theatre and political analysis) to political activism. While all their writings studied here can fall into the ever-growing category of MLN public self-criticism devoted to explaining why the Tupamaros' guerrilla war failed, Zabalza's work exceeds that narrow range because of the impact of his and others' similar attitudes on the internal development of the Frente Amplio as a whole, while Torres's critique amounts to a frontal assault on one of the holy shrines of the left in Latin America as well as Uruguay: the legacy of Ernesto 'Che' Guevara.

Torres's work is almost entirely the product of subsequent reflection on his activities as a guerrilla fighter in the 1960s since, unlike the Frente's politician-intellectuals we have just discussed, he admits to lacking the academic, theoretical and professional background his subject matter requires, but feels that 'those of us' with inside experience of revolutionary struggle and its costs have both the right and the obligation to examine that history even if the exposure of deficiencies and weaknesses runs the risk of getting them branded as traitors to the cause.[75] His book on the reasons for the MLN's failure in the 1970s is less promising than it sounds, becoming for much of its length a rather shapeless and long-winded rebuttal of outsiders' views (from the Uruguayan military to Debray) and a review of well-known MLN documents. However, Torres anticipates the later work by seeing Che's Bolivian sally as the elephant in the room for any discussion of revolution in Latin America, and suggesting that the MLN's main problem was its inability to question or think outside the premises of its own theorising, thus utterly failing to anticipate changes of direction by its enemies, or to make any preparations about what to do in the event of its own defeat.[76]

In *Cuba y el Che*, Torres retreats to an earlier unexamined premise common to all the failed revolutionary movements throughout Latin America: the 'foco' theory espoused by Che Guevara and promulgated by Regis Debray. In a nutshell, Torres accuses these two, abetted by Fidel, of distorting reality in favour of an optimistic theory of revolution that encouraged and enabled others to do likewise in their own countries, thus condemning tens of thousands to useless suffering, defeat and death. So successful was this campaign, Torres argues, that in Bolivia Che himself could not see the reality in front of him because of the ideological cloud blurring his vision, a plight exemplified in the text of Che's *Bolivian Diaries*, the main focus of Torres's short book. The real nature of the Vietnam war and the Cuban revolutionary process prior to 1959 were obfuscated so as to promote the voluntarist thesis that the whole continent would be liberated from the effects of American imperialism if just a few could acquire the romantic qualities of heroic self-sacrifice necessary to lead the way, even if, like Che himself, death in action turned them into revolutionary martyrs. Torres's view is that not only was this approach blatantly wrong-headed because it passed over the resistant facts of each individual country's situation, but also that the intensity of the counter-revolution it provoked was such that it made the resulting neoliberal economic offensive even worse than it might have been. The trinity of Guevara, Castro and Debray become partially responsible for much more than just a failed revolution and its attendant losses.[77]

It is perhaps inevitable, at a time when a de-radicalised (centre-) left is in power or making a good showing in several Latin American nations' version of the combination of electoral democracy and global capitalism, that this same left's revolutionary past and its failures and defeats should come under close scrutiny, especially from its own adherents. Torres's is a particularly aggressive instance in that it suggests that Che Guevara's legacy was actively harmful at the time as well as being irrelevant now. A more benign form of this kind of revisionism might be Castañeda's contention that in the new millennium Guevara's role is mostly nostalgic,[78] but Castañeda is (as Torres anticipates for himself) precisely one of those considered to be a traitor by those who have maintained the faith.[79]

Such considerations throw into sharp relief the contribution of Jorge Zabalza, for not only is he also largely an auto-didact[80] whose works are products of particular personal and political conjunctures, but he both retained, even deepened, his earlier revolutionary convictions and tried to put them into practice in his militancy with the MLN since 1985. Consequently, his books make little sense without an excursion into the MLN's post-dictatorship experiment with legality.[81]

When Raúl Sendic, the iconic founder of the MLN, emerged very damaged from the military's jail in March 1985, he brought with him the idea for a political front that would be to the left of the existing Frente Amplio but would include it, the embodiment of a transformed and legalised MLN devised in prison by himself and other leading members of the organisation. While this notion would, perhaps predictably, not prosper, it would become the basis of an MLN committed to electoral democracy that requested formal entry into the Frente Amplio in April 1986. This was not granted until two years later, the long wait an indication of both changes inside the Frente in part brought on by the MLN's request, but also the long-standing mutual distrust between the two movements going back to the half-hearted support offered to the Frente by the MLN in the 1971 elections. Early 1989 saw the creation of the Movimiento de Participación Popular [MPP], a more radically left voting bloc within the Frente based around the MLN but including smaller groups and a few 'independents'. In addition to Sendic (who died in April 1989), the figure that would come to symbolise this current within the MLN would be José Mujica.

However, Zabalza was committed to a more conventionally 'proletarian' trend within the legalised MLN, one increasingly at odds with it as the Frente Amplio as a whole became more openly a post-socialist centre-left reformist party. The 'proletarians' had a more traditionally Marxist conception of the people and of working class and trade union politics, and even secretly evolved plans for a 'politico-military organisation' to lead an armed population to resist any attempt at a military coup like that in June 1973. The theoretical underpinnings of the 'proletarians' extended from quasi-Leninist[82] to libertarian (Zabalza moving from the first towards the second), but at its inception it included other MLN founders such as Julio Marenales and Fernández Huidobro. At their apogee around 1989 when they controlled all the major MLN and MPP media outlets, the 'proletarians' were gradually displaced during the 1990s as the ever-improving electoral fortunes of the Frente (and the growing popularity of the MPP and Mujica within it) gradually convinced the leaders and members of both MLN and MPP that they could share power in an elected centre-left government under Vázquez's Encuentro Progresista. Zabalza was one of the few who steadfastly refused the enticements of centrist reformism, preferring resignation to what he saw as capitulation. Thus, although also within the ambit of the MLN, he represents a line of thinking that could not be more alien to Torres's.

Zabalza's four books are clearly associated with different moments in this trajectory: *Lo viejo y sabido*[83] emerges from early moves in the newly reformed MLN; *El miedo a la democracia*[84] is a product of the upswing in the fortunes of the 'proletarians' in the late 1980s; *El Tejazo y otras insurrecciones*[85] of their decline, while *La estaca*[86] follows their effective defeat, signalled by Zabalza's official withdrawal from the MLN in 1995. Zabalza can be seen, then, to be practicing what he believed: that once they had stopped being 'spectators' and joined the fray, everyone could learn to do intellectual work because ideas were essential to the struggles of daily life, anticipating the communist ideal of a society free from the need to work in which everyone could be whatever they would be (*E*, 90 and 17). He wrote merely as an 'impertinent tupamaro' hoping to reach other 'restless intellectuals' like himself, wherever they were to be found (*M*, 5).

However, much against his own intentions and against the grain of his work's surface, there is in Zabalza's writings a very strong sense of nostalgic desire. In the ferocious brief epilogue written especially to close Leicht's biography, he bemoaned the effective suicide of the values and ideas of a whole generation, vowing never to lose his 'old reference points' or take off his original 'tupamaro glasses' to look at reality. He found capitalism today pretty much as bad as it always had been, confessing: 'I miss the times of equal and simple ways of relating to one another we had in clandestinity and in prison'.[87] Elsewhere he claimed that youth was revolution's best hope because it was a period of 'permanent transgression', so, later in the same book, he proclaimed that the ideal was never to betray one's younger self: 'to be able to look at oneself in the mirror and recognise the features we had when we were young' (*E*, 26–7 and 80). The most constantly recurring feature in Zabalza's writings is a never resolved ambiguity, both fertile and constricting, admirable and frustrating, between a determination to remain faithful to a set of basic ethical and political principles and a refusal to accept that the world has changed.

In the brief 'Explanation' added to *El Tejazo*, Zabalza described the book as a 'kind of intellectual orgasm', coupled with the hope that it would contribute to all 'those little personal insurrections that, multiplied like loaves and fish, will make socialism', while debates were 'one uninterrupted National Convention' greeted with an ecstatic 'What pleasure!' (*T*, 197). As his biographer makes clear, from his days as a schoolyard bully and his adolescent drunken sprees, through his liking for reckless and heroic rescue missions during the days of student activism in the early 1960s and his romantic involvements while on military training in Cuba, to his penchant for direct action and a procession of new lovers following his separation from his comrade and wife in the late 1980s, politics for Zabalza is intimately bound up with youth, movement and the working of miracles.

The opening chapter of *El Tejazo* begins as a counter-Genesis myth and continues with a utopian pastoral vision of Uruguayan independence as permanent rebellion against incipient capitalist control through land enclosure. Outside Montevideo, because there needed to be a power centre at every ranch or crossroads, effectively 'everyone was a politician, because everyone exercised power'; nobody 'could hold down such a rebellious [insurrecta] social base' (*T*, 15). Zabalza associates all Uruguayans from Artigas, the nation's founder, to the present with the gaucho's 'untamed [cimarrón] and egalitarian spirit' that none could 'corral' [alambrarle] (*T*, 20). Not surprisingly, Zabalza found in 1997, one hundred and fifty years after the Communist Manifesto, thirty years after Che Guevara's execution, that the 'horizon' was the same:

> The same windmills and the same Quixotes, dreaming, fighting, with less security but much more uncertainty than formerly, tripping over stones they themselves put in the way, but heading, always heading towards utopias: equalling out inequalities, democratising democracies, unchaining chains, abolishing oppression; in a word, socialism, social revolution. (*E*, 20)

Like many utopians, Zabalza puts his ideal in a past far enough away to be unreachable but close enough to be imaginable as a task for the future. The principal tools will be participatory democracy and insurrection – and the unspoken demand to forget the slippery ambiguities involved in a radical left movement calling on the example of a deluded or enchanted Don Quixote.[88]

Zabalza viscerally rejects the fear of democracy he sees at the root of fascism and the armed forces rejection of unionism and all forms of self-expression by ordinary soldiers (*M*, 38 and 54–6). He sides with those who 'can wait no more' (*E*, 64) and, like him, instinctively reject bureaucratic structure and vertical chains of command in favour of direct action that emerges spontaneously from struggle (*E*, 68–71). Deliberately parodying Debray's influential 1967 book, Zabalza advocates a 'Revolution in the Revolution' more in line with the mood of 'La Movida' in the previous chapter: inorganic, fluid multitudes without representatives or leaders[89] enacting their own political choices (*E*, 72–3 and 81–6). Hence, throughout *El Tejazo*, he constantly extols what at one point he calls a 'left "counterculture"': the hormonal, epidermal[90] and enraged rejection of all forms of bureaucratism, verticalism and the cult of personality' in favour of a spontaneous 'tupamaro space' more like 'an Artigas camp or a Saravia[91] column' (*T*, 112–13). The people are natural strategists who know what is best for them (*T*, 189) and who (Zabalza here returning to his earlier interest in democratising the armed forces) would, when required, naturally obey leaders whose authority they had seen earned through their participation in the very decisions they too have helped to make (*T*, 114).

This combination of spontaneity and internally generated organisation is most fully exemplified for Zabalza in the insurrection. While he focuses on two recent Uruguayan examples, he invokes a whole tradition comprised of events and figures drawn from all over the world: slave and peasant revolts everywhere from Spartacus on, the storming of the Bastille, the Paris Communes, the 1905 soviets and the taking of the Winter Palace (*E*, 65), the barricades of the French Revolution and the Hungarian resistance to the Soviet tanks in 1956, the Palestinian Intifada and the Zapatistas in southern Mexico (*T*, 30–1 and 187), as well as a whole host of Uruguayan examples from the already mentioned Artigas and gaucho inheritance to the campaigns against the privatizations and constitutional changes by the traditional party administrations during the 1990s (*T*, 21). The catalogue of world and national acts of resistance amounts for Zabalza to an accumulated experience from which people can draw useful illustrations (*T*, 186–8), although he does not explain exactly how this learning process takes place.

Two events from recent Uruguayan history are exemplary for Zabalza. First, what became known as 'El Tejazo', 5 September 1971, the diversionary act that supposedly allowed the escape of some one hundred political prisoners from Punta Carretas prison.[92] Zabalza praises the alliance between militants and general public of La Teja to organise barricades in what became an ongoing neighbourhood defiance of the authorities narrated in a carnival-esque tone with diminutives and playful phrases such as 'here we have this poor policeman . . . ' (*T*, 25–8). His reason for singling out this apparently minor skirmish in the long campaign against state repression going back to at least 1968 becomes clear only later when he criticises the MLN's decision in 1972 to pursue the policy of direct confrontation with the security forces instead of arming the people to practice 'politics with weapons': Zabalza wanted more Tejazos, not more Pandos (*T*, 119, 131 and 192–3).[93]

La Teja, a working-class suburb that took in the main state oil refinery, hooks into Zabalza's perspective on his second event, for him the prime example of politics as insurrection: the general strike against the military coup called on 27 June 1973 and lifted fifteen days later only to prevent further loss and suffering (*T*, 194). For Zabalza this was the moment when his 'anonymous wild[94] men and women' carried out the 'act which illuminates the second half of twentieth century Uruguay' (*E*, 66), precisely because it was the event when the example of El Tejazo[95] two years earlier could have been used to extend the strike to having armed citizens disputing occupation of the streets with the military with the aim of overthrowing the coup before it took hold (*T*, 181–2). It is, then, precisely the kind of opportunity the 'proletarians' in the MLN of the 1990s wanted to be ready to take advantage of as the 'motor' of such a mass movement (*E*, 66–7).

The problem with Zabalza's examples is that they are all reactions *against* another opposing force with the upper hand, and, moreover, they are campaigns and movements that were defeated. They seem to offer little to solving problems related to what the left should do when in power. Zabalza was largely supportive of the Frente Amplio's policies of decentralisation and popular participation in Montevideo after 1989 (*E*, 31–44), but the fact is that people's involvement even in meetings to decide expenditure in their immediate neighbourhood seldom reached even 10 percent of those eligible.[96] No matter how tempting it may be to share Zabalza's determination to see the Frente Amplio's first great rally on 26 March 1971 as the 'people gathered together in assembly' (*T*, 120), this form of participatory democracy is at odds with governing a modern city. It simply takes up too much time and energy for people who need to work, maybe at several jobs, to live.

This unresolved contradiction between impeccable but inappropriate principles and unresponsive political realities was at the root of Zabalza's own troubles within the Frente Amplio. Because he felt that capitalism and bosses remained basically what they had always been, Zabalza often returned to the Communist Manifesto for inspiration (*E*, 9, 20 and 82), an unchanging conviction that led him on the eve of his faction's defeat in the MLN to see the Frente as threatening to betray the movement it had been in 1971 by becoming the party his opponents wanted it to be. His own 'political desires and expectations' would have had it 'fulfil another role'.[97] The ensuing tensions were exemplified during his stint as an ex-MLN, independent MPP town council member. Being frank in public to French president Jacques Chirac about what kind of French enterprises Zabalza was prepared to have Montevideo do business with was one thing,[98] but openly defying Tabaré Vázquez over the sale of Montevideo's most famous casino was something else again. Zabalza, along with an ever-growing majority of Uruguayans, was opposed to the privatisation of publicly owned assets, but he failed to foresee the use to which Vázquez and the pro-Vázquez elements within the MPP could make of the counter-argument: that a centre-left administration should have nothing to do with gaming houses except to regulate and tax them. When Zabalza refused to bow to the Frente's collective will, Vázquez, no doubt able reliably to anticipate the outcome, resigned the presidency of the party, thus precipitating a crisis in the MPP while it was also under pressure from the rest of the coalition's members. Fernández Huidobro, who had been fence-sitting for some time, promptly threw in his lot with Mujica, both of them activating a jointly written pro-Frente Amplio document that had been on the MPP's table for over a year since 1996.[99] The 'proletarians' found themselves outmanoeuvred and isolated, first within the MLN, and then in the MPP with a public break between Zabalza and Mujica in 1999.[100] Mujica declared that now was the time for a Frente Amplio government, not a revolution, to which Zabalza could retort he saw little point getting into government only to have your capitalist enemies as your allies.[101]

Mujica might share Zabalza's liking for Cervantes, but with a crucial difference: the Uruguayan people might have their 'Quixote moments' but they also have 'a lot of Sancho's wisdom'.[102] At the left end of the Frente's centre-left spectrum, within the MPP, it is not wholly fanciful to see Mujica playing Sancho Panza to Zabalza's Don Quixote, and not only because of their physical build. Indeed, one might say that Zabalza's whole political career lends credence to Torres's contention that, under current conditions, the Guevara legacy with which Zabalza frequently and willingly associates himself (*T*, 14 and 25; *E*, 65)[103] has become a millstone around militants' necks rather than a foundation stone on which to build anything, a form of quixotic tilting at non-existent windmills.

Torres and Zabalza are 'organic' intellectuals whose work arises as a function of a particular political context, this being especially true of Zabalza because each of his books relates to a specific juncture in his ongoing battle for 'proletarian' dominance, first in the MLN, but also in the broader MPP, so as to influence the entire Frente Amplio. Each of his essays mapped out more of his ideological and intellectual territory, extended and clarified his arguments, attempting to persuade others of the cogency of his position and of his right to the authority with which he advocated it. Torres, having long since abandoned the struggle, was more concerned with establishing the boundaries and foundations for his self-criticism in order to dismantle and throw away what had once been an essential part of himself.

In both cases, their earlier or current political beliefs largely protected them from the radical uncertainties that haunted Lechner and others in their traverse of the hazy frontiers between socialism in collapse almost everywhere and the patent deficiencies of democracy as practiced in Latin America. Couriel and Rubio, however, despite their own political activities within the Frente, could not enjoy the same degree of exemption because their professional credibility as intellectuals imposed on them a nodding acquaintance with the thinking of Barthes, Derrida or Foucault, exposing them willy-nilly to the questioning of legitimacy and authority found there. It should be clear, however, that the home-grown writing of a Zabalza loses far more than it gains from remaining free of such contamination.

The Frente Amplio, on the other hand, gains far more than it loses from having such a grand array of socialist and social democratic thinking in its camp. As shown in Chapter 2, the Frente started life precisely out of the long, slow and painful process of producing an amalgam of several different intellectual strands on the left. Consequently, one of the key elements of its 'tradition' since 1971 has been its tolerance of division and dispute within its ranks. The catch phrase 'disunity is death', so frequently and often correctly used as a warning in electoral democracies, simply does not apply to it because unity without fissures has never characterised it, so is not an expectation among its constituency. On the contrary, open discussion and disagreement seem to have encouraged participation, increased its credibility and illustrated its difference from the traditional parties (whose factions are often for electoral convenience or internal political influence). In government, they seem so far to have resulted in better policy and greater accountability.

As the Frente occupied virtually the whole space labelled 'left' on the mainstream political spectrum and as it became electorally more popular during the 1990s, the leftist intelligentsia's audience widened but only at the expense of relinquishing its own power as a group, which tended to pass more and more to the political party they adhered to.[104] The problem is, as Mujica has realised, the actual wielding of power in government is not the best atmosphere in which to create conditions ideal for the exchange of ideas.[105] This book's final chapter passes to intellectuals who, however sympathetic to the Frente Amplio or the left in general they may be, seek credibility and influence by remaining firmly outside it and standing on intellectual ground alone, though still fundamentally addressing the same basic issue that animates the centre-left government: how to be a Uruguayan in the twenty-first century.

6

Dialogue Outside Politics

Uruguay as Problem in the Twenty-First Century

Some are born lucky; others in Uruguay.
>   Graffiti from Montevideo wall during the late 1980s[1]

Uruguay = unviable.
>   Graffiti from Montevideo wall in late 1990[2]

If there is contingency and not mere necessity, there will be a place to settle accounts.
>   José Rilla (2001)[3]

On the eve of the Frente Amplio's electoral victory in 2004, two intellectuals close to the Frente could write that for the first time since the early twentieth century a majority of the nation's intellectuals would feel some 'affinity' with their country's government.[4] Caetano sees intellectuals, beset as they are by the double temptation of the facile lightness of cultural relativism on the one hand, and the self-satisfying nostalgia of playing 'guru' or 'shaman' on the other, as having no other course but the difficult one of preserving their capacity for independent critique.[5] Similarly, another of Uruguay's most respected historians saw modern Uruguayan intellectuals' chief role as 'questioning', even 'destroying', cherished but unacknowledged assumptions underpinning their society.[6] However, it was precisely this function that came under threat because of the possibilities opened up by the new political sympathies and alignments, as Garcé and Yaffé understood.[7] This chapter concentrates, first, on the difficulties facing those like Garcé, Yaffé and Caetano who seek to be the Frente's critical conscience at a key point in its electoral ascendency, and, then, shows how their concerns dovetail into the wider recent interests of intellectuals who have chosen not to have their political sympathies tested by becoming the centre-left's allies.

They prefer to suggest matters for discussion throughout society by making new variations on a topic especially important in Uruguayan intellectual and cultural history at moments of change and tension: the question of national identity.

Between Politics and Professionalism

José Rilla's preface to Garcé and Yaffé's *La era progresista* throws into sharp relief the penetration of questions of intellectual integrity into the very heart of the collective enterprise on which all of those mentioned here are engaged.[8] He points out that both have been involved in and with Uruguayan politics for years both in their lives and through their academic work ['vital y académicamente'], an attribute applicable to himself as well as them.[9] Moreover, as they matured intellectually and politically between the restoration of democracy and the economic crisis at the turn of the millennium, the ensuing sense of urgency, Rilla argues, gave them greater faith in the social sciences' capacity to provide answers than others might have. Consequently, he sees their 'academic reasoning' as walking a perilous line between 'enthusiasm' and 'distrust', 'desire' and 'suspicion'. The possibility of confusing analytical thought with wishful thinking should arouse the reader's suspicion about the authors' assessment of their own project.[10]

It is hard not to recall how much this resembles Real de Azúa's complaint back in July 1971 as he finished his book-length contribution to the collective volume *Uruguay hoy*, written during the turmoil before November's national elections: as an analyst and participant without 'sufficient space to create a gap between life and thought, between the duties of civic activism and the commitment to lucidity and objectivity, the dangers of confusing reality and desire, forecast and hope, are enormous'.[11] Garcé and Yaffé were aware of the difficulties but sought to get round them with a wish to put ideas back at the centre of political debate on the left rather than to tell any future Frente Amplio government what to do.[12] Aguirre Bayley puts aside such qualms, preferring to write a history of the Frente Amplio as its de facto 'party intellectual'. Aguirre Bayley's approach is shamelessly uncritical, and generates a positivist chronicle that sees the latest incarnation of the Frente as the best, all previous versions being steps in an inevitable march towards perfection.[13]

Aguirre Bayley has sacrificed the main factor that saved Real de Azúa in 1971 and redeems Garcé, Yaffé and their colleagues thirty or so years later: the high quality of their professionalism, determined by the quality of both their training and their abilities. All the political scientists and historians keeping a wary eye on the post-1985 centre-left are or have been students, researchers or instructors in the Faculty of Social Sciences at the Universidad de la República, even if simultaneously or subsequently they work at other tertiary institutions such as the Catholic University or the Instituto de Profesores Artigas or at privately funded research centres such as the Centro Latinoamericano de Economía Humana, where Caetano is a leading figure. Yaffé's *Al centro y adentro*, for example, started life as a master's thesis supervised by José Rilla and examined by a committee that included Caetano and Jorge Lanzaro, while those thanked for their comments and suggestions include Daniel Buquet, Daniel Chasquetti, Gustavo de Armas, Romeo Pérez, José P. Barrán, Benjamín Nahum, Juan Pablo Luna and Aldo Marchesi.[14]

As individual author, Garcé squared up to this matter even more explicitly. Honouring a long delayed intellectual debt to the MLN, Garcé was intensely aware of the controversial nature of the story he was going to develop about the two currents of thought within the ex-guerrilla movement since 1985 and of its importance for understanding the trajectory of the whole Uruguayan left as it moved towards the real possibility of attaining power by fully democratic means. He therefore self-consciously avoided all temptation to intervene polemically himself, preferring to quote wide-ranging interviews with participants and observers, giving roughly equal space to both sides, and had the text read by protagonists and specialist commentators. As narrative voice, he became, however paradoxical it sounds, ostentatiously self-effacing, preferring to exercise his 'civic duty' to Uruguayan society by offering it an 'essay written *from* the perspective of Political Science, not *in order to* do politics'.[15]

Alvaro Rico, a political scientist and historian who learned his politics in the Communist party essayed a more radical solution to this issue. One immediately noticeable feature of the title of his *Cómo nos domina la clase gobernante*[16] is its similarity to Göran Therborn's classic of 1970s western Marxism *What Does the Ruling Class Do When It Rules?*,[17] which appears in Rico's bibliography under its 1987 Spanish translation. Therborn employed a revised Marxist-Leninist analysis of the bourgeois democratic state in Europe and North America (with some asides on Japan, Chile and the Antipodes) to update the historical materialist conceptualisation of the ruling class. His book ended with a discussion of the relations between socialism and democracy which assumed that, for a Marxist, the purpose of the second could only be as a bridge to the first. Neither Therborn nor his readers could have foreseen that, just over a decade later, in two traumatic years beginning with the demolition of the Berlin Wall in late 1989, his social analysis and its theoretical underpinnings would be rendered all but redundant. This only underlines the additional difficulties facing Rico when, in peripheral, post-authoritarian Uruguay at the outset of the new millennium, he began a revision of his political credo through an examination of his country's recent return to democracy.

The cover of Rico's book speaks volumes, as it were. Casting their eyes downwards from the top, readers find first a frame from Argentina's well-known sarcastic political cartoon strip *Mafalda*. Here, the rebellious Mafalda is among a group of disgruntled, sceptical children listening to one of their demagogue peers haranguing them in dictatorial fashion, waiting for the right moment to voice her customary dissent. After the author's name, next comes the main title, in large yellow capital letters: 'How The Ruling Class Dominates Us' (without Therborn's question mark). In lower-case, smaller white italics there follows the subtitle: 'Political Order and Social Obedience in Post-Dictatorship Democracy', and last, in smaller font still, 'Uruguay, 1985–2005'. Like Therborn, historical commentary for Rico is primarily illustrative; unlike Therborn, Rico finds himself obliged to restate the obvious, rather than just extend or slightly alter an already accepted framework.

In essence, the problem Rico sees in post-dictatorship Uruguay is that neither the military regime itself nor the subsequent period of re-democratisation and its consolidation dislodged the state from its position of central importance in the way Uruguayan society is organised and in the types of discourse habitually used by the political elites to rule and by the general population to represent itself as nation or community. The effect is that all attempts at radically undermining institutions and their discursive conventions – whether anti-political like La Movida or potentially revolutionary like the MLN's 'proletarians'[18] – are either marginalised as irrelevant or neutralised through co-optation. For Rico, the transition from 'authoritarian monologue' to the 'dialogic interaction of democracy' [dialoguismo democrático] has led only to the 'depoliticising of society' and to 'defusing the passions [des-apasionar] of recent history'. His proposal consists in 're-politicising' the analysis of the dominant trends in the political and economic life of the country to replace what was an 'anti-dictatorship consensus' with a 'necessary dissent from democracy' so that it becomes possible to build some real alternative to the blueprint for Uruguay's modernisation long centred in the state and the political parties.[19] The principal weakness – and self-fulfilling justification – of Rico's propositions is the existence of his book: so difficult was it to break down the walls of this consensus that Rico could only write yet one more study of it.

The majority of intellectuals either meekly succumbed to the situation condemned by Rico, or implicitly rejected his take on it. Moreira accepted that recent history made possible political science's diversity of methods and theoretical background as well as the means to make its findings known to a wider public.[20] Lanzaro, too, wished to reach both an academic and a broader audience,[21] while Garcé and Yaffé are very specific about the multiple readership they want to address: 'informed citizens, specialist journalists, politicians and colleagues in the social sciences'.[22] This urge to reach those who wield power as well as those who suffer its effects echoes a recommendation by Barrán: that the potential of the mass media be exploited to make specialised knowledge influential in society at large.[23]

Caetano as editor underlined the role of collective intellectual endeavours that combined 'solid academic background' with a 'clear sense of civic purpose' to marry the publicising of knowledge with a critique of its current state.[24] The editors' introduction to a collection of essays based on two public seminars that brought the sensitive topic of the dictatorship from the university to the centre of Montevideo, brings all these matters into very sharp focus, illustrating clearly both the intention of specialists to reach a wider audience and the limitation put on their role as public intellectuals by an academic discourse shorn of the pretences of mastery:

> We stand before an open object of study and a book that dialogues with others in print or still to come. Consequently, we do not seek to exhaust the whole range of possible approaches to a conflictive historical period.... [The book] can only proffer some new perspectives and voices, be a contribution that does not close things off with conclusions or reduce down lived experience but rather lays them out for public discussion and opens them up for the reader.[25]

Contributors can offer only opinions based on readings of the traces left by events; they are not in a position to impose findings or recommendations arising from them. Their offerings can only combine or compete with others, all of them suffering the fate of having their effectiveness (or lack thereof) sealed by acceptance or rejection by the variously influential sections of their audience. The intellectual as interpreter loses the privileged, protected space once accorded to the 'legislator', and ideas, perspectives and thoughts, now effectively commodities, are subjected to the devices of the market place. A more optimistic perspective might liken the situation to Caetano's 'contestatory democracy', in which a consensual position is subjected to critique and counter-proposal before final adoption.[26]

For Moreira what was at stake was not just the intellectuals' relationship to the left as it got closer to power, but also the responsibility of both intellectuals and the reformed left's role in re-imagining the nation. She asked whether a 'left government' could bring forth a Uruguay with future potential, but her answer omitted part of the question: it was not clear that 'the left' could reunite all the 'fragments' of contemporary Uruguay, but 'it *is* clear' [sí es claro] that no-one else could.[27] By design or unconscious slip, the government has disappeared, leaving only an amorphous 'left', which would include those intellectuals examined here.

No single one of them exemplifies the difficulties of traversing this ambiguous terrain than the historian Gerardo Caetano. With his additional interest in ethics, Caetano often makes explicit what for others remains tacit or perhaps overlooked, an ability which has earned him comparison with the likes of Real de Azúa.[28] In a relatively early article, he observes that some events create such havoc that they break completely with the preceding period's 'system of symbols and meanings', necessitating a strategic withdrawal into theory to create a new conceptual framework,[29] while it is the succession of these 'collective imaginaries' which creates the narrative capable of motivating a unified 'us'.[30] Since, for Caetano, the Frente Amplio's election to national government in 2004 was such an event, one which, moreover, marked the official end, as it were, of Uruguay's twentieth century,[31] it is the earnestly debated notions of democracy, citizenship and memory since that date which will be examined here.

It is the opening survey in *Uruguay: Agenda 2020* that best reveals Caetano's hand through the range of its references. These run from modern classics of historiography and political science such as Nora, Ricoeur, Febvre, Bloch, Kosselleck, Gadamer, Vattimo and Arendt to contemporary political and cultural commentators and historians such as Nora Rabotnikof, Beatriz Sarlo, Manuel Castells and Norbert Lechner, as well as a whole host of Uruguayan intellectuals from Juan Carlos Onetti, Carlos Quijano and Carlos Real de Azúa to some of his current colleagues appearing in this chapter.[32] The purpose of such an impressive list is not only to anchor Caetano's own concerns in a long line of international intellectual traditions. More importantly, the re-examination of such issues as the nature of democracy and citizenship within the widest possible frame of reference reinserts Uruguay into the concerns of Western modernity, but without slavishly following inappropriate, imported models. In other words, Caetano seeks to practice as an academic historian the kind of wellfounded civic responsibility he will advocate for others.

In this context, Caetano opposes 'the historical self-awareness of a *republic*' to 'pseudo-democracies with no republic' which are closer to Machiavelli's principality tyrannised by the reflexes of habit and custom, because it is only in the former that the past can be properly and constantly weighed to give realistic prospects for a future guided by a utopian notion of perfecting 'our agora'.[33] Caetano's strategic use of the Greek word 'agora' as amalgam of forum and assembly for debate ties in with his idea of a republic in which individuals are moved to act in their own interests but only as permitted by the greater virtue, construed in quasi-Roman terms as willingness to promote and defend the greater public good, the *res publica* which transcends any one citizen's narrow aims and desires. To these ends, Caetano quotes Batlle's wish to 'demystify power'[34] for the pragmatic but honourable purposes of a citizenry that, 'tired of civic agnosticism',[35] wants a demonstration of 'republican virtue' that shifts party politics in the direction of social justice whatever the real restrictions on what can actually be done.[36]

The topic that, for Caetano, seems to bring these matters most painfully and urgently to the fore is memory and its relation to the history of the recent past. As elsewhere in Latin America, this subject has been a matter of often polarised but urgent debate in Uruguay because of the many unresolved cases of human rights abuse and extrajudicial murder or 'disappearance' during periods of authoritarian repression and dictatorship, and the subsequent post-trauma history of suffering that continues into the present. The wide spectrum of public response has varied between a wish to leave it all behind almost as if it never happened (frequently, from the military and their supporters, or representatives of conservative post-transition civilian governments) and the desire for justice through the courts and/or reconciliation through the public recognition of victims' stories.[37] A public campaign in the late 1980s to overturn the military's impunity failed in a referendum – which all but guaranteed it would be revisited later. Victory by the centre-left, which contained groups that had been targeted by security forces during the dictatorship and before, aroused hopes (in some quarters, fears) that the new government would honour promises to look again into outstanding unexplained 'disappearances'. When it did, Caetano's theoretical interest in relating memory to democracy quickly became personal and material.

The Frente Amplio government has exploited existing legislation to put on trial some retired military officers as well as ex-President Bordaberry,[38] and in 2005 it ordered the excavation of yards in former barracks and interrogation centres in search of those still missing but last seen in internal security forces custody, resulting in the disinterment of two illegally buried 'disappeared' detainees. Caetano had the chance to put theory into practice when he accepted from President Vázquez the task of leading the team responsible for a final report formally presented to him on national television in December 2006.

Caetano has been very definite about the need to evolve out of the chaos of competing personal recollections a kind of consensual civic memory that would be different from the historical record but which historians could help in nurturing into existence. Its purpose would be to aid the foundation for his idea of a new republican democratic order that would enable Uruguay to overcome its hypocritical tendency to be '*a country that masks its transformations*'.[39] There was always a potential contradiction between the personal and the political in being the most determined individual advocate of a renewed democratic society based on a reinterpretation of republican virtue, but it required close involvement with the centre of real power for Caetano to fall into something approaching hubris. In retrospect, the title of Caetano's own account of the matter courts the difficulties to come by attaching to 'memory' the demanding epithet 'exemplary'.[40] Caetano attaches great importance to the transcendental and universal nature of this notion, derived from Tzvetan Todorov and Elizabeth Jelin. Added to the 'moment of truth' taken from Hannah Arendt, it leads Caetano to claim he would have accepted the commission from any democratically elected president, and makes him urge readers not to read the report 'ideologically' as only the product of a particular political and social conjuncture rather than as a unique historical moment providing a special opportunity for Uruguayans to come to terms with their past.[41] Against the accusation that his report was just another 'official story', another exercise in whitewashing the truth, Caetano gives his most succinct summary of what drives his kind of historiography and of the social role he believes it can play:

> No 'official story', no 'hemiplegic' or 'biased' memory' can survive under the imperious demands ['imperio vital'] of a true democracy. The complete experience of republican values is incompatible with 'any' story or memory (singular) that has hegemonic pretensions, particularly when faced with traumatic pasts. Nothing like that can support the necessarily polyphonic and pluralist life of democratic coexistence ['convivencia'], least of all some story issuing from the State that hopes to monopolise the truth.[42]

Caetano confronts the dreadful problem facing Vázquez himself on this matter, namely the near impossibility of devising a way whereby Uruguayan society as a whole can face and accept the horrors of about twenty years up to 1985 (an act of reconciliation), while at the same time bringing some kind of justice to those who were victims of armed agents of the state. The very existence of such victims, let alone their rights, has barely been acknowledged,[43] but exposure runs the risk of prolonging the very social divisions the whole enterprise is designed to close. The growing stridency in tone as the essay unfolds suggests Caetano's uneasy suspicion that the report might not be the clear-cut demonstration of his deeply cherished arguments he had hoped for.

Caetano's almost messianic evangelism about an issue so central to the ethics guiding his involvement in public life was likely to arouse disquiet if not outright condemnation, and the editor is sufficiently even-handed to include two examples. Javier Miranda[44] will have none of the equation of the state's agents with the victims of their terrorism. He believes the unearthing of the secret graves of the two 'disappeared' should be the beginnings of a whole process of debate and self-examination about which it is far too soon to reach any conclusions, implying that Caetano (and the President) have sought in effect to close down a democratic discussion which would itself be evidence of the functioning of Caetano's 'exemplary memory'.[45]

However it is José Rilla, co-author with Caetano of several well-known historical works[46] and now a member of the small Independent Party[47] (as though distancing himself from conflicts of interest of this sort), who has put forward the most telling critique of Caetano's position as historian within the kind of democracy he himself proposed. Earlier, Rilla had no problem accepting with Caetano and the fellow travellers of postmodernism that historical truth was dependent on hermeneutics and therefore a matter of permanently open debate, proposing the historian as best qualified mediator between the realm of unrecoverable but ineluctable fact and the need for responsible interpretation. He then argued that the construction of truth is incompatible with the administration of justice, amnesty for all being a price victims and society at large must pay for establishing the truth.[48] Totally absent from Rilla's position was the transcendental belief that such matters can ever be finally concluded in a language not itself subject to the vicissitudes of history. His response to Caetano's report was a brief, trenchant guide to the 'teaching of recent history'. Arguing boldly that neither witness nor victim have privileged positions in the historical record and that recent history is not the exclusive patrimony of historians (thereby taking the virtue of open democratic debate about historical questions among citizens to its logical conclusion) and even less only of historians associated with the Frente, Rilla argued that all specialised knowledge should be open to questioning by the non-specialist (even by politicians in parliament!), and concluded that Uruguay's recent past was too traumatic to allow its commemoration to be so, too: 'The youngest's right to the past should not be so filtered through the past of the oldest', he tartly finished.[49] There could be no clearer demonstration of how such investigations into the function of history interconnect with the current flurry of enquiries into the way the nation sees itself.

Uruguay as a Problem

At the end of her book on the rise of the Frente Amplio since redemocratisation, Moreira asked whether the left could heal the wounds of a divided populace and address the 'Uruguay as a problem' that provoked the Frente's beginnings.[50] Her use of it confirms that *Uruguay as Problem* is a book title that sums up the way many intellectuals have been viewing the country during the period covered by this book, one that encapsulates how many Uruguayans have felt about it since independence.[51] Published in 1967, it continued a controversial view of Uruguayan history and identity its author, Alberto Methol Ferré, had begun nearly a decade earlier.[52] Methol Ferré started out with an idea shared by many: because after independence it was territory fought over by Argentina and Brazil, becoming briefly a vexatious province of first one then the other, and finally a buffer between the two only through the help or pressure of British diplomacy, Uruguay wound up constituted as a country on the map without ever really having forged itself as a nation. According to Methol Ferré, dependence on Great Britain guaranteed prosperity but deepened Uruguay's tendency to relate to an 'outside' that began with the Atlantic Ocean rather than its borders with its Latin American neighbours. By the 1960s the crisis of Uruguay's deficient attempts at modernisation coupled with the lack of an internal market big enough to sustain the costs of industrialisation meant that its only chance of becoming viable lay in abandoning its obsession with Europe and pursuing integration with the other countries connected to the River Plate Basin.

The creation of Mercosur in 1991 with an agreement initially between Uruguay, Argentina, Paraguay and Brazil suddenly made Methol Ferré's concerns seem prophetic, but it is important to realise how deeply implicated in the politics of the time his views had always been. Inspired by the anti-imperialism of the illustrious historian and National party leader Luis de Herrera, Methol Ferré wrote the first of the two books while involved with the right-wing Federación Ruralista, because the emphasis on matters which linked Uruguay to the rest of the Southern Cone seemed to him more important than the innate conservatism of most of the landowners. A dose of the National Party in power after the 1958 election changed Methol's mind, however, and in 1961, angry and disillusioned, he recanted all his hopes for a new beginning.[53] He and his fellow intellectuals such as Roberto Ares Pons and Washington Abadie, having founded the pro-Latin American federation journal *Nexo* in 1955, would gradually move leftwards to link their Agrupación Nuevas Bases with the Frente Amplio in 1971. Along the way, Methol Ferré wrote *El Uruguay como problema*, which predicted Uruguay's descent into violence, but needed an epilogue in 1971 for Methol Ferré to describe the Uruguayan situation as the most explosive on the whole continent because neither Argentina nor Brazil could afford a socialist revolution on their doorstep.[54] Underlining this urgency was a prologue by one of its dedicatees, an Argentine, the other being Brazilian, thus completing a triangle with the Uruguayan author that symbolised the author's thesis on the viability of his country. Later readers can also appreciate the irony of Methol Ferré's two friends, social scientists in their countries, seeking haven in Uruguay as political exiles from military dictatorships.

Although a regular point of reference in Uruguay, *Uruguay as Problem* is currently out of print in its home country, but it is available online as a free download. However, the still disquieting relevance of the book may have determined that those responsible for putting it on the Internet are Argentines, and the Uruguayan epilogue has been replaced by some of Methol Ferré's laudatory remarks on Perón's view of Latin American integration.[55]

The view that earlier notions of Uruguay as 'imagined community' have broken down may not be unanimous, but it is symptomatic of perspectives on the subject since the 1990s.[56] The titles of some major collective volumes that deal with various aspects of it indicate the theme's topicality and urgency as well as the range of approaches adopted towards it: *Uruguay towards 2000: Challenges and Options,*[57] *Culture(s) and Nation in End-of-Century Uruguay,*[58] *Mercosur Culture: Cultural Industries and Policies,*[59] *Uruguayan Identity: Myth, Crisis or Affirmation?,*[60] *World, Region, Village: Identities, Cultural Policy and Regional Integration,*[61] *Uruguay Towards the 21st Century: Identity, Culture, Integration, Representation,*[62] *Uruguay: Accounts Pending,*[63] *Uruguay: Cultural Imaginaries: From Indigenous Traces to Modernity,*[64] *Uruguay Today: The Landscape since October 31st*[65] (the day of the 2004 national elections), as well as Caetano's already mentioned *Uruguay: Agenda 2020.*

As these titles suggest, in Uruguay as elsewhere, the challenges to earlier views of national identity, now seen as artificially neat and exclusionary, seem to have come on two separate but interrelated fronts: changes in *how* to study the nation's past and present, and the widening scope of *what* can be included in such studies. To this must be added that only since 1985 has freedom from censorship made possible the full examination of the social and political crisis from about 1965 to the end of the dictatorship, that the gradual but consistent rise of the Frente Amplio has finally transformed a two-party system over a century old, and that the creation of Mercosur in 1991, whatever its present or future difficulties, has changed probably for ever Uruguay's relationship with its regional neighbours. There is, then, ample reason to understand why, accompanying the recent fin-de-siècle and the start of the new millennium, more than a few Uruguayan intellectuals should yet again be posing the question 'who and what are we?'

An illustration of official recognition of this changed scenario is the collective volume *Historia del Uruguay en el siglo xx* published in 2007. Its title notwithstanding, this book arises out of the Frente Amplio government's anxieties about what Uruguay is and what it might become. The product of a commission from the Department of History at the Universidad de la República by the section of The Ministry for Foreign Affairs dedicated to the Uruguayan diaspora, estimated to be about half a million, the book is aimed at providing an accurate, accessible account of twentieth century Uruguay, specifically aimed at providing sons and daughters who do not know the country and its history with a reliable account of why their parents might have left.[66] While implicitly expressing a hope that some might be encouraged to migrate back to the mother country that needs them, the book is clearly designed as a potential textbook for use at home too, probably with an eye to stemming the still damaging emigration of economically productive young people in the wake of the economic disaster of 2001–2. This book, therefore, is a fine example of cooperation between the centre-left government and its institutional specialist cultural workers, showing clearly how the humanities and social sciences can respond when offered something worthwhile to do, a project significantly wider in scope (though less clear in its possible effects) than the narrowly technical help given routinely in areas such as economics and the sciences.

A very different picture of what might be offered by such a group of intellectuals emerges from the catalogue of an exhibition on the theme of national identity held to mark the turn of the new millennium at the Fine Arts Museum in Old Montevideo during September 2000. Its title, 'Como el Uruguay no hay', is one of those set phrases dating from the bloated, self-satisfied Uruguay convinced of its uniqueness and superiority of the first half of the twentieth century, and is usually translated as 'There's nothing like Uruguay' or 'There's no country like Uruguay'. However, in the Spanish 'no hay' ['there's no(t)'] is not followed by a complement, allowing the clause's completion in common parlance with parodic reversals of this kind: 'como el Uruguay no hay . . . gracias a Dios' ['There's nothing like Uruguay . . . thank God'], leaving open whether speakers secretly agree with the sentiment but are shy about admitting it, or whether they now feel it to be an embarrassingly stupid joke about a nation no longer recognisable in the words. What the sentence opens up, then, is doubts either about what Uruguay is or about what Uruguayans feel for it.

These ambiguities were fully exploited in an exhibition which featured objects, photographs and artworks illustrating the multi-faceted entity Uruguay had been in the past and still was at the turn of the new century, while the complexities involved in organising such an event are displayed in the essays chosen for the catalogue that records it. The exhibition's curator recorded the compromise reached between his requirements as a museum director and the writers' views on the main theme as a need to walk a thin line between 'the order of sameness' often found in displays of dead things and 'the accumulation of difference' of some second-hand bazaar. The aim was to avoid a celebration of postmodern retro chic but also to abandon all claims to an objectivity that could lead to sweeping, magisterial statements instead of an invitation to viewers to question both themselves and the multiple implications of the exhibits.[67]

The catalogue editor and its three major contributors take their cue from this. Achugar asks 'What is the song . . . ?' and offers three numbered choices (perhaps implying that more are possible) ranging from pessimistic despondency in the past to open-ended but far from self-assured optimism for the future with the exhibition title as ambivalent hinge between the two; Caetano charts how political allegiance has over fifty years ceased to be a reliable guide to Uruguayans' sense of themselves, enabling a much needed re-definition of civil society; Alfaro trumpets the benefits of urban cultural anthropology to show how the decline of Angel Rama's 'lettered city'[68] has opened up space for the examination of the nation's love of soccer as a source for a renewed mythology of Uruguay as David ready to do battle with any Goliath; Porzecanski suggests that the recovered traces of indigenous, African and migrant European cultures entail the redefinition of Uruguayan national identity as an always incomplete set of parallel narratives of diverse forms of otherness.[69] Here is no professional retelling of history for quite narrowly focussed purposes as in the Frega volume, but a heterogeneous collection of essays to act as a frame for a kaleidoscopic, even splintered mirror in which any or all members of the Uruguayan public were invited to look at and reflect on themselves and each other.

In a one-page presentation, the state's representative sees the exhibition as a '*criollo* sacrarium', because in effect the state finds itself charged with looking after, as if they were holy relics, the symbols of a community currently too dispersed and vulnerable to enable the individuals who comprise it to feel confident they can hold a collective sense of identity themselves.[70] It was precisely to test presuppositions of this sort that two unrelated studies of Uruguayan identity done ten years apart used variations on consumer survey techniques to find out what at least some Uruguayans actually felt and thought about their nation. In August 1993, as a project within a postgraduate History of Historiography seminar at the Universidad de la República, Cosse and Markarian used collective interviews and individual questionnaires to discover what ideas 281 assorted inhabitants of Montevideo had about Uruguayan history.[71] Ten years later, between October 2003 and July 2005 (with the watershed national elections halfway through), San Román used online questionnaires and optional 800–word open-ended essays to ask 153 Uruguayans, of whom nearly a third lived abroad, nearly half voted for the centre-left and all had to feel familiar enough with the Internet to undertake the task, what being Uruguayan meant to them.[72] Clearly neither survey sought to be representative, both preferring a small corpus open to discursive analysis (more far-reaching in the earlier study) to a larger, sociologically more responsible one too unwieldy to permit anything except quantitative classification, which limited resources seem to have made impossible in both cases, anyway.

Despite their limitations and the differences between them, the two studies allow some general comparisons relevant to my argument here. First, there was a tension between a tendency toward nostalgia and an acknowledged need for re-examination and critique of accepted views of the past. Both studies recorded a love for the ideologically most over-determined and contested aspects of the country's origins (Artigas, the independence struggles and a romanticised image of the gaucho), coupled with a clear sense that the crisis following the military dictatorship and its aftermath required some as yet undiscovered new way forward.[73] Secondly, the intellectual and cultural elite was mostly irrelevant to the ways the majority of Uruguayans acquired their views of national identity and history unless its perspective had penetrated popular or mass culture (as in the case of protest music or the tango). Thus, San Román found that, when asked to name nationally significant writers, composers or visual artists and their works, about half those surveyed either did not answer or did not agree with any of the survey's suggested names or titles, while the remainder had no settled comparative sense of what was more or less important in the nation's inherited view of itself.[74] Finally, while the previous observation suggests that Uruguay's cherished view of itself as a culturally sophisticated exception to the Latin American semi-literate norm is under threat, a majority seem to have accepted, at least implicitly, the functional view of history passed down from Real de Azúa to Caetano and others: not only are perspectives on the past determined willy-nilly by demands in the present, but that a main purpose of historical study is exactly to provide a useable past around which to build a consensus about what is possible for the nation.[75]

The last section of this chapter turns to two intellectuals whose work amounts to a cross-disciplinary analysis of 'the nation as fruit of a permanently unfinished and renewable republican pact'.[76]

Hugo Achugar and Abril Trigo

Both Achugar[77] and Trigo[78] quote the graffiti placed at the head of this chapter: 'Some are born lucky; others in Uruguay', because they share a central theme: the enigmatic and deeply problematic nature of what it means to be Uruguayan, and the equally difficult question of the relationship, often perversely unequal, between Uruguay and its 'Other' – what surrounds or is outside it. In short, the increasingly diffuse, dispersed and fragmented notions of 'national identity' and 'national culture'.

Although Trigo is somewhat younger than Achugar, they have certain important elements in common. Both are academics, and both spend at least half of each year in universities in the United States (Achugar has taught in various institutions, Trigo consistently at Ohio State). As a result, both read several languages, and Trigo writes in at least two. This experience has influenced their writing in two crucial ways. First, the complete bibliography for both includes a typical spread of professional publications (articles in academic journals, collective volumes they have edited or to which they have contributed, seminar and conference papers, and the like), while their entire output,[79] irrespective of the intended audience in any particular case, bears the hallmarks of their quite long and successful careers in academia. Second, while both have learnt from the acknowledged masters of the '45 generation such as Carlos Quijano and Carlos Real de Azúa (in Trigo's case especially, one could add the names of inheritors of the renegade Blanco tradition such as Ares Pons and Methol Ferré), they have also absorbed and exploited more recent poststructuralist and postmodern literary and cultural theory from Europe and the United States. The different inflection they give to this shared legacy will become clear below as in each case I discuss three single-authored books.

A good illustration of the impact foreign ideas have had on Achugar can be measured by the obvious effect they have on his prose style. As he himself says, echoing Derrida and Foucault (to both of whom he frequently refers): 'The transgression or cult of transgression contained in the aesthetic of the commonplace has to do with a deconstruction of power' (*BM*, 84). The dissonance of contemporary theory will constantly be allowed to disrupt – transgress – the flowing musicality of much conventional cultural commentary in Spanish. Consequently, the 'prostitute-like, everyday image of Madonna, or its simulacrum' illustrates an all-pervasive mass culture, by offering 'another idea of aesthetics, another idea of beauty, that has little or nothing to do' with that found in the Uruguayan writers of the '45 generation (*BM*, 82). The acceptable conjunction of Baudrillard's simulacrum and the ironically named pop star Madonna clashes hopelessly, as Achugar realises, with an idealised (and now unfashionably traditional) idea of woman's beauty projected by the major Uruguayan writers of the mid-twentieth century, an opposition delightfully captured in Spanish by the juxtaposition of a modern Latinate abstraction ('masificación') with the almost colloquial Castilian phrase 'dueña y señora' ('mistress and lady'). However, this is not just passive obeisance to the imperialist demands of a globalised form of cultural critique, but the active recognition that such theorising is helpful, even necessary, to the development of a new discourse of cultural commentary in a developing country such as Uruguay, precisely because much cherished, older cultural forms are in the process of dying or mutating.

Yet, it would seem that the most pervasive influence on Achugar by late twentieth-century thinking about culture and society comes in the form of Richard Rorty's idea of conversation. In essence, this boils down to the argument that the purpose of philosophical dialogue is not to persuade 'Others' that one's own argument is better than theirs, but simply to keep the conversation going, to engage in the civilised exchange of opinions as an alternative to seeking the imposition of one set of ideas over another.[80] Rorty's impact on Achugar's thinking about Uruguay and its culture can be encapsulated in the following: 'it implies a battle' that offers the 'challenge of turning battle into debate, debate into negotiation, negotiation into conversation'.[81] While his topic here was the construction of a new national narrative (a theme to which I return below), the 'challenge' to transform struggle into conversation among equals is enacted in the style and rhetorical strategies of Achugar's own essays, especially in his acute awareness, at times bordering on fussiness, of the space or site from which he (or his voice) speaks or writes.

Indeed, it partially explains Achugar's preference for the essay itself which he describes as the 'supremely free form of writing' (*BM*, 10) and elsewhere as 'the never finished, never finishable "work in progress",[82] the eternal "rehearsal in progress" of writing, modifying, correcting oneself' (*PSB*, 14).[83] Hence Achugar's preference for books like all of his, made up of 'the fleeting, instantaneous thoughts of an accidental traveller roaming the uncertain territory of cultural, intellectual and artistic thinking' (*PSB*, 13). All he seeks is for his reflections to stimulate others (*BM*, 9), exactly as in a conversation designed to invite others to offer their own contribution. All statements should be cautious, tentative because interpretations are always made 'from one's own history, from one's own position, from one's own biases' while the access of ever more individuals to this cultural conversation serves to 'erode the arrogance' of the few who have sought to control the business of interpretation.[84] For Achugar, there can be no permanent answers to any question, no permanent conclusion to any discussion, because reading and writing always happen in an uncertain somewhere between reality and desire, and because each individual is the 'Other' for all others, making everyone's contribution precarious and transitory (*BER*, 19 and 26–29; *PSB*, 16). Achugar, therefore, characteristically rejects the imperious restrictions of binary oppositions, quoting with approval Žižek's appropriation of Groucho Marx: '"Postmodernity or class struggle? Yes, please"' (*PSB*, 14),[85] preferring questions to answers. Hence his predilection for rhetorical questions as ways to advance the discussion by suggesting further avenues for thought or investigation which others can take up if they wish (see *BM*, 95; *BER*, 17 and 123; *PSB*, 13 and 21). Achugar's whole strategy as essayist amounts to a discursive version of participatory democracy as utopia, hence the conditional tense and subjunctive mood in the following: 'the desirable thing, of course, would be that dialogue became democratic and the silencing of others an archaic, impossible practice' (*BER*, 48).[86]

In the opening title essay of *La biblioteca en ruinas* [*The Library in Ruins*], the library is simultaneously a physical place for storing and reading documents and books and a mental space for processing memories, information and aesthetic experience. The two are constantly shifting due to their vulnerability to change through additions, the impact of new information technologies and the active use in their writing that the likes of Achugar make of everything available in both locations (*BER*, 13–24).[87] It is this continuous, slippery process of transformation which allows the library to become a site of ideological struggle: with the help of Foucault and Michel Pecheux, Achugar could paint national libraries as officious and oppressive pantheons of dead knowledge, the public library as a contradictory mixture of illusory democracy and potential source of creativity and the private library as susceptible to solipsism. However, echoing the politics of subaltern studies, 'willy-nilly, every library shelters the other book which questions its legitimacy as a cathedral consecrated by the bishops of what should be known [obispos del deber saber]' (*BER*, 14 and 20).

This postcolonial answering back to power, together with a consciously anti-parochial notion of theoretical and methodological tools, informs Achugar's characteristically inclusive if not very mellifluous description of the overarching problematic the learning obtainable in libraries can be employed to examine: the 'many and multiple latin [sic] Americas' which are at the same time 'one' that is 'mine/ours', 'the one they/we wanted and we want to build, over and against the tiger from within and its velvet claws. And the tiger from without' (*BER*, 14–15). The lower case 'l' of 'latin' plus the juxtaposition of first person singular and plural with first and third persons plural serve as a reminder of the fluid nature of space generally utilised by Achugar, as well as an introduction to what it is that, in his view, the modern Latin American intellectual is to do in a world where the commonplaces of dependency theory still have some relevance.

Achugar expands on the function of intellectual work in this multiple Latin America by arguing that, since 'reading freely is desire', reading the literatures – for Achugar, this concept is plural – of Latin America is 'more an exercise for freedom than an exercise of judgement'.[88] The 'collective library', where 'readers' generosity' can point out the 'traps he has fallen into' is for Achugar a 'desirable utopia' where all assumptions and givens can be interrogated (*BER*, 23). Consequently, the periphery becomes a privileged 'space for utopian scepticism' (*BER*, 43) in which to examine the impact of 'modernity, postmodernity and avant-garde on the subject within it' (*BER*, 25). The danger is that the Latin American may be construed as the contaminated 'other' who must be contained because he is contagious (*PSB*, 15–16), an idea that must not be allowed to pollute 'the multiple other Others' (*PSB*, 23). Progressive Latin American intellectuals, in a period which is not only postmodern and postcolonial but also post-dictatorial (*PSB*, 93), must become contagious themselves, as they aid in the construction of nations and cultures that include instead of marginalising all these 'other Others'.

Achugar's analysis of nation and nationality is based around successive attempts to think through the terms so as to answer the question he first asked himself in the late 1980s: whether 'nation' is still a useful category for studying the politics and culture of Uruguay or any other country (*BM*, 38). Achugar thinks it is, but only if the nation in question assumes its proper status and dimensions, which in the Uruguayan case involves the twin notions of smallness and frontier (*BM*, 21–2), an idea he later expands into 'a space . . . I sometimes call periphery, sometimes Montevideo, Uruguay, Latin America, margin, non-space, frontier: the space of the displaced or dislocated' (*PSB*, 16). Only on the premise of 'the small utopia of being and not disappearing' in a 'porous, open frontier culture for a frontier country on the margin of the periphery' (*BM*, 27) will it be possible to construct a project for a national culture which looks backwards and ahead and is also an adequate response to the present (*BM*, 33). As we have already seen, Achugar's own writing is 'porous' and 'open' to European and North American borrowings, and he follows Fernando Calderón (and the novelist Alejo Carpentier, though he is not named here) in believing that postmodernism on the periphery involves the coexistence of times and modes of production that are modern or even pre-modern (*BM*, 40–1), making more easily periodised conceptualisations of Uruguay inherited from before 1973 irrelevant (*BM*, 42). Only with all this in mind, does Achugar feel able to approach that 'Raft of the Medusa' [balsa de la Medusa] which is national culture (*BM*, 48).

Starting from his reading of Benedict Anderson, Castoriadis, Lacan and Stanley Fish, Achugar evolves a concept of culture as 'social imaginary' and 'symbolic imagination' not restricted in class or other social terms (*BM*, 10 and 17–18). Any homogenising, monolithic idea of national culture must be replaced by one that allows the appearance of the multiple, heterogeneous, dispersed and fragmented cultures (plural) that comprise the contemporary nation (*BM*, 55–68), examples being the simultaneous availability of traditional and very recent forms of shopping (*BM*, 72) and the contrasts and contradictions permitted by modern electronic media (*BER*, 32). The emphasis on multiplicity and heterogeneity, and the characteristically tentative forms of expression, dovetail exactly with Achugar's punctilious caution regarding the site from which he speaks and his desire merely to participate in a conversation, thus rejecting that version of Uruguayan culture in which 'there is a lot of shouting but no discussion' (*BM*, 54).[89] Indeed, one real drawback to Achugar's vision is the implicit assumption that there is no social conflict that cannot be resolved by civilised people engaged in reasoned dialogue, and that all Uruguayans are, like him, willing to engage in it.

All these elements come together in the concern Achugar shares with Caetano for the articulation of memory and forgetting with the idea of a democratic national narrative.[90] Here Achugar is more forthright: a 'democratic memory' will be one that must allow itself to be 'multiple' and 'fragmentary' if it is truly to oppose the univocal, monolithic version of national history favoured by any authoritarian discourse, formally dictatorial or not (*PSB*, 121–122). Clearly, such an enterprise would involve major decisions about what should be included or omitted and how the whole would be narrated. In this context Achugar puts his reading of Rorty to good use: 'perhaps the paradox of the democratic mask or multiple faces can be resolved in . . . a mask that is successively and repeatedly negotiated and talked through [conversada]' (*PSB*, 123). There is frequently in Achugar, as we saw in Caetano, a perhaps too easy (and uneasy) slippage between narrative, history, and individual and collective memory, whose meanings are unspecified and elided, as in the following:

> The ritualised memory of State power is and has been the official memory.
> But memory is not necessarily equal to public or collective memory. In that
> sense, we must distinguish as much between those two as between popular
> memory and official memory. (*PSB*, 168)

Frustrating this imprecision may be, but it fits with another potential weakness of Achugar's essays on this theme: their tendency to become a series of commentaries on quotations from mostly foreign authors. Thus, the essay from which this passage is taken, 'Derechos de memoria' ['The Right to Memory' or 'Memory's Rights'] (*PSB*, 152–178), is almost an annotated procession of professional and academic sources on memory, history, commemoration and trauma, as well as on classics as different as Hardt & Negri's *Empire* and the final scenes of *Hamlet*. Rather than a personal deficiency, these two aspects seem to be symptoms of a double demand: that of novelty – this is new ground in Uruguay, still to be fully mapped, however well-trodden it may now be in post-Holocaust Europe; that of urgency, as illustrated already by Caetano's difficulties with his report on the 'disappeared'.

Nonetheless, having earlier asked himself whether traditional intellectuals still have a role in the twenty-first century (*PSB*, 88), Achugar is now able to give them a concrete task to perform: 'the preparation of a national historical narrative that is at the same time a democratic memory' (*PSB*, 126). As he summed up in the closing lines of *La balsa de la Medusa*, explaining collective origins and destination is how the 'social imaginary' is formed: 'to read such explanations is to read the culture/s of an imagined community. Which is exactly what we did, what we do, when writing or reading a poem, a novella, an essay' (*BM*, 113).

This quotation provides an entry into the parallels and differences between Achugar and Abril Trigo, whose principal areas of interest are summed up in the title of his first book, *Caudillo, estado, nación. Literatura, historia e ideología en Uruguay*,[91] to which I have already referred in earlier chapters. While all the terms in this title will play an ongoing part in Trigo's development, the 'caudillo' will re-emerge only from time to time,[52] and (as with Achugar) literature will become cultural studies.[93] *Caudillo* is organised into six chapters (which Trigo calls 'jornadas' as though they were stages on a journey) framed by "(Pro)logos. Protohistoria I" (*CEN*, 9–29) and "(Epi)logos. Protohistoria 2" (*CEN*, 253–260) in order to narrate a polemical alternative history of the role ideology has played in the creation of Uruguay as a nation during its experience of modernity since the late nineteenth century. Early on in the book, we find therefore what is not only an introduction to its theme but also to what will become the overarching concern of all Trigo's writing: how to explain the continued survival of 'an underdeveloped, under-populated state fenced into a corner of the world by two giants', and what sort of discourse allowed it to develop a 'national consciousness' (*CEN*, 27–8).

Trigo continues a long line of essayists and cultural historians (many of them mentioned in the course of this book) who have explored the Uruguayan version of what seems to be the inevitable lot of small nations flanked by much bigger ones: nagging doubts about their identity and even their continued existence. As if to emphasise his sense of this issue's persistent relevance in Uruguay's cultural and political history, Trigo carries a sentence first used in his second book over into his third, amplifying it in the process. Its early version reads: 'The most summary synopsis of Uruguay's intellectual history reveals a constant obsession with the problem not so much of national identity as the territory's integrity and definition (or lack thereof) [la integridad y la (in)definición territorial]'.[94] Its reappearance six years later expands the last phrase to 'the more tangible and elemental problematic of the country's geopolitical delimitation, territorial integrity and political sovereignty'.[95] The additions are significant in that it can now take in Trigo's expansion of the idea of the Uruguayan nation to include migrant communities abroad and the virtual community constructed on the Internet websites used by them.

If there is one element that is common to all three books it is the insistence on the nation's plural discursive formation and the elusiveness of the brutal realities of history brought about because the impact of ideology is registered in rhetorical moves that disguise the truth in the very act of persuading (*CEN*, 254). For Trigo, the discourse of the nation is a perpetual struggle between the state (which has a material existence in structures and institutions) and the nation, which cannot represent itself except in signs and is in a constant process of becoming. His view is that, in the Uruguayan case, the state has throttled the nation's potential in a way analogous to that in which the dominant interests of the port-capital have imposed themselves as civilised order on the more anarchic and unpredictable forces of the never quite tamed interior (*CEN*, 257). Trigo's entire work is dedicated to showing how Uruguay's experience of modernity is in large part determined by the nation's struggle to reassert its independence from the state.

It is to this end that Trigo devotes the most original aspects of his books. In *Caudillo*, he provocatively uses as illustrations of his argument examples taken from the least known and least studied genre in Uruguayan literature, the theatre. He believes this to be the genre best suited to the creation of what he calls 'ideo-myths': 'the presence, evocation of invention of "caudillos", as historical or fictional characters, people or ghosts', the '(un)confessed purpose' of which is the 'textualisation of a particular idea of the nation' (*CEN*, 28).[96] Here, we can note a number of Trigo's characteristic analytical strategies: the regular and unapologetic deployment of abstractions to carry his analysis to a level in which the particularities of individual cases can be absorbed into a whole conceived as constantly changing process, coupled with the defamiliarising use of prefixes (sometimes with brackets, as in the titles of the frame chapters given earlier) and of challenging neologisms (such as 'ideo-myths' and 'imagemes').[97] And, since his first example is Washington Bermúdez's *Artigas* [1898], Trigo is able to demonstrate how the ongoing struggle over the ideological no-man's land represented by the legendary figure of Artigas as the country's founder is central to the structuring myths that organise the nation as imagined community (*CEN*, 48–71; 194–216). From this Trigo derives the notion that the transformations of the figure of the caudillo symbolise the changes in the idea of the nation brought about by the gradual reforms or abrupt breaks in the evolution of the modern state (*CEN*, 24; 28–9).

¿Cultura uruguaya o culturas linyeras? extends his arguments in two directions: chronologically to include the dictatorship and the first years after redemocratisation (up to about 1990); more radically, it widens the meaning of culture to include Afro-Uruguayan aspects of carnival, home-grown rock music, anti-poetry and experimental narrative, graffiti, and the general changes in the streetscape of Montevideo. In other words, similar to what Roland Barthes did earlier in his *Mythologies* in the France of the 1950s and 60s, Trigo applies the lessons learned in more conventional literary and historical studies to the phenomena of popular culture. Becoming one of those cultural commentators who are 'adequately armed from the post-modern arsenal' (Trigo's theoretical masters now include Julia Kristeva, Slavoj Žižek and cultural studies pioneer Stuart Hall), he traces the new cultural practices and the celebration of difference that are the '80s generation's response to the blunt instruments of the official culture and neoliberal ideology of the new post-dictatorship democratic state (*CU*, 17). The stress is on fighting back: since 'the State levelled, mediated and razed any subculture that diverged from the hegemonic imaginary' (*CU*, 13), mostly through processes of assimilation and distortion rather than outright prohibition (except during military rule), there was no alternative for the cultural 'other'

except to snipe from the edges. Having established briefly the importance of the notion of frontier for Uruguayan development in the earlier book (*CEN*, 11 and 46), the guiding metaphor offered in the title to the first chapter of the second broadens its range and Trigo's theoretical foundations: 'Frontier-ness [frontería]; Liminality; Transculturation' (*CU*, 9–35). In other words, the idea is to turn the edge into a privileged site for observation, reflection and cultural creation. Trigo himself is prepared to work at the threshold of conventional sense-making to reinforce his point:

> It is time to smuggle frontiers: it is time to de-Uruguay ourselves in Order to Uru-understand ourselves; it is time to rethink ourselves from the margin and as margin, from the frontier and as frontier-ness, from the residual and as residue. (*CU*, 31)

These neologisms, at once playful and aggressive, are at one with the polemical tone of a volume that is an (Achugar-like) loose-knit set of essays which is intended to be 'genealogically, a zigzagging meditation on the cultures in Uruguay around the pivotal year 1985' (*CU*, 7). The margin has become not the centre but a new platform and vantage point from which to organise an intellectual assault on the nation with the aim of formulating it anew, a task continued in *Memorias migrantes*.

In many ways, Trigo's third book is his most personal and radical to date. It has a series of extracts from interviews with Uruguayan migrants from Fitchburg near Boston framed and interspersed with six essays that are theoretical, historical and analytical responses to the issues raised in the testimonial sections. Trigo explains the 'counterpoint' and 'dialogue' function of this structure as being aimed at combining 'meditation' with 'daily language', 'analytical distancing' with 'emotional commitment', the 'objective look of the subject which investigates' with the 'the subjectivity of the objects of study', because his own subjectivity finds the essay more congenial than, say, the testimonial form (*MM*, 10). As the play on subject and object suggests, the interviewees' spontaneous comments are springboards for his own preoccupations and considerations.

These are built on a historical framework which reprises that used in *Caudillo* (*MM*, 15–16 and 113–74) but becomes more stark and emphatic in the abbreviated and accelerated retelling. For example, there is a notable increase of intensity in the account of the violence at the birth of the nation and its repression in the subsequent founding myth. In *Caudillo*, once the gaucho or caudillo disappeared as 'social problem' or 'political enemy', they could be re-appropriated ideologically as 'the final triumph of the lettered city over the territory' (*CER*, 64). In *Memorias*, this becomes a 'perfect circle': 'indians, gauchos and caudillos were relegated in the imaginary [imaginariamente] to an earlier, mythic temporality, so that the danger represented by their otherness in the present was sublimated as diversity in a mythic past' (*MM*, 15). Later, Trigo adds a caustic commentary on their final resting place: 'glorification in bronze, town square and ephemeral commercial almanac' (*MM*, 127). While he remains faithful to the historical scheme first formulated in *Caudillo*, Trigo has become ever more distanced from the state's preferred version of it. What was revisionist in the first book has become oppositional hostility in *Memorias* thirteen years later.

This becomes clear in what is the book's most important argument: the diaspora is the frontier from which the new nation must be imagined. Trigo sees exile and migration as essential elements in Uruguay's self-construction as nation from Artigas onwards (*MM*, 43–6). Latterly, emigration as exported labour becomes a response to globalised capitalism (*MM*, 49), even guaranteeing the existence of the nation by functioning as a safety valve (*MM*, 55) for the failures of neoliberalism (*MM*, 166). Migrants take with them their 'cultural memory' based on their lived experience (as opposed to the official 'historical memory' and the bowdlerisations of the mass media's 'pop memory') (*MM*, 88–9). Since 'memory [is] the construction of the past in the circumstances of the present at the service of a project for the future' (*MM*, 93), migrants are those best placed to see the nation afresh, precisely because they are its distant frontier.

And they do it on computers:

> The cybernetic country can be seen as the nation's last frontier, a nowhere that is everywhere in which de-territorialised cyber-migrants re-territorialise their present by connecting to a community of ghosts whose substance is memory and whose material is language. (*MM*, 18)

On this basis, Trigo is able to end the book on an optimistic note. The 'cybernetic nation' becomes the sketch of 'a new type of community, new ways of living, feeling and imagining the nation, new ways of imagining ourselves as a people in stampede, corralled by globalisation. A laboratory for the nation to come' (*MM*, 256). There is a clear danger of empty triumphalism here. It is noticeable that it is Trigo who puts forward proposals such as this, not the migrants on the Internet themselves (with one exception, and he would appear to be a close relative of the Aldo Solari referred to earlier in this book) (*MM*, 243–244). In other words, this may be yet one more example of an intellectual taking wishful thinking for confirmed reality. However, unrealistic or not, Trigo's is one more powerfully original response to the sense that it is time to rethink Uruguay anew.

Although with different emphases, Achugar and Trigo are equally concerned with margins, however literally or figuratively construed. Achugar is more explicitly and painfully aware of the contradictions involved in being a privileged intellectual speaking and writing from a space he prefers to call the periphery, while Trigo mobilises the notion of frontier in order to reinvent questions (and possible answers) about the nature and viability of Uruguay as a sovereign state that have haunted the country's artists and intellectuals almost since independence. Achugar's ideal of a democratic history and Trigo's advocacy of the subversive force of cultural memory are the maturely considered product of the anti-political, counter-cultural attitudes of the youthful 1980s generation, a movement with which Achugar felt some sympathy and which Trigo openly admired and supported. The position of both is admirably caught in Achugar's idea of stuttering. Expanding on the title of *Planetas sin boca*, his inhabitants of underdevelopment are like planets without a sun, without a mouth that can speak the language of authority, and can only speak or write the stammerings of the periphery (*PSB*, 20):

> Who are we? There is no single reply because *we* is heterogeneous, dislocated, constantly changing, and, above all, neither is, nor should speak with, one single, solitary, authoritative voice. (*PSB*, 23, his italics)

Trigo's multiple, disembodied, diasporic voice that is nowhere and everywhere exemplifies this collective 'we' without a centre. Despite the Frente Amplio government's attempts to reach out to this significant fraction of the population, only time will tell whether its peripheral, dispersed diffuseness merely confirms its powerlessness.

In his introductory summary of the findings from a 2002 survey on culture and consumption in Uruguay, Achugar incidentally describes the role he and all intellectuals working on the borders between culture, society and politics can have at the start of the twenty-first century. In an observation he is characteristically at pains to clarify as being his own alone, he finds that the Uruguay that emerges from the statistics can no longer be singular because it is even more fragmented and culturally diverse than most politicians and commentators are prepared to admit. Since that is so, the pre-dictatorship Uruguay described by the likes of Carlos Real de Azúa and Germán Rama quite simply no longer exists, if it ever existed except in their and others' imaginations and desires. As though taking the advice implied in this blunt assessment, Achugar limits the role of the survey he helped coordinate to providing information those responsible for running the country might find useful.[98] Clearly, Achugar finds this limited but realistic judgement of intellectuals' impact in society more congenial than the rather more heady and grandiose hopes entertained by those writing amid the turmoil of the 1960s and 1970s, despite the fact that his survey was done in mid-2002, when Uruguay was in the grips of its worst economic depression since the 1930s.

Achugar's perspective can be seen as part of a broader view. All the intellectuals examined in this chapter are academically trained and work at least part of the time in universities in Uruguay or abroad, mostly in the social sciences, though sometimes (as in the cases of Achugar and Trigo) in the hinterland between them and the humanities. The political scientist Nora Rabotnikoff, although not referring at all to Uruguay and focusing specifically on the role of academic historians in the construction of public memory, illuminates the role of intellectuals generally in a situation where their very legitimacy is questioned. Because the public sphere is now a field of competing points of view in which no single one can automatically claim authority over any of the others, Rabotnikoff implies that the opportunities for specialist intellectual workers to influence public debate by exploiting the modern media to get their opinions heard and debated is greater than ever before.[99] A further inference is that there exists a clear moral obligation to ensure that such expertise is of the highest possible level and that its relay in forms accessible to an informed lay public is not unnecessarily distorted by vested interests. Whether it is Jaime Yaffé or Adolfo Garcé trying to account for the changes in the Frente Amplio since 1985, or Abril Trigo proclaiming the need for an expanded sense of what the Uruguayan nation is, the politically non-aligned but progressive intelligentsia in contemporary Uruguay have embraced this disenchanted evaluation of their position in society. It may be a long way from the vision of those literary intellectuals who signed the document in *Marcha* urging people to vote for the Frente in November 1971, and it may tacitly accept the limited role assigned to intellectual activities in the current capitalist market place. Yet what may appear as passive acquiescence in a severely circumscribed position masks the real possibility of having a limited but measurable influence on society as it is, and that is what the intellectuals studied here have settled for.

CONCLUSION

Politics is not only a battle for power. Fortunately, it is also a dispute between principles, values, ideals and doctrines. In Uruguay, too.

Gustavo de Armas, Adolfo Garcé & Jaime Yaffé (2003)

This book has featured four stories: two failed projects, and two others as yet undecided. The two failures were both militarist. The MLN-Tupamaros believed that Uruguayan democracy was too compromised to produce the socialism they believed necessary to solve the country's ever more serious social and economic crisis in the interests of the majority. Their attempt to impose the conditions conducive to their aims was defeated by the armed forces in late 1972. The 1973 coup was staged by a military that thought the ruling political elite was as corrupt as the democratic institutions themselves, and that the only force capable of saving Uruguay from itself was themselves.

Whatever the other many differences between them, both these options were anti-democratic in that they placed little or no faith either in the people's ability to choose for themselves how they were governed or in the institutions designed to represent them. In this sense, the reluctant support given by the MLN to the Frente Amplio in the lead-in to the 1971 national elections is parallelled by the military being willing to negotiate a return to democracy only after its defeat in the constitutional referendum of 1980, and then only with politicians chosen by themselves.

However, this same dual tale suggests how weak this militarist option is in Uruguay, and how correspondingly much stronger are the assumptions underlying its political traditions, eventually even within the armed forces themselves. Germane here is Alain Touraine's reminder that it was intellectuals and soldiers who 'invented' Latin American countries,[1] for this book's main focus has been the continuing story of intellectuals' relationship with the political alternative to militarism in Uruguay. Since the late 1950s, in Uruguay this has all but entirely been the developing involvement of the progressive intelligentsia with forces on the centre-left, for the straightforward reason that the repression of the late 1960s and the dictatorship between 1973 and 1985 only postponed a reformist social and political agenda for which the Uruguayan electorate initially expressed a mild and ambiguous preference when, for the first time in nearly a century, it chose the National party ahead of the Colorados in the national poll of 1958. Just short of fifty years later, the final step in the transformation of the Uruguayan political scene heralded by that tentative opening move was the inauguration in March 2005 of the centre-left government of a restructured Frente Amplio in which the now legalised MLN-Tupamaros were the most voted sector.[2] Whatever happens in November 2009, when the Frente faces the electorate again after its first period of national government, the options available to the Uruguayan people will be much wider than they were in November 1958.

It has been this book's contention that progressive intellectuals have been instrumental in bringing about this reality, and the second as yet incomplete project is precisely their relationship to mainstream politics. Up to 1973, the need was to promote dialogue among the different forces on the left, and then between them and their potential constituency to counteract the increasingly reactionary propaganda and repressive actions of a militarised state. Over and above whatever specifically intellectual work they did, the left-wing intellectuals' most important task was that symbolised by the hundred and sixty odd signatures on the open letter inviting people to vote for the fledgling Frente Amplio in the 1971 national poll. Part I examined stages in this journey from acrimonious debates on a fragmented and frustrated left to the line of independent left-wing journalists, social historians and political commentators such as Oscar Bruschera and Carlos Quijano who were major players in founding the Frente Amplio in late 1970.

After the military failed in their attempt to set themselves up as, in effect, the intellectual founders of a new Uruguayan nation, the repressed returned. It first took the form of a release of pent up energy that turned its back on all conventional forms of political action or representation, finding outlets in marginalised or – in Uruguay – novel manifestations such as rock music, shapeless, barely organised artistic 'events' and the commercial graphics and anti-writing of underground magazines.

After the return to democracy in 1985, this contestatory outburst symbolised or permitted the arrival of what the military had tried to expel or keep out: the foreign or alien, which came in two forms. First, surreptitious and ambiguous, was the fertile if indefinite potential of thinking associated with poststructuralism; second were the much more visible and unavoidable effects of globalised economics and its accompanying neoliberal near orthodoxy, which converted everything, including ideas, into marketable commodities. The effect of both on the Uruguayan left and the progressive intellectuals was definitive.

The erosion of the philosophical foundations of long-held forms of authority and legitimisation combined with the lessons learned from the collapse of right and left kinds of militarism to bring about a total rethinking of the relations between socialism, or other types of re-distributive social reform, and the principles and mechanisms of electoral democracy. José Mujica might have thought, before the 2004 elections that made him a senator and a minister, that being in government did not promote the 'freedom and respect' necessary for the exchange of ideas essential to intellectual work.[3] However, many of his colleagues within the Frente, whether parliamentary representatives or group militants, became 'organic' intellectuals by contributing to debates on politics and policy either as part of a simultaneous academic position or as a direct result of the possibilities and difficulties occasioned by their activism. Such participation was in part encouraged by the internal negotiation and disagreement that reflected the Frente's functioning as a coalition of groups that stretched from ex-Christian Democrats at one end of the spectrum, to ex-guerrilla fighters and ex-revolutionary socialists at the other.

It was also an effect of the increased professionalisation and specialisation noticeable in all capitalist societies in the West. Progressive intellectuals who have gone alongside the Frente Amplio as it has moved from opposition to government over the last twenty-five years have been professional researchers or academics. This does not mean that artists and writers no longer support, work for and write about the Frente, but rather that it is no longer necessary for them to do so. Victims of the same division of intellectual and artistic labour that has long been the norm in the West's most developed countries, Uruguay's artists and writers can pursue careers whose parallel history would touch the one told here at frequent but not always predictable points. The Frente's more established status as a party and the declining generalised role as social commentators of literary intellectuals in postmodernity have meant that the former no longer relies on the latter as it did in 1971 and before.

Consequently, where Blixen finds that the kind of intellectual as social critic that existed up to the 1980s has now 'practically disappeared', to be only partially replaced by novelists, memoirists and social scientists,[4] I have found that such endeavours are now undertaken in Uruguay among academic historians and cultural critics. This book's last chapter was devoted, therefore, to showing how critiques and interpretations of the Frente's policies and way of working made from positions close to (but not within) the Frente itself link up with the wider concerns of those continuing the long line of essayists who have over the decades examined the constantly repeated issue of 'Uruguay as problem'.

One such political historian remarked that the past was both a political no-man's land to be fought over and a 'quarry' of resources to be used for action.[5] In a sense, this book has followed left-wing intellectuals who put this idea into practice in their search for ways to transcend the limitations of critique and to address directly what was to be done, a painful question first addressed publicly to his elders and betters by a young Juan Flo back in 1952: 'What shall we do, then?'[6] For much of the last half century, this has led many intellectuals on the left to subordinate their purely cultural or philosophical concerns to more immediate social or political needs. It seems legitimate to hope that their efforts have served to ensure that such a sacrifice will not become necessary again.

NOTES

Introduction: Uruguay as a Question

1   The most frequently cited source for this view is Carina Perelli & Juan Rial, *De mitos y memorias políticas: la represión, el miedo y después* (EBO, 1986), chapter 1. See also Constanza Moreira, *Democracia y desarrollo en Uruguay: una reflexión desde la cultura política* (Trilce, 1997), 84–5, and Rafael Bayce, *Cultura política uruguaya desde Batlle hasta 1988* (FCU, 1989), 25–37.

2   José de Torres Wilson, *La conciencia histórica uruguaya* (Feria del Libro, 1964), 35.

3   Among reliable general sources for this period are the following: Martha Machado Ferrer & Carlos Fagúndez Ramos, *Los años duros: cronología documentada (1964–1973)* (Monte Sexto, 1987); Benjamín Nahum et al., *Historia uruguaya tomo 8, 1959–1973: El fin de la era liberal* (EBO, 1992); Gerardo Caetano & José Rilla, *Historia contemporánea del Uruguay: de la colonia al Mercosur* (2nd ed., Fin de Siglo, 2005); Benjamín Nahum, *Manual de historia del Uruguay Tomo II: 1903–2000* (11th ed., EBO, 2003); Instituto de Ciencia Política, *El Uruguay del siglo xx – la política* (EBO, 2003); Carmen Appratto et al., *El Uruguay de la dictadura* (EBO, 2004); Oscar Brando (ed.), *Uruguay hoy. Paisaje después del 31 de octubre* (Ediciones del Caballo Perdido, 2004). Other more detailed sources will be used as required.

4   In this I follow a host of other commentators on the role and nature of intellectuals in Latin America. See, for example, Roderic A. Camp, *Intellectuals and the State in Twentieth Century Mexico* (Austin, Texas UP, 1985); Jorge G. Castañeda, *Utopia Unarmed: The Latin American Left After The Cold War* (New York, Knopf, 1993), 20–1, and chapter 6.

5   Nicola Miller, *In the Shadow of the State: Intellectuals and the Quest for National Identity in Twentieth-Century Latin America Latin America* (London, Verso, 1999), 5–6.

6   See Roberto Ares Pons, 'Militancia y desarraigo de la intelligentsia uruguaya' [1955], in his *La intelligentsia uruguaya y otros ensayos* (EBO, 1968), 38–9. The importance attributed locally to this essay is shown by the fact that it was published first as an article in 1955, and then as a separate pamphlet in 1961, before being collected in the volume to which I refer.

7   Ulíses Graceras, *Los intelectuales y la política en el Uruguay* (El País, 1970), 7.

8   Angel Rama, *La generación crítica, 1939–1969* (Arca, 1972), 12.

9 Castañeda, *Utopia Unarmed*, 201. Enrico Mario Santi, 'Politics, Literature and the Intellectual in Latin America', in David W. Foster & Daniel Altamiranda (eds.), *Theoretical Debates in Spanish American Literature* (New York, Garland, 1997), 339.

10 See, for example, Manuel Durán, 'The Beleaguered Latin American Intellectual', *Ventures*, 7 (Fall 1967), 60, and Michel Baud & Rosanne Rutten in the introduction to their edited volume *Popular Intellectuals and Social Movements: Framing Protest in Asia, Africa and Latin America*, in *International Review of Social History*, 49 (2004), Supplement 12.

11 Here I use the terms in Zygmunt Bauman, *Legislators and Interpreters. On Modernity, Postmodernity and Intellectuals* (Cambridge, Polity Press, 1987).

12 Fortunately, there is now a preliminary history of this whole process in two books, of which the second from its title onwards sets out to complement the first: Angel Rama, *La ciudad letrada* (Hanover, Ediciones del Norte, 1984) [in English as *The Lettered City* (trans. John C. Chasteen, Duke UP, 1996)]; and Jean Franco, *The Decline and Fall of the Lettered City: Latin America in the Cold War* (Cambridge [MA], Harvard UP, 2002).

13 At least two commentators shared the author's opinion. See Ruben Cotelo, 'Repentinismo y mito', *El País* (9 January 1961), 16, and Mario Benedetti, 'Arturo Sergio Visca y la contemplación activa' [1961] in his *Literatura uruguaya siglo xx* (3rd ed., Arca, 1988), 237–42, especially 239.

14 See Arturo Sergio Visca, *Un hombre y su mundo* (Asir, 1960), 27–31, an unpaginated prefatory note, and 75.

15 The quoted phrase occurs in an open letter from the Federación Anarquista del Uruguay of May 1971 in Rodrigo Vescovi, *Ecos revolucionarios. Luchadores sociales, Uruguay 1968–1973* (Nóos, 2003), 59.

16 Mauricio Maidanik, 'Por un diálogo militante', *Marcha*, 1279 (5 November 1965), 31.

17 *La generación crítica* (Arca, 1972), 214–15.

18 Of the five members of the jury, four were well-known writers and critics associated closely with *Marcha*: the intellectual and cultural historians Arturo Ardao and Manuel Claps were born in 1912 and 1920 respectively, the political historian Carlos Real de Azúa in 1916 and the literary critic Emir Rodríguez Monegal in 1921, while the other, Hector Caselli, represented the Young Christian Association. See Carlos Real de Azúa (ed.), *Problemas de la juventud uruguaya* (Marcha, 1954), 11.

19 Juan Flo, 'Problemas de la juventud en nuestro país', in Real de Azúa, *Problemas*, 143–56.

20 Mario Benedetti, a major supporter of and frequent contributor to *Marcha*, would take up some of these issues in an exercise in self-criticism included in his *El país de la cola de paja* [1960]. Because of its influence, *Marcha* itself has been extensively studied: Angel Rama, 'La lección intelectual de *Marcha*', *Cuadernos de Marcha*, 2nd series, 19 (May/June 1982), 53–8; Pablo Rocca, '35 años en *Marcha*: escritura y ambiente literario en *Marcha* y en el Uruguay, 1939–1974', *Nuevo Texto Crítico*, vi, 11 (1993), 3–151; Luisa Peirano Basso, *"Marcha" de Montevideo* (Buenos Aires, Javier Vergara, 2001); Mirian Pino, 'El

semanario *Marcha* de Uruguay: una genealogía de la crítica de la cultura en América Latina', *Revista de Crítica Literaria Latinamericana*, xxviii, 56 (2002), 141–56; Mabel Moraña & Horacio Machín (eds.), *MARCHA y América Latina* (Biblioteca de América, 2003).

21 Flo. 'Problemas', 146, 150–2, 155–6.

22 Rama, *Generación crítica*, 214.

1 From Alienation to Integration: Intellectuals, Politics and Polemics

1 Carlos Real de Azúa, '¿Adónde va la cultura uruguaya?', *Marcha*, no. 885 (25 October 1957), 22–3.

2 Carlos Real de Azúa, 'Legatarios de una demolición', *Marcha*, 1186 (27 December 1963), 7–8. The pugnacious reputation of this essay can be seen in the description by a conservative senator twenty years later of one generation of intellectuals having been 'promoted as the "legatees of a demolition" carried out by an earlier generation of malcontents' (in Alfredo Lepro, *Refrescando la memoria: Jorge Pacheco Areco, Presidente de la República 1967–1972* [no publ., 1983], 75).

3 Angel Rama, 'Los nuevos compañeros', *Marcha*, 1186 (27 December 1963), 2–3.

4 Fernando Ainsa, 'Catarsis liberadora y tradición resumida: las nuevas fronteras de la realidad en la narrativa uruguaya contemporánea', *Revista Iberoamericana*, lviii, 160/161 (1992), 811. See, similarly, Pablo Rocca, '35 años en *Marcha*: escritura y ambiente literario en *Marcha* y en el Uruguay, 1939–1974', *Nuevo Texto Crítico*, vi, 11 (1993), 107. Rocca also points out that the first writers to fall foul of the new climate of general political repression did so in 1968–9 (113–14).

5 Alberto Zum Felde, *Proceso intelectual del Uruguay* (Vol. 1, Librosur, 1985), 182. This is a reprint of the much expanded third edition of 1967, the last to be prepared during the author's lifetime.

6 Alvaro Barros-Lémez, 'La larga marcha de lo verosímil: narrativa uruguaya del siglo xx', *Casa de las Américas*, 170 (1988), 42.

7 Carlos Real de Azúa, 'Partidos políticos y literatura en el Uruguay', *Tribuna Universitaria*, 6–7 (1958), 102. See also Mario Benedetti, *Literatura uruguaya siglo xx* (3rd ed., Arca, 1988), 34, and Ulises Graceras, *Los intelectuales y la política en el Uruguay* (El País, 1970), 134.

8 See Graceras, *Los intelectuales*, 89, and Aldo Solari, *El tercerismo en el Uruguay* (Arca, 1965), 100. The same case has been made much more recently in the opening sections of Gerardo Caetano & Adolfo Garcé, 'Ideas, política y nación en el Uruguay del siglo xx', in Oscar Terán (ed.), *Ideas en el siglo: intelectuales y cultura en el siglo xx latinoamericano* (Buenos Aires, Siglo XXI, 2004), 309–422.

9 Hugo Achugar, 'Vanguardia y batllismo: el intelectual y el estado', *Río de La Plata*, 4–6 (1987), 420–1.

10 Abril Trigo, *Caudillo, estado, nación. Literatura, historia e ideología en el Uruguay* (Gaithersburg, Hispamérica, 1990), 80.

11 Reliable accounts of the Terra coup, its antecedents and aftermath can be found

in Raúl Jacob, *El Uruguay de Terra* (EBO, 1984); Carlos Machado, *Historia de los orientales: tomo III* (EBO, 1997), chapters 22–24; Benjamín Nahum et al, *Historia uruguaya, tomo 7: crisis política y recuperación económica, 1930–1958* (EBO, 1989), 11–87.

12   As eventually did the population at large. In June 1938, a pro-democracy rally brought 200,000 people on to the streets of Montevideo, a phenomenal number given that the capital's total population at the time was only 700,000. See Jacob, *El Uruguay*, 65 and Germán W. Rama, *La democracia en Uruguay* (Buenos Aires, Grupo Editor Latinoamericano, 1987), 53, n. 23. Jacob (*Uruguay de Terra*, 75) names painter Pedro Figari and novelist Carlos Reyles as among the few well-known intellectuals to support the coup.

13   Gonzalo Varela, *De la república liberal al estado militar: Uruguay 1968–1973* (Ediciones del Nuevo Mundo, 1988), 41.

14   See Jacob, *Uruguay de Terra*, 75–6. The history of the organised left in Uruguay can be really said to start with the foundation of the Socialist Party in 1911, and the Communist Party in 1920. However, earlier but not so successful attempts to organise radical groups can be found among socialists and anarchists in the last quarter of the nineteenth century. See Carlos Zubillaga, 'Luchas populares y cultura alternativa en Uruguay', *Siglo XIX*, iii, 6 (1988), 11–39.

15   José A. de Torres Wilson, *La conciencia histórica uruguaya* (Feria del Libro, 1964), 27, building on remarks in Flo's 1952 essay analysed in the Introduction above.

16   Roberto Ares Pons, 'Militancia y desarraigo de la intelligentsia uruguaya' [1953], quoted from his collection *La intelligentsia uruguaya y otros ensayos* (EBO, 1968), 45.

17   This will be the theme of the next two chapters.

18   Real de Azúa, 'Legatarios', 7.

19   Angel Rama, 'Testimonio, confesión y enjuiciamiento de 20 años de historia literaria y de nueva literatura uruguaya', *Marcha* (3 July 1959), 20B.

20   Mario Benedetti, *El país de la cola de paja* [1960] (7th ed., Arca, 1968), 56.

21   This may be why a writer from the interior such as Julio C. Da Rosa felt the need to write a collection of essays called *Civilización y terrofobia: apuntes de campo y ciudad* (Diálogo, 1968), where the neologism 'terrofobia' means fear of the land. This city/country hostility goes back to the civilisation versus barbarism and port versus hinterland disputes in the nineteenth century, and is at the heart of the history of modernisation in the River Plate region as a whole, not Uruguay alone.

22   Mario Delgado Aparaín, 'Reflexiones sobre una generación desgeneracionada', *La Hora* (1 November 1986), 8. He goes on to say pithily that while Montevideo-based intellectuals were bemoaning the collapse of the Uruguayan welfare state, he and his friends in Minas were wondering when it was ever going to reach them, and quotes the critic and publisher Heber Raviolo to the effect that the Europeanised Uruguay which had turned its back on the rest of Latin America ended with the capital's outer suburbs since much of the interior resembled it only too closely! (8–9). Achugar has also confirmed that the tendency to see Montevideo as though it were the country as a whole severely

limited intellectuals' ability to analyse the country's ills (see Hugo Achugar, *La balsa de la Medusa* [Trilce, 1992], 59).

23 See Carlos Machado, *Historia de los orientales: Tomo III (De Batlle a los'70)* (EBO, 1997), 188–91, and Francisco Panizza, *Uruguay: Batllismo y después* (EBO, 1990), 103–4.

24 Alberto Methol Ferré, 'La parroquia entra en la historia', *Marcha* 940 (5 December 1958), 6. Many years later, he would greet the creation of Mercosur in similarly unrestrained terms: Alberto Methol Ferré, 'La pérdida de un visible sistema de referencias', *Diplomacia en Acción*, i, 1 (1991), 37–40.

25 For a summary of Methol Ferré's views over the years, see the interview with Ignacio Palacios Videla, 'Conversación con Methol Ferré: un profeta realizado: del Uruguay opulento al Mercosur', *Todo es Historia*, xxv, 297 (1992), 33–47.

26 Ruralism would later be called 'the countryside's critical conscience' in Caetano & Garcé, 'Ideas, política', 343.

27 Fernando Butazzoni, *Seregni-Rosencof, mano a mano* (Aguilar, 2002), 247. This is a book-length series of conversations between Líber Seregni (by 2002, ex-President of the Frente Amplio) and Mauricio Rosencof, one of the founders of the MLN, popularly known as the Tupamaros.

28 The previous paragraphs were compiled from the following sources: Julio A. Salinas, 'La ofensiva ruralista de la década del 50 y las relaciones entre el estado y la sociedad uruguaya', *Estudios Rurales Latinoamericanos*, ii, 1 (1979), 56–76; Rosa Alonso Eloy & Carlos Demasi, *Uruguay 1958–1968. Crisis y estancamiento* (EBO, 1986); Gustavo Cosse, 'Acerca de la democracia, el sistema político y la movilización social: el caso del 'ruralismo' en Uruguay', *Estudios Rurales Latinoamericanos*, v, 1(1983), 77–100; Germán D'Elía, *El Uruguay neo-Batllista, 1946–1958* (EBO, 1983); Raúl Jacob, *Benito Nardone: El ruralismo hacia el poder* (EBO, 1981); Abril Trigo, *Caudillo, estado*, 169–77; and, for some pithy judgments and anecdotes, Julio L. Clericetti, *Historia política uruguaya 1938–1972* (no publ., 1984), and César di Candia, *Tiempos de tolerancia, tiempos de ira* (Fin de Siglo, 2005), 127–44.

29 Tomás Berreta, like Nardone, son of Italian migrants, stood up for the small rural landowners and tenants in the course of a long career in public service and politics. He became Colorado president in March 1947 but died only six months later. In addition to trying to modernise agricultural production, he was a conservative who thought strikes in the public sector should be made illegal. He was succeeded by his vice president Luis Batlle Berres from the more conventionally 'Batllista' minority Colorado faction, who remained in power till the historic Nationals' win in 1958.

30 Alberto Methol Ferré, '¿Quién gana las elecciones?', *Marcha* 941 (12 December 1958), 6 and 10.

31 Carlos Rama, '¿Es posible un fascismo uruguayo?', *Marcha* 941 (12 December 1958), 6 and 10.

32 A reader was to suggest in the letters column of the following issue that Rama's article was typical of 'spirits inclined to the speculative disciplines, and disposed . . . unwittingly to disconnect themselves from reality', and that democracy was too deeply entrenched to give way in Uruguay to fascism Europe-style, while if

anything resembled fascism at all it was precisely the defeated Colorado government! See 'Quidam', 'Fascismo uruguayo', *Marcha* 942 (19 December 1958), 2.

33   Niko Schwartz, 'La unión de las izquierdas', *Marcha* 942 (19 December 1958), 3.

34   Eduardo Hughes Galeano, 'Los partidos obreros resisten el impacto', *Marcha* 942 (19 December 1958), 6. It is worth noting that the future author of the best-selling 'bible' of the Latin American Left, *Las venas abiertas de América Latina* [1971], had not yet dropped his potentially embarrassing English, patrician first surname.

35   Albert Methol Ferré, 'Terciarios y moralismo', *Marcha*, 942 (19 December 1958), 6 and 10.

36   Alberto Methol Ferré, 'Otra vuelta de tuerca', *Marcha* 943 (26 December 1958), 6–7.

37   Eduardo Hughes Galeano, 'Nueva parte del tema', *Marcha* 943 (26 December 1958), 6.

38   Albert Methol Ferré, 'Adiós, Señor Nardone', *Marcha* 1047 (24 February 1961), n. p. See also the differences between his *¿Adónde va el Uruguay?* (no. publ., 1958) and its republication as *La crisis del Uruguay y el imperio británico* (Buenos Aires, A. Peña Lillo, 1960).

39   See his *Uruguay, ¿provincia o nación?* (Buenos Aires, Coyoacán, 1961).

40   Roberto Ares Pons, 'Es imposible un fascismo uruguayo', *Marcha*, 943 (26 December 1958), 7.

41   Carlos Rama, '¿Es posible un fascismo uruguayo?' [part 2], *Marcha* 947 (13 February 1959), 6.

42   Apart from the exaggerated comparison of Uruguay with the small Central American republics, Rama largely anticipated the whole political history of the next decade or so. The period of serious repression would not begin, however, until Pacheco took over the reins of the Colorado government in December 1967.

43   In fact, both Methol Ferré and Ares Pons would vote in 1962 for the Unión Popular, a coalition based around the more radical elements of the Socialist party (see next chapter for more details).

44   Roberto Ares Pons, 'Sobre fascismo y ruralismo', *Marcha* 949 (27 February 1959), 6.

45   It did not. Ares Pons, like Methol Ferré, was forced to eat his words. In June 1961, he wrote that the government had abandoned all that was progressive or radical in the National Party's heritage. See the 'Advertencia' to his *Uruguay, ¿provincia o nación*? 7. The main essay had been finished in 1959.

46   MB [ME?], 'Fascismo y otras yerbas', *Marcha*, 950 (6 March 1959), 2.

47   *Marcha* 951 (13 March 1959), 6. Rama's three articles are grouped together under the title of the first in his *Uruguay en crisis* (El Siglo Iliustrado, 1969), 43–59.

48   Trigo, *Caudillo, estado, nación*, 177.

49   In Spanish, either 'la tercera posición' or, referring to the whole movement that developed around it, 'el tercerismo'.

50 See Graceras, 97; G. W. Rama, *Democracia*, 64 and Varela, *República liberal*, 41–2. Mauricio Rosencof remembers university students organising protest marches against both Soviet and American imperialism. See Butazzoni, *Seregni-Rosencof*, 280.

51 A. F. S., 'Lo que no es y lo que es la Tercera Posición', *Marcha*, 580 (15 June 1951), 8.

52 Roberto Ares Pons, 'Sobre la tercera posición', collected in his *La intelligentsia uruguaya*, 59–68. This is an essay to which no-one in the debate to follow made any acknowledgement.

53 Aldo Solari, *El tercerismo en el Uruguay* (Alfa, 1965). Further references to this book will appear in the text, preceded by the letter *T*.

54 Trigo seems to be largely following Solari when he calls the 'Third Position' 'more a subjective reaction than a systematic position' and Real de Azúa in seeing in it an example of 'ideological schizophrenia' (*Caudillo, estado*, 179).

55 Aldo Solari, 'Réquiem para la izquierda' [1962], in his *Estudios sobre la sociedad uruguaya* (vol. 2, Arca, 1965), 135–55. See Chapter 2 below for further remarks on this essay, and on the left's results in 1962.

56 Aldo Solari, *El desarrollo social del Uruguay de la postguerra* (Alfa, 1967), 121–2, 126–7 and 131.

57 In fact, over the next twenty years Solari's view of the role the progressive intelligentsia played in the mid-late 1960s was to become even more negative. In a 1986 paper, 'El proceso de redemocratización en el Uruguay' (collected in his *Uruguay: partidos políticos y sistema electoral* [El Libro Libre / FUCCYT, 1988], 227–53), he repeated some of the points outlined here but goes on to suggest that the net result of the intelligentsia's trenchant criticism of the main political parties was to undermine even further the very notion of democracy itself (229–30), a view shared in the late 1980s by intellectuals on the left not only in Uruguay but throughout Latin America, as will be shown in Part Two below.

58 Ruben Cotelo, 'Introducción: dramatis personae', in Carlos Real de Azúa, *Tercera posición, nacionalismo revolucionario y tercer mundo* (Cámara de Representantes de la República Oriental del Uruguay, 1997), Vol. 3, 814.

59 For the complete debate, see Real de Azúa, *Tercera posición*, Vol. 3, 825–1025. All further references will appear in the text preceded by the letters *TP*. Despite Cotelo's assurance that Ardao (the only survivor of the three at the time) oversaw the production of this volume (*TP*, 824), one of his own contributions has been omitted: Arturo Ardao, 'Segunda respuesta a un tercero', *Marcha*, 1289 (20 January 1966), 8.

60 It is this study that makes up the first two volumes of the publication whose third volume, besides the debate discussed here, usefully reprints Solari's original text (641–809).

61 Solari himself was out of the country so could not defend his book.

62 See Hebert Gatto, *El cielo por asalto* (Taurus, 2004), 98–9, note 92. Also very pro-Ardao are Carmen de Sierra Nieves, 'Intelectuales y universitarios uruguayos frente a la "Guerra Fría" y la "Tercera Posición"', *Ciclos*, viii, 16 (1998), 125–41, and Yamandú Acosta, 'Arturo Ardao: la inteligencia filosófica y el discernimiento del tercerismo en *Marcha*', in Horacio Machín & Mabel

Moraña (eds.), *'Marcha' y América Latina* (Pittsburgh, Instituto Internacional de Literatura Iberoamericana, 2003), 123–61.

63 Later, some left-of-centre historians and political scientists would vindicate Solari's approach to the 'Third Position' and to the progressive intelligentsia, generally. See Caetano & Garcé, 'Ideas, política', 343–5, and Adolfo Garcé, 'Tres fases en la relación entre intelectuales y política en Uruguay (1830–1989)', in Gustavo de Armas & Adolfo Garcé (eds.), *Técnicos y política* (Trilce, 2000), 59 and 73.

64 Collected in his *Uruguay en crisis* (El Siglo Ilustrado, 1969), 9–42.

65 See the identically titled volume in English, edited by Solari and Seymour M. Lipset (New York, Oxford UP, 1967). The colloquium was held in June 1965.

66 Rama, *Uruguay en crisis*, 14–15.

67 On the Congress for Cultural Freedom, see Francis Stonor Saunders, *Who Paid The Piper? The CIA and The Cultural Cold War* (London, Granta, 1999).

The whole debate in Uruguay over the nature and role of the Congress can be read in articles and letter columns in *Marcha* between May 1965 (i.e. during the preparations for the colloquium on elites) and May 1967 (when the truth finally became public knowledge). The international brouhaha had a strong Uruguayan flavour for two reasons other than the seminar on Elites in Latin America. First, Benito Milla's Editorial Alfa, influential because of its dedication to publishing new Uruguayan writing, was shown to have received funds indirectly from the CIA, a revelation that destroyed it (Milla, an exiled Spanish republican, migrated to Caracas and set up Monte Avila, perhaps even more important a publishing venture than Alfa had been in Montevideo). Secondly, one of the renowned journals to disappear in the fallout of the affair was *Mundo Nuevo*, edited in Paris by none other than Emir Rodríguez Monegal, who had vacated his position at *Marcha* to do the job. His political and intellectual standing with his erstwhile colleagues was not good before he left (as the tone and the odd acid comment in parts of his *Literatura uruguaya del medio siglo* make clear), but the revelation of the CIA's involvement in the funding of his magazine sent it to rock bottom (Rodríguez Monegal would not return to Montevideo until 1984, an event I record below in Chapter 4).

A judicious selection of documents can be found in Barros-Lémez, *Intelectuales y política*, 34–107.

There seems no evidence whatever that Solari wrote *Tercerismo* 'for the Congress for Cultural Freedom' other than that Editorial Alfa published it and that Carlos Rama disapproved of them all. He also omitted all reference to Solari's pivotal work in Uruguayan sociology during the 1960s.

68 Solari did indeed leave Uruguay to teach in various parts of the Americas and to work for the United Nations and the Centro Económico para América Latina (CEPAL), but returned at the close of the military dictatorship to hold responsible posts in the administration of public education until his death in 1989. See Rubén Cotelo's introduction to the Real de Azúa/Arturo Ardao debate (*TP*, 822).

69 Real de Azúa, 'Partidos y literatura', 117.

70 Real de Azúa, 'Legatarios', 8.

71 'Praxis' Editorial Board, 'De redacción', *Praxis*, 1 (1967), 4–5.
72 Angel Rama, *La generación crítica* (Arca, 1972), 21.
73 Varela, *República liberal*, 41.
74 See C. Real de Azúa (ed.), *Problemas de la juventud uruguaya* (Marcha, 1954) for some early complaints on this subject.
75 Rama, *Democracia*, 90–2.
76 Graceras, *Los intelectuales*, 132.
77 Solari, *Desarrollo social*, 123.
78 Rama, *Generación crítica*, 59. See Graceras *Los intelectuales*, 139–40, for a report on the fears aroused through unfamiliarity by a sociological survey of university students in 1966. Martorelli dates the rise of the social sciences between 1963 and 1967 and their peak in the years up to 1973 (*La promesa de las ciencias sociales* [CLAEH, 1983], 133).
79 It is worth pointing out that this movement was originally founded by intellectuals: students of law, engineering and visual arts (see Luis Costa Bonino, *Crisis de los partidos tradicionales y movimiento revolucionario en el Uruguay* [EBO, 1985], 60). Two of its leaders, Raúl Sendic and Julio Marenales were, respectively, a law graduate and a teacher at the School of Fine Arts (Alain Labrousse, *The Tupamaros* [London, Penguin, 1973], 37).
80 Regis Debray, *The Revolution on Trial* (London, Penguin, 1978), 203.
81 Rama, *Generación crítica*, 84–5.
82 Costa Bonino, *Crisis de los partidos*, 37.
83 Varela, *República liberal*, 42.
84 Rama, *Democracia*, 100.

2 From Fidel to the Frente: the Uruguayan Left Searches for Someone to Talk to

1 Regis Debray, *The Revolution on Trial* (Harmondsworth, Penguin, 1978), 14.
2 Carlos Real de Azúa, *Partidos, política y poder en el Uruguay (1971 – coyuntura y pronóstico)* [1971] (Universidad de la República, 1988), 46.
3 Carlos Real de Azúa (ed.), *Antología del ensayo uruguayo contemporáneo* (2 vols., Universidad de la República, 1964). See the editor's introduction (vol. 1, 11–59), and the presentations of individual items throughout.
4 Albert Methol Ferré, *El Uruguay como problema* (Diálogo, 1967). I comment on this book in some detail in Chapter 6 below.
5 I refer here among many possible examples to Arturo Ardao, 'La independencia uruguaya como problema', *Cuadernos de Marcha*, 38 (1967), 83–96, and Carlos Real de Azúa, *El impulso y su freno* (EBO, 1964). However, much of the work of both writers comprises analyses of intellectual, cultural, social or political history designed to throw light on Uruguay's current problems through re-readings of its past.
6 See Carlos Maggi, *El Uruguay y su gente* (Alfa, 1961) and Mario Benedetti, *El país de la cola de paja* (Asir, 1960). Maggi's book had a third printing in 1967, while more overtly political, extended editions of Benedetti's volume appeared throughout the decade, culminating in the ninth edition of 1970, which was the one banned by the military in 1973 (along with all his other books).

7   Mario Benedetti, 'La literatura uruguaya cambia de voz' [January 1962], in his
    Literatura uruguaya siglo xx (4th ed., Buenos Aires, Seix Barral, 1997), 31.

8   For accounts of the ideological and cultural impact of creative writing and
    other intellectual endeavours, see Stephen Gregory, 'Uruguay as a Problem and
    the National Book Industry, 1960–1973', *Anales* [Sydney], iii, 2 (1994), 75–92;
    Gustavo San Román, 'La *Enciclopedia Uruguaya*: nacionalismo paradójico', *Río
    de la Plata*, 26/7 (2003), 89–102, and Abril Trigo, 'El proyecto de *Capítulo
    Oriental* y *Enciclopedia Uruguaya* (Reflexiones sobre las publicaciones en
    fascículo de los años 60)', *Hispamérica*, 94 (2003), 13–24.

9   Debray, *Revolution*, 14.

10 See Carlos Real de Azúa, 'Política, poder y partidos en el Uruguay de hoy', in
    Luis Benvenuto et al., *Uruguay hoy* (Buenos Aires, Siglo XXI, 1971), 145–321.

11 Real de Azúa, *Partidos, política*, 24–5.

12 *Marcha*, 1572 (26 November 1971), 7. Reproduced in Alvaro Barros-Lémez,
    Intelectuales y política (Monte Sexto, 1988), 214–15.

13 Moisés Lasca, 'Los artistas e intelectuales en el Frente Amplio', *Estudios*, 59
    (1971), 93–4, 97.

14 Ruben Yáñez, '1971: un salto cualitativo en la cultura uruguaya', *Estudios*, 62
    (1972), 90, 93.

15 Aldo Solari, *El desarrollo social del Uruguay en la postguerra* (Alfa, 1967), 166.
    Solari could not sign the *Marcha* document as he had already left the country
    to work abroad.

16 Hebert Gatto, *El cielo por asalto. El Movimiento de Liberación Nacional
    (Tupamaros) y la izquierda uruguaya (1963–1972)* (Taurus, 2004), 113.

17 Julio Castro, 'El Frente Amplio, un horizonte de esperanza', *Cuadernos de
    Marcha*, 53 (September 1971), 6.

18 Fernando Urioste Braga, 'La gran tarea del Frente', *Cuadernos de Marcha*, 47
    (March 1971), 66–9, quote on p. 66.

19 Real de Azúa, *Partidos, política*, 120.

20 Aldo Solari, 'Elecciones 1966: cambio sin cambiar', reprinted in *Uruguay:
    partidos políticos y sistema electoral* (El Libro Libre/ FUCCYT, 1988), 194.

21 General accounts of Uruguayan political history used for the following para-
    graphs are: Germán Rama, *La democracia en Uruguay* (Buenos Aires, Grupo
    Editorial Latinoamericano, 1987), Gonzalo Varela, *De la república liberal al
    estado militar: Uruguay 1968–1973* (Ediciones del Nuevo Mundo, 1988), Carlos
    Zubillaga, *La democracia atacada* (EBO, 1988), Benjamín Nahum et al, *El fin
    del Uruguay liberal* (EBO, 1998), Instituto de Ciencia Política, *El Uruguay del
    siglo xx: la política* (EBO, 2001), and César di Candia, *Memoria: el camino de la
    violencia uruguaya (1940–1973)* (6 vols., El País, 2006).

22 All writers agree that the Cuban Revolution received the virtually unanimous
    support of the Uruguayan intelligentsia. As Carlos Rama put it, you did not
    need even the fingers on one hand to count those hostile to it (*Uruguay en crisis*,
    88). As reported above, one of the few not wholeheartedly to applaud it or unre-
    servedly condemn the US's attacks on it, was Rodríguez Monegal, as is made
    clear in the opening chapter of his *Literatura uruguaya del medio siglo* (Alfa,
    1966). Not surprisingly, then, July 1959 was the last time Angel Rama and

Rodríguez Monegal appeared in the pages of the same issue of *Marcha* (see Pablo Rocca, '35 años', 72).

23 See figures quoted in M. Machado Ferrer & C. Fagúndez Ramos, *Los años duros: cronología documentada (1964–1973)* (Monte Sexto, 1987), 51 and 77.

24 See de Torres Wilson, *Conciencia histórica*, 26 and 33–5, for clear evidence of 1958 conceived as a watershed in the nation's affairs. It is also worth recalling the tone of Methol Ferré's remarks on the 1958 election results quoted above in Chapter 1.

25 See Julio Castro, 'Una larga marcha' [originally in *Marcha*, 12 February 1971], *Cuadernos de Marcha*, 3rd series, 7 (1985), 53.

26 See Clara Aldrighi, *La izquierda armada. Ideología, ética e identidad en el MLN-Tupamaros* (Trilce, 2001), 79–80.

27 Quoted in Miguel Aguirre Bayley, *El Frente Amplio: historia y documentos* (EBO, 1985), 11–12.

28 See 'Una declaración', *Marcha*, 1100 (23 March 1962), 15.

29 See 'El Popular', 'Mesa redonda de escritores en el FIDEL', *El Popular* (10 August, 1963), n. p. Graceras gives a long list of adherents from the fields of journalism, literature, theatre, fine arts and the academy stretching to two pages (*Los intelectuales y la política* [El País, 1970], 135 and 141).

30 For assessments of the effects these new coalitions had on the traditional organisations of the Communist and Socialist parties, see Gerardo Caetano, Javier Gallardo & José Rilla, *La izquierda uruguaya: tradición, innovación y política* (Trilce, 1995), 42–6 and 96–108.

31 'Unión Popular', 'Llamamiento al pueblo uruguayo', *Marcha* (24 August 1962), 2.

32 See Carlos Machado, *Historia de los orientales* (tomo 3, EBO, 1997), 181–96, *passim*. An interesting and full, if also biased, account of the groups participating in these alliances is Ariel Collazo, 'El Uruguay no es excepción', *Pensamiento Crítico* [Havana] (July, 1967), 83–109. The author's own organisation, the Movimiento Revolucionario Oriental (MRO), which had broken away from the National Party, had first attempted to align itself with the Unión Popular but, after ideological disputes, ended up with FIDEL, giving Collazo an insider's view of both coalitions. The article's title parodies the pro-Batlle, rather smug assumption of Uruguay's social and cultural superiority to the rest of Latin America, and also reflects its author's controversial contention that, contrary to the view put forward by Debray in his famous *Revolution in the Revolution?* [1967], Uruguay could indeed be part of a successful continent-wide revolutionary armed struggle, and was, therefore, 'not an exception'.

33 See INDAL, *Partido Comunista del Uruguay y la formación del Frente de Izquierda* (Heverlee-Louvain, INDAL, 2nd. ed., 1972), 63–4, and Luis Touron, 'La brega unitaria: una constante del Partido Comunista', *Estudios*, 57 (1970), 47–59, collected in INDAL, *Partido comunista*, 211–19. An example of earlier entreaties is the 'Llamado a todas las fuerzas antimperialistas, democráticas y avanzadas del país', *Estudios*, 18 (December 1960), 9–12. It makes special reference to the Socialist Party on the first page.

34 Eduardo Galeano, '¿El partido socialista nace de nuevo?', *Marcha* (30 March 1962), n.p.

35 Eduardo Payssé González, 'Vivián Trías: la crisis y la unidad de las izquierdas' [interview], *Marcha* (20 October 1961), 7 and 22. Perusal of the editorials in the Communist Party's paper *El popular* and the Socialists' *El sol* for 1962–3 reveals just how deep the divisions were over such issues as the relative importance of the class struggle nationally as against Uruguay's place as a dependent economy within the international capitalist system. It should also be remembered that such disagreements had strong historical roots, since the Communist Party had been founded in 1920 by a dissident group that had broken away from the Socialist Party, formed nine years earlier.

36 See Galeano, 'El partido socialista', and MRO: 'Habla el Movimiento Revolucionario Oriental', *Marcha* (10 November 1961), n.p., Eduardo Payssé González, 'Ariel Collazo: "Artigas no era Blanco ni Colorado"' [interview], *Marcha* (8 December 1961), 8 and 26, the already mentioned interview with Vivián Trías, and INDAL, *Partido Comunista*, 83.

37 The figures are taken from Carlos Zubillaga & Romeo Pérez, *Los partidos políticos* (CLAEH, 1983), 115, as will be those for the 1966 poll.

38 See Julio L. Clericetti, *Historia política uruguaya* (no publ., 1984), 67.

39 Mario Benedetti, 'Posdata 1963', in his *El país de la cola de paja* (7th ed., Arca, 1968), 127–149. Further page references appear in the text.

40 Aldo Solari, 'Réquiem para la izquierda', in his *Estudios sobre la sociedad uruguaya* (Vol. 2, Arca, 1965), 135–55. Further page references appear in the text.

41 Senator Erro and his followers had been important in the 1958 National Party victory and their vote had partially decided the majority fraction within the party as a whole. His defection to the Unión Popular in 1962 was electoral suicide for his group. Solari, echoed by many political commentators since, makes the general point that to be a dissident faction within a main party can be an advantage electorally, whereas a disagreement that takes the faction right outside it is nearly always fatal ('Requiem', 137). Benedetti's friend Zelmar Michelini was also to know both sides of this coin: he polled well in 1962 and 1966 as leader of a separate faction within the Colorado Party, but did considerably less well when he joined the Frente Amplio in 1971.

42 The importance Solari and Benedetti give to the middle class vote becomes clear when one remembers that they comprised between 60 and 65 percent of the population. See Isaac Ganón, *Estructura social del Uruguay* (Editorial As, 1966), 203 and Aldo Solari, 'Partidos políticos y clase social', in his *Estudios*, vol. 2, 124. However, exactly what constituted the middle class in Uruguay during the 1960s is extremely difficult to determine given the paucity and unreliability of statistics about Uruguayan society at the time. For accounts that reveal the obviously very real difficulties in assessing class distribution in Uruguay, see Carlos M. Rama, *Sociología del Uruguay* (Buenos Aires, Eudeba, 1965), 81–95 and Solari, *Desarrollo social*, 55–96.

43 Thus illustrating how pivotal Benedetti's experience of the 1962 elections was in his evolution towards the adoption of the Tupamaros and Cuban

Revolution's version of the armed struggle. In 1971, he co-founded the Movimiento de Independientes 26 de Marzo, a legalised shop front for the clandestine Tupamaros, a radical politics that informs all his books of the early 1970s. As well as being forced into exile in 1974, it is my contention that Benedetti paid a very high intellectual price for his commitment to a revolutionary politics he in effect borrowed from elsewhere. However, the trajectory he followed, as self-undermining as it turned out to be, is a clear example of the kind of fate that the advent of the Frente Amplio was intended to make unnecessary. On Benedetti's militancy, see my 'The Road or the Inn? Mario Benedetti as Activist and the Movimiento de Independientes 26 de Marzo', forthcoming in *Journal of Iberian and Latin American Research* [Melbourne] (July 2008).

44 At the turn of the new millennium, Solari's position with regard to the Uruguayan left would be vindicated by a historian sympathetic to the Frente Amplio (see Gerardo Caetano, 'Pasado-futuro: una polaridad crucial y resistente', in Caetano (ed.), *Uruguay: Agenda 2020* [Taurus, 2007], 36–7), and economist and Frente Amplio senator Alberto Couriel in 'La izquierda y el "réquiem para la izquierda"', chapter 6 in his *La izquierda y el Uruguay del futuro* (2nd ed., EBO, 2004), which had previously appeared in a general re-evaluation of Solari's work: Rolando Franco (ed.), *Sociología del desarrollo, políticas sociales y democracia* (Mexico, Siglo XXI, 2001). I discuss Couriel and Caetano further in Chapters 5 and 6 below.

45 Quoted in Samuel Blixen, *Sendic* (Trilce, 2000), 78. The failure of the Unión Popular fed directly into the foundation of the MLN (Tupamaros) by Sendic, Huidobro and others a year later.

46 See César Reyes Daglio, 'El congreso del FIDEL y los caminos de la unidad total de las izquierdas', *Estudios*, 26 (1963), 62–4.

47 FIDEL, 'Un llamado a la unidad', *El Popular* (1 July 1963), 1.

48 Quoted in an anonymous editorial, 'La hora de la unidad ha sonado ya', *El Popular* (9 July 1963), 3.

49 Reyes Daglio, 'El congreso del FIDEL', 64.

50 Comité Ejecutivo Nacional del Partido Socialista, 'Declaración', quoted with approval in *El Popular* (2 September 1963), n. p.

51 Graceras, *Los intelectuales*, 125.

52 Whether such a provision promoted stability by discouraging the proliferation of new parties or instability and stagnation by virtually ensuring the fragmentation and continual search for compromises within the established ones was a matter of fierce debate. There have been significant changes to Uruguayan electoral law since 1985. See Carlos O. Pisani, *Sistema político-electoral del Uruguay, siglo xxi* (Arca, 2004).

53 Julio Castro, 'La unión de las izquierdas', *Marcha* (30 September 1966), 6.

54 M. H. J. Finch, *A Political Economy of Uruguay since 1970* (London, MacMillan, 1981), 20.

55 Y. González Sierra, *Cronología histórica del movimiento sindical uruguayo. Hechos, resoluciones políticas y eventos sindicales, 1870–1984* (CIEDUR, 1989), 44.

56 For some general sources on Uruguayan trade unionism up to the dictatorship,

see José R. Bottaro, *25 años de movimiento sindical uruguayo* (Acción Sindical Uruguaya, 1985), Rosa Alonso Eloy & Carlos Demasi, *Uruguay 1958–1968. Crisis y estancamiento* (EBO, 1986), Carlos Rama, 'Historia del movimiento obrero y social uruguayo', *Cuadernos Americanos*, ccxix, 4 (1978), 129–45, Héctor Rodríguez, *Sindicatos: participación y negociación* (FCU, 1985), Hugo Cores, 'La lucha de los gremios solidarios', *Brecha* (11 August 1989), 15–18, and Universindo Rodríguez et al., *El sindicalismo uruguayo* (Taurus, 2006). A reliable summary in English can be found in the introductory pages of Martín Gargiulo, 'The Uruguayan Labor Movement in the Post-Authoritarian Period', in Edward C. Epstein (ed.), *Labor Autonomy and the State* (Boston, Unwin Hyman, 1991), 219–46.

57 Héctor Rodríguez, 'El Congreso del Pueblo', *Marcha*, 1263 (16 July 1965), 6.
58 González Sierra, *Cronología*, 41.
59 CUI, *CNT: 1964–1965. Documentos sindicales*, I (CUI, 1984), 18–21.
60 Héctor Rodríguez, *Nuestros sindicatos (1865–1965)* (Ediciones Uruguay, 1965), 81–3.
61 See Varela, *República liberal*, 36; Rama, *Democracia*, 102, and Howard Handelman, 'Labor-Industrial Conflict and the Collapse of Uruguayan Democracy', *Journal of Interamerican Studies and World Affairs*, xxiii, 4 (1981), 371–94.
62 *República liberal*, 38 and *Democracia*, 106.
63 For documents relating to the preparatory stages of the Congress, see Centro Uruguay Independiente [CUI], *El pueblo delibera. El Congreso del Pueblo veinte años después* (CUI, 1985), 13–35.
64 Rodríguez, 'Congreso', 6–7. For a comprehensive account of the attacks on the Congress, see CUI, *El pueblo*, 201–27.
65 Vladimir Turiansky, *El movimiento obrero uruguayo* (Ediciones Pueblos Unidos, 1973), Appendix 1, 209–12.
66 Congreso del Pueblo, 'Llamado al Pueblo Uruguayo', *El Popular*, 3062 (16 August 1965), 10, and reproduced as 'Mensaje al Pueblo Uruguayo' in Turiansky, 213–18, from which all quotations are taken.
67 According to Héctor Rodríguez, 'El elefante y la caja de fósforos: después del Congreso del Pueblo', *Marcha*, 1268 (23 August 1965), 6. For blow-by-blow accounts of the Congress, see CUI, *El pueblo*, 65–104.
68 CUI, *El pueblo*, 237, 240, 245 and 251.
69 Graceras, *Intelectuales y política*, 122, and Abril Trigo, *Caudillo, estado, nación. Literatura, historia e ideología en Uruguay* (Gaithersburg, Hispamérica, 1990), 188, note 14.
70 Eloy & Demasi, *Uruguay 1958–1968*, 57.
71 See, respectively, Gatto, *El cielo por asalto*, 143, note 124, and Jaime Yaffé, *Al centro y adentro. La renovación de la izquierda y el triunfo del Frente Amplio en Uruguay* (Linardi y Risso, 2005), 136.
72 The document exists in at least three widely differing versions. The first was published in *El Popular*, 3062 (16 August 1965), 9, and was reproduced in Turiansky (218–32). The second and most polished appears in CUI, *CNT: programa y estatutos* (CUI, 1984), 15–29 and in Héctor Rodríguez, *Sindicatos:*

participación y negociación (FCU, 1985), 80–102. It is to this more recent and accessible republication that all references are made. However, a considerably longer and more unwieldy version which shows all the signs of being the probably hastily devised document passed on the floor of the Congress itself is in CUI, *El pueblo*, 113–50.

73 However, not all published versions of the Program include all categories. It is not clear whether the very important differences between them are due to errors arising from the urgency and haste with which the documents were originally assembled and published, or from subsequent attempts by different groups to alter or lay claim to them. It does seem plausible to suppose that different versions circulated at different times (especially during the Congress itself) and that, leaving aside any vested interests, a particular organisation might genuinely not know that their version varied significantly from others.

74 So much was their passive role taken for granted that the armed forces merited not so much as a single mention.

75 Rodríguez, *Sindicatos*, 80–102. Quotations are from pp. 80 and 82.

76 Rodríguez, 'El elefante y la caja', 7.

77 Graceras, *Intelectuales*, 124.

78 Twenty-five years later, Rodríguez, remembering his earlier image of the elephant in the matchbox, summed up this sad state of affairs: 'the elephant died'. Cited in Marta Harnecker (ed.), *Frente Amplio: los desafíos de una izquierda legal* (Vol. 1, La República, 1991), 33.

79 CUI, *CNT*, 5 and CUI, *El pueblo*, 233–4.

80 See, for example, the wrangle between the Communists and Socialists over the supposed brake on revolutionary action applied by the Soviet Union's official policy on Latin American Communist parties. Some relevant documents are in Carlos Machado (ed.), *Izquierdas y derechas en América Latina. Documentos* (Editorial Patria Grande, 1968), 152–65.

81 See his *Mística, desarrollo y revolución* [1969], published twice abroad during the dictatorship, and again in Uruguay during the transition (Librosur, 1985).

82 See the introduction to INDAL, *Democracia cristiana del Uruguay y la formación del Frente Amplio* (2nd ed., Caracas, INDAL, 1973), 9. A short history of the party can be found in José L. Cogorno [then General Secretary], 'Visión organizativa a través del análisis histórico del PDC', in the same volume (103–10).

83 Oscar Bruschera, '¿Qué hacer?', parts 1–3, *Marcha*, (25 October, 1 and 8 November 1968). Just before that, another journalist, from the more Cuba-inspired section of the left, had been asking whether it was time for a third party. See Carlos María Gutiérrez, '¿Hacia un tercer partido?', *Marcha* (18 October 1968), 11.

84 See Oscar Bruschera, *Las décadas infames* (Linardi y Risso, 1986) for an involved insider's account of the whole turbulent period.

85 Juan P. Terra, 'El PDC y las raíces del Frente', *Cuadernos de Marcha*, 47 (1971), 13–14. This article quotes extensively from the television speech.

86 Juan P. Terra, 'En los comienzos del Frente', *Cuadernos de Marcha*, 46 (1971), 46–7.

87 Oscar Bruschera, *Los partidos tradicionales* (Librosur, 1984), 39. This book reprints two seminal essays from the late 1950s.

88 Hence Gustavo de Armas & Adolfo Garcé's contention that most of the criticisms launched in the 1960s against the way Uruguay was governed were empirically correct (*Uruguay y su conciencia crítica: intelectuales y política en el siglo xx* [Trilce, 1997], 76).

89 PDC, 'Una salida hacia el Uruguay nuevo', INDAL, *Democracia cristiana*, 99–102, quotations from pp. 100 and 102.

90 See Aguirre Bayley, *Frente*, 17 and Romeo Pérez, 'La izquierda en la fase post-autoritaria', in Charles Gillespie et al., *Uruguay y la democracia* (EBO, 1984), I, 131, note 2.

91 According to José L. Massera, 'Libertad y democracia: contraseña unificadora', *Estudios*, 48 (December 1968), 50–1.

92 PDC, 'Una salida', 102.

93 See, for example, Carlos María Gutiérrez, 'La ilusión frentista, 1: la propuesta del PDC', *Marcha* (28 June 1968), 8–9 and José M. Quijano, 'La ilusión frentista, 2: entre diálogo y represión' in the same issue, 9–10, and Massera, 'Libertad y democracia', 52–3.

94 Terra, 'PDC y las raíces', 15–16 and 'En los comienzos', 49. Terra reflects on his and the PDC's role in founding the Frente, as well as the PDC's later difficulties with the coalition during the first years after redemocratisation, in Harnecker, *Frente Amplio*, vol. 1, 11–15.

95 See the PDC's 'Fundamentos' and 'Programa de principios' (INDAL, *Democracia cristiana*, 31–5 and 37–42) for illustrations of how the Party's ideology dovetailed with Terra's personal qualities as a negotiator on the future Frente's behalf. He also gives his own account in Juan P. Terra, '¿Por qué impulsamos el Frente?' in the same volume, 155–6.

3 Dialogue Engaged: The Frente Amplio as Coalition

1 Quoted in José Rilla, *La actualidad del pasado* (Debate, 2008), 373–4, note 33.

2 See Gerardo Caetano, Javier Gallardo & José Rilla, *La izquierda uruguaya: tradición, innovación y política* (Trilce, 1995), 49, and Samuel Blixen, *Sendic* (Trilce, 2000), 180. Seregni remembered later that the whole issue of 'exclusions' was the main topic of debate during this period of the Frente's gestation. See Fernando Butazzoni, *Seregni-Rosencof, mano a mano* (Aguilar, 2002), 274. Scott Myers also mentions the encouraging example of Allende's 1970 victory in Chile (*Los años oscuros. Uruguay 1967–1987* [Editorial Latina, 1997], 80).

3 INDAL, *El Frente Amplio del Uruguay y las elecciones del 1971* (Heverlee-Louvain, INDAL, 1973), 91.

4 Juan Pablo Terra, 'El PDC y las raíces del Frente', *Cuadernos de Marcha*, 47 (1971), 16.

5 INDAL, *Frente Amplio*, 96–7.

6 The secretary of this group was José A. de Torres Wilson, a young historian quoted elsewhere in this book.

7 INDAL, *Frente Amplio*, 113–15, 125, 17 and 155, respectively.

8   INDAL, *Frente Amplio*, 92.
9   INDAL, *Frente Amplio*, 139.
10 INDAL, *Frente Amplio*, 93–5. For a rather partisan account of the whole preliminary process from Líber Seregni's perspective, including his protracted but eventually thwarted negotiations with like-minded high ranking army officers, see Samuel Blixen, *Seregni* (Ediciones de Brecha, 1997), 61–8.
11 On the number of founding groups, compare Aguirre Bayley, *Frente*, 21 and INDAL, *Frente Amplio*, 49–50.
12 According to Pablo Rocca, '35 años en *Marcha*: escritura y ambiente literario en *Marcha* y en el Uruguay, 1939–1974', *Nuevo Texto Crítico*, vi, 11 (1993), 138, note 83.
13 See Terra, 'El PDC y las raíces', 16.
14 INDAL, *Frente Amplio*, 156.
15 Alba Roballo, '"Para salvar al Batllismo, me voy del Batllismo"', *Cuadernos de Marcha*, 46 (1971), 70.
16 Alvaro Barros-Lémez, *Seregni* (Monte Sexto, 1989), 68–73, quote on p. 79.
17 Butazzoni, *Seregni-Rosencof*, 94.
18 See Carlos Real de Azúa, *Partidos, política y poder en el Uruguay (1971 – coyuntura y pronóstico)* (Universidad de la République, 1988), 121.
19 Líber Seregni, *La autoridad del pueblo* (ed. Germán Wettstein, Editorial Indice, 1984), 27. In the paragraphs that follow, further references will appear in the text preceded by the word *Autoridad*.
20 Barros-Lémez, *Seregni*, 78.
21 According to Gonzalo Varela, *De la república liberal al estado militar: Uruguay 1968–1973* (Ediciones del Nuevo Mundo, 1988), 114.
22 Líber Seregni, *Una línea coherente* (Vol. 1, Libros para La Patria Nueva, 1988), 73. Further references in this section will appear in the text preceded by *Una línea*.
23 See also Germán W. Rama, *La democracia en Uruguay* (Buenos Aires, Grupo Editor Latinoamericano, 1987), 116–17.
24 This unwieldy hybrid term refers to the fact that the preferred election formula for the ruling faction of the governing Colorado Party involved the reelection of Pacheco as president, a procedure forbidden by the constitution. When the necessary constitutional amendment to permit it failed to get the required number of votes, Pacheco's chosen successor, Bordaberry, was elected on the same faction's back-up ticket.
25 Seregni is probably referring to the July 1969 decree that prohibited all reference to the Tupamaros except by use of certain pejorative terms.
26 Omar Prego, *Reportaje a un golpe de estado* (La República, 1988), 11.
27 On Batlle's notion of a secular, social harmony and its limitations, see Carlos Real de Azúa's classic if far from exhaustive study *El impulso y su freno* (EBO, 1964).
28 Gerardo Caetano & José Rilla, 'Izquierda y tradición en Uruguay', La Lupa section, *Brecha* (1 July 1988), n.p.
29 INDAL, *Frente Amplio*, 66–7.
30 INDAL, *Frente Amplio*, 55–8.

31 Gerónimo De Sierra, 'La izquierda de la transición', in Charles Gillespie et al., *Uruguay y la democracia* (Vol. 1, EBO, 1984), 153.

32 Butazzoni, *Seregni-Rosencof*, 74–5.

33 According to the standard work on the subject, Germán Rama, *El club político* (Arca, 1971), and Aldo Solari, 'Requiem para la izquierda', in his *Estudios sobre la sociedad uruguaya* (vol. 2, Arca, 1965), 148–9. For a more recent discussion of how club and committee have changed over time, see Juan P. Luna, *La política desde el llano: Conversaciones con militantes barriales* (EBO, 2004).

34 Analogously, in the constitutive document of February 5, the people were asked to 'exhaust' all democratic forms of opposition to the Pacheco administration (INDAL, *Frente Amplio*, 50).

35 INDAL, *Frente Amplio*, 56–7.

36 INDAL, *Frente Amplio*, 64–5, but reproduced in Aguirre Bayley, *Frente*, 119–22 as 'Político Commitment'.

37 Barros-Lémez, *Seregni*, 72.

38 A point emphasised in Julio Castro, 'Una elección diferente' [originally in *Marcha* (1 October 1971)], *Cuadernos de Marcha*, Tercera Epoca, i, 7 (1985), 57.

39 Aguirre Bayley, *Frente*, 29–31.

40 The governing Colorado Party, for example, put up seven different presidential formulas for the 1971 elections.

41 Castro,' Una elección diferente', 57.

42 INDAL, *Frente Amplio*, 63.

43 Oscar Bruschera, *Las décadas infames* (Linardi y Risso, 1986), 67.

44 Frente Amplio, 'Bases programáticas', INDAL, *Frente Amplio*, 51–4.

45 Frente Amplio, 'Bases', 51–3.

46 Frente Amplio, 'Bases', 53.

47 INDAL, *Frente Amplio*, 59–63, quotes on p. 62. Aguirre Bayley (*Frente*, 17) points out that the '30 primeras medidas de gobierno' were modelled on the 40 measures of Salvador Allende's Unidad Popular in Chile. This may well be the case, but the social welfare reforms bear a striking resemblance to some of the 'soluciones immediatas' and 'soluciones de fondo' inserted into the version of the Congreso del Pueblo's proposals as they were readopted by the Convención Nacional de Trabajadores at its founding conference in 1966. See CUI, *CNT: programa y estatutos* (CUI, Documentos Sindicales No. 2, 1984), 23–6.

48 Frente Amplio, 'Bases', 54 and 57. The military would generate their own vision of Artigas, however. See Isabel Cosse & Vania Markarian, *1975: Año de la Orientalidad. Identidad, memoria e historia en dictadura* (Trilce, 1996).

49 See, for example, Trigo *Caudillo, estado*, 221–2 and Rilla, *Actualidad*, 359.

50 There was considerable disagreement on this score even among the participants. See, for example, Juan Pablo Terra, '¿Por qué impulsamos el Frente?', INDAL, *Democracia cristiana del uruguay y formación del Frente Amplio* (2nd ed., Caracas, INDAL, 1973), 155–6; Mario Benedetti, 'La transformación empieza en las bases', *Cuadernos de Marcha*, 41 (1971), 25–8; Oscar Bruschera, 'Las líneas fundamentales del Frente Amplio', *Cuadernos de Marcha*, 47 (1971), 3–7; Rodney Arismendi, 'La revolución uruguaya en la hora del Frente Amplio'

and 'Un avance sustancial del proceso revolucionario uruguayo' in his *Uruguay y América en los años 70* (Mexico, Ediciones de Cultura Popular, 1979), 41–58 and 59–67, respectively; Fernando Urioste Braga, 'La gran tarea del Frente', *Cuadernos de Marcha*, 47 (1971), 66–70.

51 And not from any wish to imply a critique of existing socialism or Marxist theory, as claimed in Nelson Argones & Pablo Mieres, 'La polémica en el Frente Amplio, ¿pugna por contenidos organizacionales o institucionales?', *Cuadernos del CLAEH*, 49 (1989), 53.

52 Bruschera, *Décadas infames*, 60–2.

53 Rama, *Democracia*, 114–16 and Trigo, *Caudillo, nación*, 219.

54 Adolfo Garcé & Jaime Yaffé, *La era progresista* (Fin de Siglo, 2004), 26.

55 Trigo, *Caudillo, estado*, 219.

56 Enrique Iglesias, *Uruguay: una propuesta de cambio* (Arca, 1966). For a recent reassessment of the whole enterprise which suggests the report's continuing relevance to Uruguay's economy, see Adolfo Garcé, *Ideas y competencia política en Uruguay (1960–1973): Revisando el "fracaso" de la CIDE* (Trilce, 2002).

57 Iglesias, *Uruguay*, 24 and 47–9.

58 Iglesias, *Uruguay*, 30–1 and 76.

59 Juan Rial, 'Makers and Guardians of Fear: Controlled Terror in Uruguay', in Juan E. Corradi, Peter Weiss Fagen, Miguel A. Garretón (eds.), *Fear at the Edge: State Terror and Resistance in Latin America* (California UP, 1992), 90.

60 With no provocation from the Tupamaros, who observed a truce for the whole election period.

61 Thus confronting the same hurdle that defeated those involved in the 1966 discussions referred to earlier. As Carlos Mártinez Moreno, wearing his lawyer's hat instead of his more familiar novelist's cap, has made clear, the obstacles to getting a new party officially recognised tended to make it easy for parliamentarians to make sure intruders did not threaten their powerbase. See his 'Crepúsculo en Arcadia: la institucionalidad y su derrumbe a la uruguaya', in Benvenuto, *Uruguay hoy*, 412.

62 Which for Varela (*República liberal*, 110) showed how clearly the executive was under the control of the right. However, it is worth noting that Seregni does not share this general view, believing that all irregularities were removed in the second count. Rosencof remains unconvinced (Butazzoni, *Seregni-Rosencof*, 209–10).

63 It is estimated that some 5 to 10 percent of Uruguay's population (from 150,000 to nearly 300,000 people) became economic or political refugees during the 1960s and 1970s and that these included an alarmingly high proportion of economically active people and individuals of childbearing age. See José L. Petrucelli, 'Consequences of Uruguayan Emigration: Research Note', *International Migration Review*, xiii, 31 (1979), 519–26; César A. Aguiar, *Uruguay: país de emigración* (EBO, 1982); César A. Aguiar & Antonio Cravotto, *Población, territorio, ciudades* (CLAEH, 1983); and Abril Trigo, *Memorias migrantes. Testimonios y ensayos sobre la diáspora uruguaya* (Rosario/Montevideo, Beatriz Viterbo/Trilce, 2003), 37–61.

64 See Rolando Franco, *Democracia a la uruguaya* (El Libro Libre, 1984), Ch. 4.

65 See INDAL, *Frente Amplio*, 244–7, 267–70 and 277–85. These pages contain closely argued editorials from *Marcha* and the journal *Cuestión*, an official request from the National Party for an investigation into some of the irregularities, and an interview with National Party leader Wilson Ferreira Aldunate, who remains remarkably calm and collected, given that the swindle undoubtedly deprived him of a presidency he would otherwise have won easily.

66 Constanza Moreira, *Final de juego. Del bipartidismo tradicional al triunfo de la izquierda en Uruguay* (Trilce, 2004), 42.

67 They were Enrique Rodríguez (a Communist), Francisco Rodríguez Camusso (leader of the MBPP), Juan Pablo Terra (PDC), Zelmar Michelini (MGP) and Enrique Erro (UP).

68 Some of whose names are familiar, if only as authors of books and articles mentioned in this book: Rodney Arismendi, Vladimir Turiansky, Oscar Bruschera and Vivián Trías.

69 This represents a reasonable spread of candidates across the major groups within the Frente, but it is noticeable that none from the smaller groups were elected. They were not the only losers. Alba Roballo's defection from the Colorado Party cost her a seat in the Senate. In defeat, she remained determined and unrepentant. See the interview in INDAL, *Frente Amplio*, 256–9.

70 Aguirre Bayley, *Frente*, 31–3.

71 Ernesto González Bermejo, 'Encuentro de compañeros y la unidad crítica', *Marcha*, 1575 (24 December 1971), 10–11. Eighteen years later, Seregni was to highlight this problem in his own recollections of the period, and maintained that it had still not been solved for the election campaign in 1984 (Barros-Lémez, *Seregni*, 85 and 178–9). It would not be until the turn of the century that the Frente really began to make inroads into the electorate of the interior.

72 Arismendi, 'Un avance sustancial', 60.

73 See Debray, *Revolution on Trial*, 147.

74 For example, de Sierra, 'La izquierda', 154 and Argones & Mieres, 'La polémica', 49.

75 See Varela, *República liberal*, 117.

76 Arismendi, 'Un avance', 65.

77 Julio Castro, 'La lucha recién empieza' [originally in *Marcha* (3 December 1971)], *Cuadernos de Marcha*, Tercera Epoca, 7 (1985), 58.

78 Seregni, *Autoridad*, 38.

79 Rama, *Democracia*, 114.

80 It also recalls Real de Azúa and Flo's description of the entrants to the 1952 essay competition mentioned in the Introduction.

81 See Debray, *Revolution on Trial*, 150. This is a lesson the Frente would learn in the period after the dictatorship. As José Mujica, a leader of the original Tupamaros who in the 1990s became a senator for its legalized successor, the Movimiento por la Participación del Pueblo sector of the Frente (see Chapter 5 below), put it in an interview in 2003: 'Political strategy should not be confused with electoral strategy'. Quoted in Jorge Lanzaro (ed.), *La izquierda entre la oposición y el gobierno* (Fin de Siglo, 2004), 197.

82 Castro, 'La lucha', 59 and Debray, *Revolution on Trial*, 152.

83 González Bermejo, 'Encuentro de compañeros', 10–11.
84 See Butazzoni, *Seregni-Rosencof,* 42–3, 45, 162 and 176.
85 González Bermejo, 'Encuentro de compañeros', 10–11.
86 Bruschera, *Décadas infames,* 74–5.
87 Bruschera, 'Las líneas fundamentales', 4.
88 See Blixen, *Seregni,* 103.
89 Francisco Panizza, *Uruguay: Batllismo y después* (Montevideo, Ediciones de la Banda Oriental, 1990), chapters six to eight. In a similar vein, Rafael Bayce discusses Pacheco's contribution to the polarisation of Uruguayan politics and its role in mobilising and politicising the armed forces in his *Cultura política uruguaya* (Montevideo, Fondo de Cultura Universitaria, 1989), 31–7. Students and trade unions have likewise been reported as conceptualising the national political scene in black-and-white terms (see Nahum, *El fin del Uruguay liberal,* 164 and 168).
90 Varela, *República liberal,* 122–3.
91 Quoted in Bruschera, *Décadas infames,* 82.
92 For later recollections and analytical reflections on the Frente's early days up to the military coup by a number of leading figures from a representative sample of its member groups and parties, see Harnecker, *Frente Amplio,* vol. 1.
93 See also Luis Costa Bonino, *Crisis de los partidos tradicionales y movimiento revolucionario en el Uruguay* (EBO, 1985), 83. Here, the Tupamaros and the military are seen as espousing symmetrically opposed versions of 'a conspiratorial and anti-democratic nationalism', the first trying to destroy the nexus 'traditional parties-oligarchy-US imperialism', while the other led a crusade against 'parliament-the Left-the insurrection-USSR and international communism'.
94 Rama, *Democracia,* 116 and 154.
95 Varela, *República liberal,* 164 and 171.
96 Rama, *Democracia,* 166.
97 Carina Perelli, 'Youth, Politics and Dictatorship in Uruguay', in Corradi et al, *Fear at the Edge,* 212.
98 Bruschera, *Décadas,* 73.
99 See INDAL, *Frente Amplio,* 166–7.
100 From the 'Document no. 5', quoted in Alain Labrousse, *Los Tupamaros* (Buenos Aires, Tiempo Contémporaneo, 1971), 290.
101 INDAL, *Frente Amplio,* 161.
102 Mario Benedetti, *Crónicas del 71* (Arca, 1972), 152 (from an essay first published in *Marcha* [1 October 1971]).
103 Mario Benedetti, *Terremoto y después* (Arca, 1973), 146 (from an essay first published in *Marcha* [24 August 1972]).

Interlude: The Armed Forces and Failure

1 Other than the general histories already used in Part One, for the period including the last years of the breakdown of Uruguayan democracy, see Luis Macadar (ed.), *La crisis uruguaya y el problema nacional* (CINVE/EBO, 1984); Juan Rial, *Partidos políticos, democracia y autoritarismo* (2 vols., CIESU/EBO,

1984); Francois Lerin & Cristina Torres, *Historia política uruguaya (1873–1980)* (Ed. Del Nuevo Mundo, 1987); (Servicio Paz y Justicia [SERPAJ], *Uruguay nunca más* (SERPAJ, 1989); Carmen Appratto et al., *El Uruguay de la dictadura* (EBO, 2004); Alcides Abella (coord.), *1968 Uruguay 1985* (4 vols., EBO, 2006–8). On the dictatorship itself, see Gerardo Caetano & José Rilla, *Breve historia de la dictadura* [1991] (2nd ed., EBO, 2006); Carlos Demasi, 'La dictadura militar: un tema pendiente', in Hugo Achugar (ed.), *Uruguay: cuentas pendientes. Dictadura, memorias y desmemorias* (Trilce, 1995), 29–49; Paul W. Drake, *Labor Movements and Dictatorships* (Baltimore, Johns Hopkins UP, 1996), 91–116; Carlos Demasi (ed.), *El régimen cívico-militar* (1973–1980) (FCU, 2004) [vol. 2 of an ongoing *Cronología comparada de la historia reciente del Uruguay* begun in 1996]; Aldo Marchesi et al., *El presente de la dictadura. Estudios y reflexiones a 30 años del golpe de Estado en Uruguay* (Trilce, 2004); Virginia Martínez, *Tiempos de dictadura 1973/1985. Hechos, voces, documentos. La represión y la resistencia día a día* (EBO, 2007).
Quotations and references, as well as specific or contentious matters, will be footnoted separately.

2 Scott Myers, *Los años oscuros. Uruguay 1967–1987* (Editorial Latina, 1997), 55.

3 The number of 'civilians at their service' (José Rilla, *La actualidad del pasado* [Debate, 2008], 453) remains unclear but was probably substantial to start with, diminishing over time as the military showed their true colours, but difficult to gage accurately because any discontent at the time had to be disguised to avoid suspicion, while since redemocratisation, admission of earlier support for the military would itself risk censure in at least some quarters.

4 See Silvia Dutrénit Bielous, 'Se cruzan los relatos: memoria personal y reconstrucción histórica', *Estudios Sociales*, 25 (2003), 119–46, and Vivian Markarian, *Left in Transformation: Uruguayan Exiles and the Latin American Human Rights Networks* (London and New York, Routledge, 2005).

5 See Luis González, *Uruguay: una apertura inesperada* (CIESU/EBO, 1984); José Rilla, 'Uruguay 1980: transición y legitimidad plebiscitaria', *Nueva Sociedad*, 150 (1997), 77–83; Daniel J. Corbo Longuiera, *El plebiscito constitucional de 1980* (Puerta del Sol, 2006); Gastón Goicoechea Pérez, 'El recurso del miedo', in Abella, *1968 Uruguay 1985*, vol. 3, 45–59.

6 On social movements in Uruguay, see Carlos H. Filguiera (ed.), *Movimientos sociales en el Uruguay de hoy* (EBO, 1985) and Carmen Midaglia, *Las formas de acción colectiva en Uruguay* (CIESU, 1992).

7 On the economy under the military, see CINVE, *La crisis*; Jorge Notaro, *La política económica en el Uruguay 1968–1984* (EBO, 1984); Luis Bértola, 'La dictadura, ¿un modelo económico?', in Marchesi, *El presente*, 201–4; Danilo Astori, 'La política económica de la dictadura', in Appratto, *El Uruguay*, 147–77.

8 See Hugo Achugar, 'Balances y desbalances culturales a comienzos del siglo xxi', in Marchesi, *El presente*, 209–13. This would be confirmed, at least in the political arena, if it is correct that, from 1971 to 1999 (thus including the twelve years of dictatorship), the Frente Amplio grew annually by just over two percent, whereas the Colorados and Nationals each contracted annually by just

over one percent. See José Rilla, 'Cambiar la historia. Historia política y elite política en el Uruguay contemporáneo', *Revista Uruguaya de Ciencia Política*, 11 (1999), 110, note 9.

9 Gustavo de Armas and Adolfo Garcé, *Uruguay y su conciencia crítica: intelectuales y política* (Trilce, 1997).

10 Junta de Comandantes en Jefe [JCJ], *Las Fuerzas Armadas al pueblo oriental. Tomo 1: La subversión; Tomo 2: El proceso político* (Fuerzas Armadas Uruguayas, 1976 and 1978, respectively).

11 For general background and relevance to Latin America of the national security doctrine, see Mauricio Ruz F., 'Doctrina de seguridad nacional: contribución a un debate', *Mensaje* [Chile], 261 (August 1977), 418–26, and Jorge Tapia Valdés, 'La doctrina de la seguridad nacional y el rol político de las fuerzas armadas', *Nueva Sociedad*, 47 (1980), 23–46. On its Uruguayan variant, see Carina Perelli, *Someter o convencer: el discurso militar* (EBO, 1987) (a study of the armed forces magazine *El Soldado* in the mid- to late-1970s); José Luis Castagnola & Pablo Mieres, 'La ideología política de la dictadura' and Carmen Appratto & Lucila Artagaveytia, 'La educación', in Appratto, *El Uruguay*, 113–44 and 213–49, respectively.

12 JCJ. *La subversión*, 12, 4–5, 13, 79 and 12.

13 JCJ. *La subversión*, 13, 1–4.

14 From 'El educador oriental: su fe', published originally in *El soldado* (October 1978), quoted in Caetano & Rilla, *Breve historia*, 87–8, capitals in original. The entire list comprises 24 items.

15 JCJ. *La subversión*, 11.

16 Of the 89 signatories to the public letter of support welcoming the Frente Amplio (see the opening to Chapter 2 above) who also feature in Alberto Oreggioni (ed.), *Diccionario de literatura uruguaya* (2 Vols., Arca/Credisol, 1987), only seventeen published major books in Uruguay between 1973 and 1983, with seven others producing minor work or offering contributions on safe topics such as the classics or recognised and acceptable figures of more recent world literature. In the same period, twenty-five of the authors produced important publications in exile, while a further twenty-five published nothing in book form until after the dictatorship. The difference is made up by those who died or seem to have stopped writing.

17 Such as Miguel Aguirre Bayley, *Frente Amplio. Uno solo dentro y fuera de Uruguay en la resistencia a la dictadura* (Cauce, 2007) and Juan Pedro Ciganda, *Sin desensillar . . . y hasta que aclare. La resistencia a la dictadura, AEBU, 1973–1984* (Cauce, 2007).

18 See José Pedro Díaz, 'La cultura silenciosa', in Saúl Sosnowski, *Represión, exilio y democracia* (EBO, 1987), 201–219; Mabel Moraña, *Memorias de la generación fantasma. Crítica literaria 1973–1988* (Monte Sexto, 1988), especially pp. 17–72 and 97–117; Gerardo Albistur, 'Autocensura o resistencia. El dilema de la prensa en el Uruguay autoritario', in Abella, *1968 Uruguay 1985*, vol. 1, 111–36, and Jaime Yaffé, 'El insospechado papel de las "aspirinas blancas"', in Abella, *1968 Uruguay 1985*, vol. 3, 87–106. Leo Masliah, 'La música popular. Censura

y represión', in Sosnowski, *Represión, exilio,* 111–25, and Moraña, *Memorias,* 119–30, show how matters eased after 1980.

19 See Alvaro Rico (coord.), *15 días que estremecieron al Uruguay* (Fin de Siglo, 2005), a collective effort that is a fine example of historiography understood as the recovery of the repressed history of the recent past.

20 Caetano & Rilla, *Breve historia,* 113.

21 See Carina Perelli during a discussion session in Sosnowski, *Represión, exilio,* 271; Appratto, 'La educación', 241–3, and Virginia Martínez, *Tiempos de dictadura 1973/1985* (EBO, 2007).

22 Rafael Bayce, *Cultura política uruguaya. Desde Batlle hasta 1988* (FCU, 1989), 39–47.

23 Roberto Appratto, *Se hizo de noche* (Amulato, 2007).

24 Carina Blixen, for example, recalls that while being employed at a private school after being sacked from her teaching position at a state institution, the principal was telephoned and asked to dismiss her on the grounds that she was persona non grata for the military. See her *Palabras rigurosamente vigiladas: dictadura, lenguaje, literaura. La obra de Carlos Liscano* (Ediciones del Caballo Perdido, 2006), 23.

25 A full assessment of such organisations remains to be done, but some details can be found in Carlos Zubillaga, 'Historiografía y cambio social: el caso uruguayo', *Cuadernos del CLAEH,* 24 (1982), 37, and *Historia e historiadores en el Uruguay del siglo xx* (Facultad de Humanidades y Ciencias de la Educación, 2002), 209–16; Díaz, 'Cultura silenciosa', 211–12; Macadar, *La crisis,* 7–10, and Ana Ribeiro, *Historia e historiadores nacionales (1940–1990)* (Academia Nacional de Letras, 1991), 58–9.

26 As in James Petras & Morris Morley, 'The Metamorphosis of the Intellectuals', in their *US Hegemony Under Seige: Class, Politics and Development in Latin America* (London, Verso, 1990), 146–56.

27 See Vania Markarian, *Left in Transformation: Uruguayan Exiles and the Latin American Human Rights Networks* (New York and London, Routledge, 2005). To sample the spectrum of perspectives among the Uruguayan left in exile, see Federico Fasano Mertens, *Después de la derrota. Un eslabón débil llamado Uruguay* (Mexico, Nueva Imagen, 1980), Mario Benedetti, *El desexilio y otras conjeturas* (Madrid, El País, 1984), and Nelson Caula (ed.), *El diario de Enrique Erro. La cárcel, el exilio y la transición* (Rosebud, 1998).

28 For a detailed study of the negotiations between politicians and military, see Charles Gillespie, *Negotiating Democracy: Politicians and Generals in Uruguay* (Cambridge UP, 1991).

29 The current vogue for publishing memoirs or testimonies among the now ageing participants in the political and social upheavals of the 1960s and '70s is gradually opening up this area.

30 This needs to be kept separate from the very public exercise in self-analysis undergone by the Tupamaros, legalised after the dictatorship first under their more formal name of Movimiento de Liberación Nacional [MLN], and then the more electorally friendly Movimiento de Participación Popular, on their way to becoming the most voted group within the Frente. See Chapter 5 below.

31 Although, as Nahum reminds us, Pacheco's repressive policies were as much a blight on Uruguayan democracy as anything the Tupamaros or other left groups did. See Banjamín Nahum, *Breve historia del Uruguay independiente* (EBO, 2003), 119.

32 In Lawrence Weschler, *A Miracle, A Universe: Settling Accounts with Torturers* (Chicago UP, 1998), 213.

33 On the left's difficulties with defeat, see Angel Rama, 'Otra vez la utopía, en el invierno de nuestro desconsuelo', *Cuadernos de Marcha*, 2nd Series, 1 (1979), 75–81; Fasano Mertens, *Después*, 213–18; Gerardo Caetano, Javier Gallardo & José Rilla, *La izquierda uruguaya: tradición, innovación y política* (Trilce, 1995), 116–18; Jaime Yaffé, 'Memoria y olvidos en la relación de la izquierda con el pasado reciente', in Marchesi, *El presente*, 184–98, and Diego Sempol, 'La historiografía blanca sobre el pasado reciente: entre el testimonio y la historia', in Abella, *1968 Uruguay 1985*, vol. 2, 23–8.

34 Híber Conteris, 'El Uruguay postmoderno y la pérdida de la memoria', in Adrina J. Bergero & Fernando Reati (eds.), *Memoria colectiva y políticas del olvido: Argentina y Uruguay, 1970–1990* (Buenos Aires, Beatriz Viterbo, 1997), 107.

35 See Wilfredo Penco's prologue to Oreggioni, *Diccionario*, vol. 1, n.p.

36 See Garcé & De Armas, *Uruguay*, 75–6, and Oscar Brando, 'Hacia una nueva cultura democrática', in his *Uruguay hoy. Paisaje depués del 31 de octubre* (Ediciones del Caballo Perdido, 2004), 234–7.

37 Alvaro Rico, 'El orden de los simulacros y el orden social en la restauración democrática' in Rico, *Uruguay: cuentas pendientes*, 63–120.

4 The Revenge of the Foreign: Uruguay on the Eve of De(con)struction

1 Pablo Fernández, who was there, remembered 'hallucinatory conversations in Villa Biarritz'. See his 'El poder de la irreverencia', *Brecha*, 920 (17 June 2003), 25.

2 Fernando Leicht, *Cero a la izquierda. Una biografía de Jorge Zabalza* (Letraeñe, 2007), 159. I return to Zabalza in the next chapter where his writings are seen in the context of the internal struggles of the legalised MLN within a streamlined Frente Amplio readying itself for national government.

3 Among leftist intellectuals, evidence of an understandable desire to pick up where they had all been forced to leave off can be found in otherwise very different examples such as Jorge Notaro, *La política económica en el Uruguay 1968–1984* (CIEDUR/EBO, 1984), 255, and the preface to Mario Benedetti, *Escritos políticos (1971–1973)* (Arca, 1985), 5. As late as 12 June 1992, *Brecha* could republish unchanged on its back page an editorial by Carlos Quijano that first appeared in *Marcha* on 16 July 1965.

4 Gerardo Caetano, 'El árbol y el bosque en el Uruguay de la recesión', *Estudios Internacionales* [Chile], xxxv, 139 (October–December 2002), 117. For more generalised discussion of the phenomenon, see Beatriz Stolowicz, 'El desprestigio de la política: lo que no se discute', *Política y cultura*, 17 (2002), 165–92.

5 Rafael Bayce, *Cultura política uruguaya. Desde Batlle hasta 1988* (FCU, 1989), 78. Elsewhere Bayce reports on Gallup surveys that placed politicians fifth on

a list of nine professions in 1985 with a score of +17, dropping to last, along with car dealers, large landownwers and the military, with a negative score of -44 by 1992. See Rafael Bayce, 'Legitimidad y crisis política. Microformas perversas de macrlegitimidad en el Uruguay', *Cuadernos del CLAEH*, 78/9 (1997), 354.

6 Abril Trigo, *¿Cultura uruguaya o culturas linyeras? (Para una cartografía de la neomodernidad posuruguaya)* (Vintén, 1997), 21. Trigo is an important figure in his own right to whom I return in Chapter 6.

7 Gabriel Sosa, *Qué difícil es ser de izquierda en estos días y otras historias de amor* (Planeta, 2004). The epigraph is from page 144.

8 Bank employees had to be 'militarised' by force to prevent economically damaging strikes in this volatile sector during the oppressive late 1960s.

9 Compare 'El escritor y la crítica en el contexto del subdesarrollo', written at the turn of 1976–77, and 'Algunas formas subsidiarias de la penetración cultural', written a year or so later (see Mario Benedetti, *El recurso del supremo patriarca* [8th edition, Mexico, Nueva Imagen, 1990], pp. 33–67 and 151–75).

10 Some lamented Benedetti's aloofness from more organised protest. See Nelson Caula [ed.], *El diario de Enrique Erro* (Trilce, 1998) and Federico Fasano Mertens, *Después de la derrota* (Mexico, Nueva Imagen, 1980).

11 Verónica D'Auria & Sivia Guerrera, *Conversaciones oblicuas entre la cultura y el poder. Entrevistas a diez intelectuales uruguayos* (Ediciones Caracol al Galope, 2001), 69. Achugar also included Eduardo Galeano here, but there is some indication, as we will see later, that Galeano still enjoyed the approval of readers infuriated by Benedetti.

12 Hugo Achugar, 'Entre dos orillas. Los puentes necesarios', in Saúl Sosnowski (ed.), *Represión, exilio y democracia: la cultura uruguaya* (EBO, 1987), 241–7.

13 Earlier in the conference, the social anthropologist and novelist Teresa Porzecanski had also indicated the relevance to her of the work of young experimental writers of the late 1960s, thus suggesting (correctly, in my view) that there was no difficulty in getting such work published prior to 1973. See Teresa Porzecanski, 'Ficción y fricción de la narrativa de imaginación escrita dentro de fronteras', in Sosnowski, *Represión, exilio*, 221–30. See also the seminal 1969 essay by Angel Rama, 'El estremecimiento nuevo en la narrativa uruguaya', in his *La generación crítica 1939–1969* (Arca, 1972), 220–45.

14 Amanda Berenguer, 'Los signos sobre la mesa', in Sosnowski, *Represión, exilio*, 171–8.

15 Maslíah's comments are in Sosnowski, *Represión, exilio*, 272–3. That the situation of writers and artists who stayed at home under authoritarianism was not as imagined by those who did or could not remain in Uruguay is also suggested in the same exchange by critics Mabel Moraña and Alvaro Barros-Lémez (270) and the much younger social scientist Carmen Perelli (271), and earlier by the older novelist José Pedro Díaz, 'La cultura silenciosa', 201–9.

16 Sosnowski, *Represión, exilio*, 273 and 277.

17 For example, in what was a kind of personal mini-manifesto for intellectuals reaching maturity in the 1980s, Gustavo Wojciechowski wrote that Benedetti had 'covered himself up', throwing 'spadefuls of mediocrity over his own

discoveries. Farewell office poems'. See his 'Tics culturales', *La Revista del Sur*, 1 (August 1987, supplement), 87. *Poemas de la oficina* [1956] was a groundbreaking book by Benedetti.

18 Miguel A. Campodónico, '"Escribir es para mí una función natural y es mi oficio". Entrevista con Mario Benedetti', *Aquí*, 231 (1987), 12–13.

19 See *Cuadernos de Marcha*, 3rd series, 29 (March 1988), 78.

20 'Today', 'Sobre una entrevista', *Aquí* (16 December 1987), 4.

21 Tomás Linn, 'El turno de las nuevas generaciones: ¿Parricicidas éstos o filicidas aquéllos?', *Cuadernos de Marcha*, 3rd series, 28 (February 1988), 69–71.

22 Jorge Castro Vega, 'Hacia una cultura de la restauración', *Cuadernos de Marcha*, 28 (February 1988), 63–8, quotations from pp. 66–7. An editorial note in the next issue (29 [March 1988], 80) clarified that the title should have been enclosed between question marks.

23 'Cartas de los lectores', *Cuadernos de Marcha*, 29 (March 1988), 76–78. The reference here is to Benedetti's collection of poems *Yesterday y mañana* (Arca, 1987), as well as to *El país de la cola de paja* [1960], particularly concerned with what Benedetti saw as the very Uruguayan tendency to be constantly other than what one really knew oneself to be. Ironically, in one of the poems, 'Letter to a Young Poet', Benedetti included the following lines: 'I like it that you feel parricidal/it does us all good . . . Whereas how sad/it would be for us all/that you should feel/an orphan' (*Yesterday y mañana*, 92). Unfortunately, that was exactly how 'Today' and the '80s generation would feel – isolated and marginalised by the cultural power brokers. Benedetti seemed to forget the generosity in his verse when it came to dealing with real young poets who directed their 'parricidal' attitudes at him.

24 Omar Prego, '¿Hacia una cultura de la degradación?', *Cuadernos de Marcha*, 3rd series, 29 (March 1988), 59–63.

25 César di Candia, 'Reportaje a Mario Benedetti', *Búsqueda* (5 January 1989), 31.

26 Bayce, *Cultura política*, 78.

27 Hugo Achugar, *La balsa de la medusa* (Trilce, 1992), 48, note 52.

28 Aldo Mazzuchelli, 'Los auténticos decadentes', originally in *Postdata*, 287 (2000). Accessed at <www.henciclopedia.org.uy/autores/Mazzuchelli/Benedetti.htm>.

29 See throughout the essays of the periodically extended editions of *Perplejidades de fin de siglo* [originally 1993].

30 Mario Benedetti, *Memoria y esperanza, Mensaje a los jóvenes* (Buenos Aires, Planeta, 2004), quotations from pp. 7 and 77.

31 Gustavo Verdesio, Gabriel Peveroni & Eduardo Roland, 'La movida de los 80 II', henciclopedia.org.uy/autores/Verdesio/MovidaII.htm. This is, unusually, a *Henciclopedia* original, only available here.

32 Gabriel Peveroni, 'Rock que me hiciste mal', <www.henciclopedia.org.uy/Peveroni/RockUruguayo.html>.

33 First by Bayce in *Cultura política*, and later with appreciative acknowledgement in Trigo, *¿cultura uruguaya?*, 156–190, republishing an essay from 1995.

34 In Sosnowski, *Represión, exilio*, 253. The paper's full title was 'Uruguay: redemocratización, cultura, desexilio (¿se puede volver a casa?)', 249–60.

35 For a brief survey of some of them, see Lauro Maurada, 'Revistas "subte" sin subterfugios', *Brecha* (22 April 1988), 30–1.
36 The most influential of the many studies of this phenomenon is the often-cited essay by Juan Rial: 'El imaginario social. Los mitos políticos y utopías en el Uruguay. Cambios y permanencias durante y depués del autoritarismo', in Sosnowski, *Represión, exilio*, 63–89. The relevant section is on pages 70–80. An earlier version of the same essay appears as Chapter 1 of Juan Rial & Carina Perelli, *De mitos y memorias políticas. La represión, el miedo y después* (EBO, 1986).
37 Milita Alfaro, 'Con Rafael Bayce: "Uruguay es un gran avestruz"', *Brecha* (22 September, 1989), 2–3.
38 See Raúl Zibechi, *La revuelta juvenil de los 90* (Nordan Comunidad, 1997), especially pp. 173, 224–7, and 229–30.
39 The highpoint in the political practice derived from La Movida would be the community and neighbourhood campaign of sit-ins and occupations against the proposed education reforms of 1996. See Zibechi, *La revuelta*, 199–234.
40 See summaries of some aspects of these elements in Jorge Ruffinelli, 'Uruguay: dictadura y redemocratización. Un informe sobre la literatura 1973–1989', *Nuevo Texto Crítico*, 5 (1990), 37–66; Ernesto Gonzalez Bermejo, 'Al término del banquete' [interview with semiotician Fernando Andacht], *Brecha* (4 December 1992), 15–17; and from one of the participants in La Movida, Aldo Mazzuchelli, '"El país" como sujeto de frases vacías', <www.henciclopedia.org. uy/autores/Mazzuchelli/Frases.htm>.
41 This is a constant theme throughout Bayce's and Trigo's writings on La Movida, and reappears in various guises throughout Zibechi, *Revuelta juvenil*. See also Peveroni, 'Rock', and Fernández, 'El poder'.
42 Rafael Bayce, 'La lógica del miedo 1968–1984: génesis y consolidación', *Relaciones*, 20/21 (January 1986), 8. A third category, the 'autistas', were those during the dictatorship who meekly accepted the military regime and, after it, yearned to put the clock back to what they imagined were the good old days before the social and political upheaval of the late 1960s and early 1970s. See also his *Cultura política uruguaya. Desde Batlle hasta 1988* (FCU, 1989), 39–47.
43 Bayce, *Cultura política*, 74–9 and 88.
44 Literally 'popular song'. This movement, related very loosely to the new song movements in Chile and Cuba and to the protest folk song wave elsewhere, used a depoliticised, zany, corrosive humour to become the constantly hassled focus of resistance during the dictatorship. In this it joined up with other tradi-tional forms of popular protest associated with carnival. See, in addition to Trigo, *¿Cultura uruguaya?*, Coriún Aharonián, *Conversaciones sobre música, cultura e identidad* (Tacuabé, 2000); Ernesto Donas & Denise Milstein, *Cantando la ciudad: Lenguajes, imaginarios y mediaciones en la canción popular montevideana (1962–1999)* (Nordan Comunidad, 2003); María Figueredo, *Poesía y canción popular: su convergencia en el siglo xx, Uruguay 1960–1985* (Linardi y Risso, 2005); Guillermo Lamolle, *Cual retazo de los suelos. Anécdotas, invenciones y meditaciones sobre el Carnaval en general y la murga en particular* (Trilce, 2005); Leo Maslíah, 'La música popular: censura y represión', in

Sosnowski, *Represión, exilio*, 113–25 [by one of 'canto popular's leading practitioners]; Gustavo Remedi, *Carnival Theater. Uruguay's Popular Performers and National Culture* (trans. Amy Ferlazzo, Minneapolis, Minnesota UP, 2004 [Spanish original, 1996]).

45 Gustavo Espinosa, "Trampas para cazar al otro", <www.henciclopedia.org.uy/ autores/Espinosa/Trampasotro.htm>. Originally published in *La República de Platón*, 11 (1993). Note the somewhat ironic reference to Carlos Maggi, *El Uruguay y su gente* [1963].

46 Angel Rama, *La ciudad letrada* (Hanover [USA], Ediciones del Norte, 1984), translated by John C. Chasteen as *The Lettered City* (Duke UP, 1996). Jean Franco has updated Rama's famous book in one that knowingly recalls its title: *The Decline and Fall of the Lettered City* (Harvard UP, 2002).

47 The last words of Héctor Bardanca, 'Cultura nacional: los puntos sobre las jotas de joven y de jodido', *Cuadernos de Marcha*, 3rd Series, 13 (October 1986), 84–6.

48 Eduardo Milán, 'Pequeñas notas sobre una gran depresión cultural', *Cuadernos de Marcha*, 3rd series, 11 (September 1986), 78–80, the quotations from the last page.

49 The whole issue of modernity and postmodernity on the periphery was a matter of very considerable debate throughout Latin America during the 1980s and 1990s. See, among many examples, Fernando Calderón (ed.), *Imágenes desconocidas: la modernidad en la encrucijada postmoderna* (Buenos Aires, CLACSO, 1988); George Yúdice, Jean Franco & Juan Flores (eds.), *On Edge: The Crisis of Latin American Culture* (Minneapolis, Minnesota UP, 1992); John Beverley, José Oviedo & Michael Aronna (eds.), *The Postmodernism Debate in Latin America* (Durham, Duke UP, 1995).

50 Tomás Linn, 'La necesaria mudanza interior', *Cuadernos de Marcha*, 3rd series, 35 (September 1988), 3.

51 Carlos Muñoz & Gustavo Escanlar, 'Uruguay: ¿Algo más que rock and roll?', *Cuadernos de Marcha*, 3rd series, 30 (April 1988), 65.

52 Several of the essays in Abril Trigo, *¿Cultura uruguaya* implicitly make clear the important link between rock lyrics and what Trigo calls the 'Lumpenpoesía' of the time (123–55), as the Movida poets sought to free themselves from what they saw as the chains of the legacy of the 45 and 1960s generations that had preceded both them and the authoritarian break with the past. Trigo has summed up and extended his earlier thoughts on Uruguayan rock music in English: 'The Politics and Anti-Politics of Uruguayan Rock' in D. Pacini Hernández, E. Zolov & H. Fernández L'Hoeste (eds.), *Rockin' Las Americas: The Global Politics of Rock in Latin/o America* (Pittsburgh UP, 2004), 115–41. See also Zibechi, *La revuelta*, 99–115, Fernando Peláez & Gabriel Peveroni, *Rock que me hiciste mal. El rock uruguayo desde los 60 hasta nuestros días* (EBO, 2006), and Víctor Nattero [songwiter and lead guitarist with Los Traicores/The Traitors], *Viviendo en Uruguay*, <www.freewebs.com/rockuruguayo80/ Nattero.htm> (accessed December 2007).

53 See Peveroni, 'Rock'.

54 Zibechi, *La revuelta*, 14.

55 Muñoz & Escanlar, '¿Uruguay?', 66.

56 Gustavo Escanlar, Rosario González & Carlos Muñoz, 'Arte en la lona. Un cross a la mandíbula', *Cuadernos de Marcha*, 3ra época, 31 (May 1988), 75–8. To sample the 80s contribution to more conventional literary forms, see Alberto Gallo, 'Jóvenes jóvenes 1 (en literatura)", *Brecha*, La Lupa section (21 July 1989), n.p.; Abril Trigo, 'Joven narrativa uruguaya', *Hispamérica*, 58 (1991), 87–112, and 'Poesía uruguaya actual (los más jóvenes)', *Hispamérica*, 64/65 (1993), 121–47.

57 Zibechi, *La revuelta*, 153–8.

58 Escanlar & Muñoz, 'Arte', 77.

59 'Arte en la lona' could be the kind of event (on a larger scale, no doubt) that Rosalía and her friends were trying to organise in 'Qué difícil es ser de izquierda en estos días'. When she told Martín they were rehearsing for a 'recital', he asked 'A poetry recital?', and got this reply: 'No, nothing like that; we call it an attitude recital. It's a bit like performance art, but it's not that really, either. You'll see on our first night!' (Sosa, *Qué difícil*, 125). A show, then, as shape-less and indefinable as 'Arte en la lona', but one that also blurs the boundaries between life and art. Also, like Rosalía, Escanlar was a writer as well as working in advertising (according to the entry in Alberto Oreggioni (ed.), *Nuevo diccionario de literatura uruguaya*, Vol. 1 [EBO, 2001], 197).

60 For comments from other participants in La Movida which support Muñoz and Escanlar's account of it, see Alberto Gallo, 'Jóvenes jóvenes I', *Brecha* (21 June 1989), unpaginated La Lupa section. Those interviewed are Aldo Mazzuchelli (poet), Eduardo Roland (teacher, musician, poet), Andrea Blanqué (poet and fiction writer) and the editorial collective of a 'little maga-zine', *Inédito viable*, published at the Instituto de Profesores 'Artigas', as well as Escanlar himself. Fourteen years later, Blanqué still saw the 'Arte en la lona' event as La Movida's highpoint in Riesgopaís, 'Escribir en el páramo', *riesgopaís* (26 June 2003), 9.

61 Eduardo Roland, *Contra cualquier muro: graffiti de la transición 1985–1989* (Ediciones de UNO/Vintén, 1990), pages unnumbered throughout.

62 In two parts, the conversation can be found at henciclopedia.org.uy/autores/ Verdesio/Movida80.htm and henciclopedia.org.uy/autores/Verdesio/ Movida80II.htm.

63 Alfaro, 'Con Rafael Bayce', 3.

64 Lisa Block de Behar (ed.), *Diseminario. La deconstrucción: otro descubrimiento de América* (XYZ Editores, 1987). The editor's introduction is pp. 5–20 (the quotation being from p. 7) and her remarks about Derrida are on 23–5.

65 Block de Behar, *Diseminario*, 27–47 and 49–106, respectively.

66 Block de Behar repeated her approach in her paper at the Sosnovski seminar, where she got terms such as silence, eloquence, 'critical resistance' and 'discourse in crisis' into her title alone (see Sosnowski, *Represión, exilio*, 179–191), and popularised it in the weekly Montevideo cultural press: see her 'Una hipótesis de lectura: la verdad suspendida entre la repetición y el silencio', *Jaque* (10 August 1984).

67 See, for example, his sometimes barbed *Literatura uruguaya del medio siglo*

(Alfa, 1966) and the occasional corresponding retorts in Angel Rama, *La generación crítica 1939–1969* (Arca, 1972).

68 In addition to many journal articles, see his *Narradores de esta América* (Arca, 1969) and *El boom de la novela latinoamericana* (Caracas, Tiempo Nuevo, 1972).

69 See M. E. Mudrovcic, *Mundo nuevo: cultura y guerra fría* (Rosario, Beatriz Viterbo, 1997). For Uruguayan coverage of the impact of the exposure of CIA involvement in the Congress for Cultural Freedom and famous journals such as *Encounter*, see Alvaro Barros-Lémez (ed.), *Intelectuales y política: polémicas y posiciones, años '60 y 70* (Monte Sexto, 1988), 33–107. Probably the most important Uruguayan casualty was the expatriate Spanish republican Benito Millá's publishing house Alfa, home to much that was best in new Uruguayan literature from the early 1960s.

70 Borges's letter is dated 22 October 1985. One month later, as part of a clearly organised plan, he would leave for Geneva, where he would die and be buried in June the following year, thereby frustrating those many of his compatriots who would have wanted to use his death and funeral as vehicles for the effusions of an Argentine nationalism he reviled.

71 Emir Rodríguez Monegal, *Jorge Luis Borges. A Literary Biography* (New York, Dutton, 1978).

72 Homero Alsina Thevenet, 'Presentación de Emir Rodríguez Monegal' and Jorge Luis Borges, 'Borges y Emir', in Block de Behar, *Diseminario*, 109–15 and 117–18. Borges himself was, as is widely recognised, more than familiar with the theme of the self as other, as attested by two of his own canonical short fictions: 'Borges and I' [1960] and 'The Other' [1975].

73 Block de Behar, *Diseminario*, 119–23.

74 Block de Behar, 'Del silencio', in Sosnowski, *Represión, exilio*, 180.

75 Teresa Porzecanski, 'Ficción y fricción de la narrativa de imaginación escrita dentro de fronteras', in Sosnowski, *Represión, exilio*, 221–30, the quoted passages appearing on 224–6.

76 Here Hamed made fun of Methol Ferré's famous 1967 book *El Uruguay como problema*, to which I return below in Chapter 6. As Hamed undoubtedly knew perfectly well, one of Methol Ferré's persistent arguments in his writings on Uruguay is that it is too small to be viable as an independent state.

77 Amir Hamed, 'Uruguay versus los buenos: minimanual para evadir toda emergencia', <www.henciclopedia.org.uy/autores/Hamed/Emergente.html>. Hamed, one of whose major themes is precisely the diluting effect of the virtual world of cyberspace on our notion of the real, is one of the chief editors of this important website.

78 Amir Hamed, *Retroescritura* (Fin de Siglo, 1998).

79 Hamed, *Retroescritura*, 100, punctuation as in original.

80 Sandino Núñez, *Disneywar. Apuntes sobre la violencia territorial en la aldea global* (Lapzus, 2006), the quotations being on pages 83, 50, 69, 21, 72 and 71 respectively.

81 Fabián Giménez & Alejandro Villagrán, *Estética de la oscuridad: posmodernidad, periferia y mass media en la cultura de los noventa* (Trazas, 1995), 57.

The italicised Latin word is in the original.

82   Mersault was the protagonist (or anti-hero) of the 1942 novel *L'étranger* (in English *The Outsider*) by the French writer Albert Camus. Throughout the novel, Mersault seems alienated from his surroundings and behaves in ways others perceive as irrational or inappropriate. The perhaps self-important point that Tani was trying to make is that he saw himself as an intellectual out of tune with the almost universally held values of the society he lived in.

83   See Ana María Araujo & Horacio Tejera (eds.), *La imaginación al poder 1968–1988. Entrevistas a protagonistas de la insurrección juvenil de 1968* (FCU, 1988), 63 and 73–4.

84   This was a weekly cultural supplement of the left wing, pro-Frente Amplio daily *La República*. For a study of it, see Susana Draper, 'Cartografías de una ciudad posletrada: *La república de Platón* (Uruguay, 1993–1995)', *Revista Iberoamericana*, lxix, 202 (January-March 2003), 31–49.

85   Susana Draper & Orlando Betancor, 'Filosofía, ¿crítica cultural? Un diálogo con Ruben Tani', *Relaciones*, 206 (2001), 4.

86   Bayce, *Cultura política*, 57, 55 and 79.

87   Rafael Bayce, *5 tareas de Hércules. Para gobernar en el siglo xxi: Uruguay como ejemplo* (Trilce, 2005). Further page references appear in the text.

88   Alfaro, 'Con Rafael Bayce', 3.

5   Dialogue Resumed: Democracy, Intellectuals and the Frente Amplio in Post-Dictatorship Uruguay

1   It won when still inconveniently renamed the Encuentro Progresista/ Frente Amplio-Nueva Mayoría (with its equally unfriendly acronym EP/FA-NM) but since then has officially been rechristened with its original name.

2   Zygmunt Bauman, *Intimations of Postmodernity* (London and New York, Routledge, 1991), 19 and 24 respectively.

3   Joanaldo A. Burity, 'The Impertinence of Intellectuals, Democracy and Postmodernity in Latin America', *Angelaki*, ii, 3 (1997), 59.

4   Claudia Ferman, 'In Defense of Modernity: its Utopian Idea, its Revolutionary Memory and its Cultural Criticism. An Interview with Nicolás Casullo', in Ferman (ed.), *The Postmodern in Latin and Latino American Cultural Narratives* (New York and London, Garland, 1996), 67 and 69.

5   Norbert Lechner, 'Introducción', in his *Estado y política en América Latina* (2nd ed., Mexico, Siglo XXI, 1983), 7–24, quotations on pp. 10–11 and 21. This and the epilogue (300–34) offer a succinct summary of Lechner's thinking at the time on how the Latin American left intelligentsia should not only revise *what* it thought about in the area of politics, but also *how* it thought about it.

6   See, among many examples, Manuel A. Garretón, 'From Authoritarianism to Political Democracy: A Transition That Needs Rethinking' and Norbert Lechner, 'In Search of the Lost Community', both in Luis Albala-Bertrand (ed.), *Democratic Culture and Governance* (New York/Gaithersberg, UNESCO/Hispamérica, 1992), 21–33 and 63–8, respectively, through to Francisco Panizza, 'Unarmed Utopia Revisited: The Resurgence of Left-of-Centre Politics in Latin America', *Political Studies*, 53 (2005), 716–34, and

Franklin Ramírez Gallegos, 'Mucho más que dos izquierdas', *Nueva Sociedad*, 205 (2006), 30–44.

7   The wide range of the now voluminous literature on Latin American social movements can be sampled in Sonia E. Alvarez, Evelina Dagnino & Arturo Escobar (eds.), *Cultures of Politics and Politics of Cultures. Revisioning Latin American Social Movements* (Boulder, Westview Press, 1998). A vigorous restatement of their radical potential can be found in Sara Motta, 'Utopias Reimagined: A Reply to Panizza', *Political Studies*, 54 (2006), 898–905. For a succinct argument against overstating their relevance, see Manuel A. Garretón, 'Modelos y liderazgos en América Latina', *Nueva Sociedad*, 205 (2006), 102–113.

8   Juan Flo, 'Problemas de la juventud en nuestro país', in Carlos Real de Azúa (ed.), *Problemas de la juventud uruguaya* (Marcha, 1954), 145–56. The question is on the final page.

9   See Chapter 1 above.

10 Benjamín Arditi, 'Intelectuales y política. Una perspectiva socialista latinoamericana', *David y Goliat*, 56 (April 1990), 27–34.

11 Norbert Lechner, *La democratización en el contexto de una cultura postmoderna* (Santiago, FLACSO, Documento de Trabajo no. 292, 1986), 8.

12 See also the elegiac tone of the Moreiras epigraph at the head of this chapter, as well as Idelber Avelar, *The Untimely Present: Postdictatorial Latin American Fiction and the Task of Mourning* (Durham and London, Duke University Press, 1999), especially pp. 1–21 and 79–84. Avelar's main argument is precisely that the dictatorships in the Southern Cone made possible the path to postmodernism and neoliberal economics, which in turn entailed 'mourning' the loss of the revolutionary enthusiasm (as well as the lost lives) that had preceded them. Arditi later uses Derridean poststructuralism to show that mourning the demise of a utopia can be the first step to clarifying how imagining the impossible enables any politics as an art of the possible. See his 'Talkin' 'bout a Revolution: The End of Mourning', *Parallax*, 9, 2 (2003), 81–95, later expanded as chapter 5 in his *Politics on the Edges of Liberalism* (Edinburgh UP, 2007).

13 Martin Hopenhayn, *No Apocalypse, No Integration: Modernism and Postmodernism in Latin America* (trans. Cynthia M. Tomkins & Elizabeth R. Horan, Durham, Duke University Press, 2001). Hopenhayn uses the terms 'apocalypse' and 'integration' in a way quite different from Arditi, but both acknowledge a debt to Umberto Eco's application of the concepts in his 1964 essay, 'Apocalyptic and Integrated Intellectuals: Mass Communications and Theories of Mass Culture', found in English in Umberto Eco, *Apocalypse Postponed* (ed. Robert Lumley, London, Flamingo, 1995), 27–52. Other later essays related to the topic are on pages 65–80 of the same volume.

14 José Joaquín Brunner, *América Latina: Cultura y modernidad* (Mexico, Grijalbo, 1992), 192 and 200–1. He also recognises the importance of Eco's use of 'apocalyptic' and 'integrated' intellectuals (180, note 6).

15 Beatriz Sarlo, *Escenas de la vida posmoderna. Intelectuales, arte y videocultura en la Argentina* (Buenos Aires, Ariel, 1995), chapter 5. Also in English: *Scenes from Postmodern Life* (trans. Jon Beasley-Murray, Minneapolis, Minnesota UP, 2001).

16 Norbert Lechner, 'De la revolución a la democracia: el debate intelectual en América del Sur', *Opciones*, 6 (1985), 57–72.

17 Evelina Dagnino, 'Culture, Citizenship and Democracy: Changing Discourses and Practices of the Latin American Left', in Alvarez et al, *Cultures of Politics*, 40.

18 Fernando Coronil, 'El estado de América Latina y sus Estados', *Nueva Sociedad*, 210 (2007), 214.

19 James Petras & Morris Morley, 'The Metamorphosis of Latin America's Intellectuals', in their *US Hegemony Under Siege: Class, Politics and Development in Latin America* (London and New York, Verso, 1990), 147–56, and James Petras, 'Intellectuals: a Marxist critique of post-Marxists', in his *The Left Strikes Back: Class Conflict in Latin America in the Age of Neoliberalism* (Boulder, Westview, 1999), 58–79.

20 See Chapter 1 above.

21 Neil Larsen, 'Postmodernism and Imperialism: Theory and Politics in Latin America' [1990], in his *Reading North by South. On Latin American Literature, Culture and Politics* (Minneapolis, Minnesota University Press, 1995), 164–85.

22 *Reading North*, 170. Larsen declares himself at the outset a Marxist-Leninist (164). The reasons for his choosing Laclau & Mouffe's *Hegemony and Socialist Strategy. Towards a Radical Democratic Politics* [1985] as his target become clear in the Forward to the second edition of their book, where they write as follows of 'the monolithic transvestite that Marxism-Leninism presented as the history of Marxism. It has to be clearly stated: the lasting theoretical effect of Leninism has been an appalling impoverishment of the field of Marxian diversity' (London, Verso, 2001), viii. Larsen could not have seen these words, but he would have understood the thrust of the argument well enough from the text, suggesting that there is something more than a little personal in the virulence of his remarks. As early as Laclau and Mouffe's original introduction, their 'intellectual project' is described as '*post*-Marxist' and 'also post-*Marxist*' (4). On the link between Leninism and authoritarianism, see 59–65.

23 Marta Lagos, 'A apearse de la fantasía: Hugo Chávez y los liderazgos en América Latina', *Nueva Sociedad*, 205 (2006), 99.

24 Carlos M. Vilas, 'La izquierda latinoamericana. Búsquedas y desafíos', *Nueva Sociedad*, 157 (1998), 73, italics in original.

25 Alberto Couriel, *Globalización, democracia e izquierda en América Latina* (EBO, 1996), 68.

26 Jorge Lanzaro, in the long opening chapter of his own edited volume *La izquierda uruguaya entre la oposición y el gobierno* (Fin de Siglo, 2004), 56.

27 My account of the development of the transformation of the Frente Amplio since 1984 is largely drawn from the following sources: Gerardo Caetano, Javier Gallardo & José Rilla, *La izquierda uruguaya. Tradición, innovación y política* (Trilce, 1995); Instituto de Ciencia Política, *El Uruguay del siglo xx, Tomo 2: La política* (EBO, 2003); Carlos Demasi, Alvaro Rico & Marcelo Rossal, 'Hechos y sentidos de la política y la pospolítica: Transición y postransición democrática', in Oscar Brando (ed.), *Uruguay hoy: Paisaje después del 31 de octubre* (Ediciones del Caballo Perdido, 2004), 7–77; Nelson Fernández, *Quién es quien en el*

gobierno de la izquierda (Fin de Siglo, 2004); Adolfo Garcé & Jaime Yaffé, *La era progresista* (Fin de Siglo, 2004; 2nd ed. 2005); Lanzaro, *La izquierda uruguaya*; Constanza Moreira, *Final de juego. Del bipartidismo tradicional al triunfo de la izquierda en Uruguay* (Trilce, 2004); Jaime Yaffé, *Al centro y adentro* (Linardi y Risso, 2005). Special mention is worth making of Jaime Yaffé, 'Del Frente Amplio a la Nueva Mayoría. La izquierda uruguaya (1971–2004)', *Secuencia* [Mexico], 60 (September/December 2004), 175–210, and Daniel Chavez, 'Del Frente Amplio a la Nueva Mayoría. La izquierda uruguaya ante la perspectiva del gobierno', in César A. Rodríguez Garavito et al., *La nueva izquierda en América Latina* (Bogotá, Norma, 2005), 147–90, since both offer succinct accounts designed for a non-Uruguayan audience. Quotations and references to specific details in my account will be separately noted as required.

28 Lanzaro, *La izquierda uruguaya*, 74.

29 Such as *La República*, *Brecha*, *Caras y Caretas*, *Zeta*, and *Cuadernos de Marcha*, plus the publications of many of the Frente's constituent groups, all this before the attentions of the opposition press.

30 Crottogini's difficult position has begun to be recognised. See Alberto Silva, *Profesor Juan José Crottigini: Una vida alumbrando vida* (La Rueda de Amargueando, 2004).

31 According to Samuel Blixen, *Sendic* (Trilce, 2000), 314 and Gerardo Tagliaferro, *Fernández Huidobro. De las armas a las urnas* (Fin de Siglo, 2004), 187.

32 See José 'Pepe' Mujica & Rodrigo Arocena, *Cuando la izquierda gobierne* (Trilce, 2003) and Mario Mazzeo, *Charlando con Pepe Mujica* (Trilce, 2002). Both interviews offer good examples of Mujica's ability to combine a sharp, university-trained intelligence with a typically colloquial speaking style.

33 Hebert Gatto, 'Izquierda tradicional y nueva izquierda: un debate ineludible', *Zeta*, 15 (May 1987), 14–19.

34 Manuel Laguarda, 'Reflexiones acerca de la ruptura', *Alternativa Socialista* (30 March 1989), n.p.

35 Hebert Gatto, 'Democracia y revolución', *Cuadernos de Marcha*, 3rd series, 43 (May 1989), 43–9.

36 Manuela Laguarda, 'Socialismo o reformismo desde lo alto', *Cuadernos de Marcha*, 3rd series, 44 (June 1989), 59–65.

37 Manuel Laguarda, 'Socialismo o reformismo desde lo alto (segunda parte)', *Cuadernos de Marcha*, 3rd series, 45 (July 1989), 27–30.

38 Marta Harnecker (ed.), *Frente Amplio: los desafíos de una izquierda legal* (4 vols., La República, 1991).

39 Harnecker, *Frente Amplio*, Vol. 4, 72–3.

40 Achim Wachendorfer (ed.), *La izquierda uruguaya frente a la crisis del socialismo real* (FESUR, 1991).

41 See 'La caída de los "socialismos reales" y el destino de la izquierda', *Brecha*, 333 (16 April 1992), a special Forum section page-numbered i–xx.

42 Nelson Caula & Hugo Machín (eds.), *¿Izquierda?* (Rosebud, 1994). In similar vein, see Rosario Queirolo, 'La tradicionalización del Frente Amplio: la con-

flictividad del proceso de cambio', in Eduardo González (ed.), *Los partidos políticos uruguayos en tiempos de cambio* (FCU, 1999), 87–111.

43 Nelson Argones & Pablo Mieres, 'La polémica en el Frente Amplio: ¿pugna por contenidos organizacionales o institucionales?', *Cuadernos del CLAEH*, 49 (1989), 41–59.

44 Alfredo Falero & Angel Vera, 'Transformaciones sociales y campo popular en Uruguay: construcción de alternativas y escenarios posibles', in Brando, *Uruguay hoy*, 159.

45 On the persistence and transformation of 'clientelismo' in recent Uruguayan political history, see Fernando Filgueira et al., 'Los dos ciclos del Estado uruguayo en el siglo xx', Instituto de Ciencia Política, *El Uruguay*, 197–201, and Juan Pablo Luna, *La política desde el llano. Conversaciones con militantes barriales* (EBO, 2004), especially 203–13.

46 On the Frente's experience in running the municipality of Montevideo, see Peter Winn & Lilia Ferro-Clérico, 'Can a Leftist Government Make a Difference? The Frente Amplio Administration of Montevideo, 1990–1994', in Douglas A. Chalmers et al (eds.), *The New Politics of Inequality in Latin America* (OUP, 1997), 447–68, Eduardo Canel, 'Municipal Decentralization and Participatory Democracy: Building a New Mode of Urban Politics in Montevideo City?', *European Review of Latin American and Caribbean Studies*, 71 (October 2001), 25–46, Benjamin Goldfrank, 'The Fragile Flower of Local Democracy: A Case Study of Decentralization/Participation in Montevideo', *Politics & Society*, xxx, 1 (2002), 51–83 and Salvador Scheletto, 'Por el ojo de una cerradura. Una mirada sobre la experiencia de gobierno municipal de la izquierda en Montevideo (1990–2004)', in Lanzaro, *La izquierda uruguaya*, 381–434. The Intendencia of Montevideo also puts out relevant material on its website.

47 See Mariano Arana & Oscar Destouet (eds.), *5 vertientes de la izquierda* (EBO, 2004).

48 Astori's story is engagingly told in Miguel Angel Campodónico, *Radicales y moderados: Danilo Astori. Vida y pensamiento político* (Linardi y Risso, 2004). The title is slightly misleading: some half of the book is made up of Astori's own words from a series of interviews conducted by the author.

49 Tabaré Vázquez's political ideas and personal attitudes can be gleaned from the engaging replies in Carlos Liscano, *Conversaciones con Tabaré Vázquez* (Ediciones del Caballo Perdido, 2003) and, more formally, in Tabaré Vázquez, *El gobierno del cambio* (La República, 2004). See also Daniel Esquibel's sometimes frivolous, often cynical but always pretentious *Tabaré Vázquez: seductor de multitudes* (Fin de siglo, 1997) on Vázquez as media image, Edison Lanza & Ernesto Tulbovitz, *Tabaré Vázquez: misterios de un liderazgo que cambió la historia* (Alcierre, 2005), an attempt at a full political biography, and Abril Trigo, 'De Artigas a Tabaré Vázquez, o de cómo se hace un imaginario (pos)nacional', <www.henciclopedia.org.uy/autores/Trigo/ ArtigasTabare .htm>, which analyses him within the Uruguayan tradition of the 'caudillo'.

50 On the 1996 reforms, see Moreira, *Final de juego*, 37–40 and 43–49; Guillermo Waksman, 'La izquierda avanza hacia el gobierno', *Nueva Sociedad*, 148 (1997),

12–19; Pablo Mieres, 'La reforma constitucional de 1996 en Uruguay y sus posibles efectos sobre los partidos y el sistema de partidos', *Cuadernos del CLAEH*, 80 (1997), 5–29; Daniel Buquet Corleto, 'Uruguay fin de siglo. Tiempos de coalición', *Nueva Sociedad*, 155 (1998), 6–14.

51   See Moreira, *Final de juego*, 134.

52   The most complete account of the changes to the Frente's political platform over the last two decades is Garcé & Yaffé, *La era progresista*, chapters 2 and 3, plus their appendix of extracts from relevant documents.

53   For examples of vigorous disagreement on these matters, see Harnecker, *Frente Amplio*, Vols. 3, 23–95 and 4, 40–73.

54   José Rilla, 'Cambiar la historia. Historia política y elite política en el Uruguay contemporáneo', *Revista Uruguaya de Ciencia Política*, 11 (1999), 107–27.

55   Caetano, Gallardo & Rilla, *La izquierda*; Moreira, *Final de juego*, 15 and 51; Jaime Yaffé, 'Izquierda, historia y tradición en Uruguay. La tradicionalización del Frente Amplio y el nacimiento de la tercera divisa', *Cuadernos del CLAEH*, 86/7 (2003), 155–92.

56   See especially Moreira, *Final de juego*, 95–118.

57   Filgueira et al., 'Los dos ciclos', 200–1.

58   Jaime Yaffé, 'Réquiem para el "Réquiem para la izquierda". El triunfo del FA: de la competencia interpartidaria al desempeño electoral', in Daniel Buquet (ed.), *Las claves del cambio: ciclo electoral y nuevo gobierno 2004/5* (EBO, 2005), 43–62.

59   I look at Aldo Solari's unsolicited and unwelcome advice to the left during the 1960s in Chapter 1 above.

60   On the Frente Amplio in government, I have used Garcé & Yaffé, *La era progresista* (2nd ed.), 129–62, Buquet, *Las claves del cambio*, the same editor's *¿Y ahora? El primer ciclo del gobierno de izquierda en Uruguay* (EBO, 2006), and Gerardo Caetano et al., *La hora de las reformas. Gobierno, actores y políticas en el Uruguay 2006–2007* (EBO, 2007).

61   In 2005, for example, the two presidents wrote a joint open letter to all their continental counterparts advocating regional unity. See *Diplomacia Estrategia Política*, i, 3 (2005), 194–8).

62   See Caetano, *La hora de las reformas*, 21–47, for the controversy surrounding its publication.

63   Enrique Rubio, 'Coyuntura: aproximación a la teoría', in Rubio, Hebert de Souza & Marcelo Pereira, *Coyuntura: respuesta y cambio* (CUI, 1985), 77–131, especially 82–4.

64   Enrique Rubio & Marcelo Pereira, *Utopía y estrategia; democracia y socialismo* (Trilce, 1994), 8. Further page references will appear in the text preceded by the initials *UE*.

65   Enrique Rubio, *La izquierda del futuro* (Marcha, 1999), 8 and 17. Further references will be given in the text preceded by the initials *IF*.

66   Enrique Rubio, *Izquierdas y derechas en la mundialización* (EBO, 2007), referred to henceforth in the text as *ID*.

67   Enrique Rubio, *Saber y poder. La cuestión democrática en la sociedad del conocimiento* (2003).

68 The two terms Rubio uses in Spanish ('globalización' and 'mundialización') are usually considered to be synonyms.

69 Alberto Couriel, *La izquierda y el Uruguay del futuro* (2nd ed., EBO, 2004).

70 *Izquierda y Uruguay*, 201, 11 and 9–10.

71 See 'La izquierda y el "réquiem para la izquierda"', *Izquierda y Uruguay*, 191–202. On Solari, see Chapter 1 above.

72 'Criterios básicos de una propuesta de la izquierda', *Izquierda y Uruguay*, 203–29, also published as 'Uruguay: basic criteria for a left project', *Diplomacy, Strategy & Politics*, 3 (2005), 144–70.

73 Quoted in Juan Pablo Luna, "¿Entre la espada y la pared? La transformación de las bases sociales del Frente Amplio y sus implicaciones de cara a un eventual gobierno progresista", in Lanzaro, *La izquierda uruguaya*, 229, note 36.

74 The Economist, 'The Next Chile', *Economist*, 382, 8514 (3 February 2007), 2.

75 See Jorge Torres, *Cuba y el che: la ruta mágica* (Fin de Siglo, 2007), 5, 50, 71, 13–15.

76 Jorge Torres, *La derrota en la mira* (Fin de Siglo, 2002) 62, 93, 392–399, 320–323.

77 Torres, *Cuba*, 78–9, 23–4, 16–19, 49–52, 150–6, 10–11.

78 Jorge Castañeda, *Compañero: The Life and Death of Che Guevara* (London, Bloomsbury, 1997), especially the prologue and final chapter.

79 See, for example, Petras, *Left Strikes Back*, 80–93, an attempted demolition of Castañeda's earlier *Utopia Unarmed*.

80 He seems to have been a capable but indifferent student at high school and in qualifying as a solicitor's clerk. See Federico Leicht, *Cero a la izquierda. Una biografía de Jorge Zabalza* (Letraeñe, 2007).

81 I rely in what follows primarily on Mario Mazzeo, *MPP: orígenes, ideas y protagonistas* (Trilce, 2005) and Adolfo Garcé, *Donde hubo fuego* (Fin de Siglo, 2006). Leicht's biography emphasises Zabalza's own activities, of course, and largely praises his perspective on all political matters.

82 See, for example, Andrés Cultelli, *La revolución necesaria. Contribución a la autocrítica del MLN* (Buenos Aires, Colihue, 2006).

83 Edición de autor, 1986. I have been unable to obtain a copy of this privately published book. According to Leicht, it was written under the influence of Lenin's *What To Do?* (*Cero a la izquierda*, 165). Zabalza re-uses its title for the preamble to *La estaca* (see below).

84 TAE, 1989. Further references will appear in the text preceded by the letter *M*.

85 TAE, 1995. Further references will appear in the text preceded by the letter *T*.

86 Ediciones del Cerro, 1998. Further references will appear in the text preceded by the letter *E*.

87 Leicht, *Cero a la izquierda*, 195–6.

88 The political platform of the MLN's legal shopfront in 1971, the Movimiento de Independientes 26 de Marzo, opens with a far from crystal clear epigraph from *Don Quixote*: "'The important thing is the road and not the inn'", quoted in INDAL, *El Frente Amplio del Uruguay y las elecciones de 1971* (Heverlee-Louvain, INDAL, 1973), 159. Coincidentally or not, Zabalza refers with

approval to the activities and publications of the Movimiento 26 de Marzo (*T*, 110, 113, 120–1).

89 Unlike the intellectuals of La Movida, Zabalza lampoons what he calls post-modernism (which he characteristically associates with those he sees as having betrayed the 'New Left' thrust of the 1960s for their own sordid, selfish ends [see, for example, *E*, 79]), but some might see in his idealisation of 'multitudes' shades of Deleuze and Guattari's notion of the 'rhizome'.

90 Elsewhere Zabalza also describes these political choices as 'a matter of skin' (*E*, 71).

91 Aparicio Saravia headed the Blanco rebellion in the last Uruguayan civil war in 1904, when he lost out to the Colorados under Batlle y Ordóñez, who then went on to structure the first wholly modern version of the Uruguayan state.

92 The alternative, less enchanted version is that it was deliberately permitted by the authorities to justify the armed forces being put in charge of internal security matters, which occurred during the week or so that followed.

93 For a selection of perspectives on the Punta Carretas escape and the MLN's highly controversial (and self-defeating) increasingly militarist policies from 1971 onwards, including the far from wholly successful occupation of the rural town of Pando, see Samuel Blixen, *Sendic* (Trilce, 2000), Clara Aldrighi, *La izquierda armada* (Trilce, 2001), Alfonso Lessa, *La revolución imposible* (Fin de Siglo, 2003) and Hebert Gatto, *El cielo por asalto* (Taurus, 2004). Eleuterio Fernández Huidobro, *Historia de los Tupamaros* (Vol. 3, TAE, 1990) offers a privileged insider's view. Eduardo Rey Tristán, *A la vuelta de la esquina: la izquierda revolucionaria uruguaya 1955–1973* (Fin de Siglo, 2005) includes other movements closer to Zabalza's libertarian ideal.

94 Zabalza's Spanish word 'silvestres' can mean 'rustic', recalling the legacy that Zabalza extends back to Uruguay's earliest days, but the strike was initiated in urban centres, especially the capital.

95 That the district of La Teja provided clear examples of solidarity between militants, strikers and the wider community seems confirmed in Alvaro Rico et al., *15 días que estremecieron al Uruguay* (Fin de Siglo, 2005), 92, 213, 237–42, 380, 391, 409–11, 438, 516, 617.

96 See Intendencia Municipal de Montevideo, 'Presupuesto participativo ciclo 2007' at <www.montevideo.gub.uy>, and more generally, the essays mentioned above in note 46.

97 Rosario Queirolo, 'Entrevista al edil Jorge Zabalza', in Luis Eduardo González (ed.), *Los partidos políticos uruguayaos en tiempos de cambio* (FEU, 1999), 115–6.

98 See Leicht, *Cero a la izquierda*, 188–9.

99 See Mazzeo, *MPP*, 109–20.

100 Garcé, *Donde hubo fuego*, 133–60 and Leicht, *Cero a la izquierda*, 189–92.

101 See extracts from 1999 interviews contrasted in Mazzeo, *MPP*, 67–8.

102 In Mario Mazzeo, *Charlando con Pepe Mujica* (Trilce, 2002), 15.

103 See also Leicht, *Cero a la izquierda*, 55.

104 As implied in Gatto, *El cielo por asalto*, 134, note 118.

105 José Mujica & Rodrigo Arocena, *Cuando la izquierda gobierne* (Trilce, 2004), 12.

6   *Dialogue Outside Politics: Uruguay as Problem in the Twenty-First Century*

1   In the unpaginated collection of graffiti by Eduardo Roland, *Contra cualquier muro: graffiti de la transición 1985–1989* (Ediciones de UNO/Vintén, 1990).

2   Quoted in Gerardo Caetano, 'Notas para una revisión histórica sobre la cuestión nacional en el Uruguay', *Revista de Historia*, 3 (1992), 77.

3   José Rilla, 'Historia, memoria y ciudadanía', in Laura Gioscia (ed.), *Ciudadanía en tránsito. Perfiles para el debate* (EBO, 2001), 78.

4   Adolfo Garcé & Jaime Yaffé, *La era progresista* (Fin de Siglo, 2004), 109.

5   Gerardo Caetano, 'Democracia y cultura: reflexión en torno a algunos desafíos contemporáneos', in Hugo Achugar & Sonia D'Alessandro (eds.), *Global/local: democracia, memoria, identidades* (Trilce, 2002), 117 and 128–9.

6   Gerardo Caetano & José Rilla, 'La juvenil madurez: conversación con José Pedro Barrán', in Fernando Pita (ed.), *Las brechas en la historia, 2: los temas* (Brecha, 1996), 141.

7   Garcé & Yaffé, *La era progresista*, 109.

8   The list could be lengthened by widening the range of disciplines to include, say, sociology and psychology. I have restricted myself to political science and history because, by being closer to the Frente Amplio's concerns as an agent on the political scene, they display the commitments and compromises associated with doing intellectual work under such conditions with particular intensity.

9   For example, he and Caetano were 'independent' signatories to the influential 'Documento de los 24', published as an open letter from interested members of the Frente at the height of its internal struggles over socialism in 1991, while Alvaro Rico (of whom more below) signed as a member of the Communist Party. Garcé and Yaffé's own names do not appear. See *La era progresista*, 143.

10 José Rilla, 'Prólogo', in Garcé & Yaffé, La era progresista, 8.

11 Carlos Real de Azúa, 'Política, poder y partidos en el Uruguay de hoy', in Luis Benvenuto (ed.), *Uruguay hoy* (Buenos Aires, Siglo XXI, 1971), 256. Real de Azúa's essay has since appeared separately as *Partidos, política y poder en el Uruguay (1971 – Coyuntura y pronóstico)* (Universidad de la República, 1988), the quotation being from p. 111. I look at the circumstances in which Real de Azúa and other intellectuals found themselves in 1971 in Chapter 3 above. Garcé and Yaffé's own book was printed about a month before the 2004 elections.

12 See *La era progresista*, 12 and 91.

13 Miguel Aguirre Bayley, *Frente Amplio: "la admirable alarma de 1971"* (Cauce, 2005). The tone is clearly set in the preface (7–15).

14 See Jaime Yaffé, *Al centro y adentro* (Linardi y Risso, 2005), 9–10.

15 Adolfo Garcé, *Donde hubo fuego* (Fin de Siglo, 2006), 11 and 14–16. The quotations are on p. 15, Garcé's italics.

16 Alvaro Rico, *Cómo nos domina la clase gobernante* (Trilce, 2005).

17 First published in English by New Left Books in 1978.

18 See the previous two chapters.

19 Rico, *Cómo nos domina*, 66–70, 136, 163 and 176. Other attempts to summarise all or part of Rico's aims are on pp. 21, 42, 177 and 186–7.

20 Constanza Moreira, *Final de juego* (Trilce, 2004), 8. Her book just missed the national election campaign, being printed in November.

21 Jorge Lanzaro (ed.), *La izquierda uruguaya: entre la oposición y el gobierno* (Fin de Siglo, 2004), 8. This book, too, was published just in time for the elections in October.

22 *La era progresista* (2nd ed), 7.

23 Caetano & Rilla, 'Juvenil madurez', 141.

24 Gerardo Caetano (ed.), *20 años de democracia, Uruguay 1985–2005: miradas múltiples* (Taurus, 2005), 11.

25 Aldo Marchesi et al., 'Pensar el pasado reciente: antecedentes y perspectivas', in their *El presente de la dictadura. Estudios y reflexiones a 30 años del golpe de Estado en Uruguay* (Trilce, 2004), 5–32, quotation on p. 16.

26 Caetano, 'Democracia y cultura', Achugar & D'Alessandro, *Global/local*, 130–1.

27 Moreira, *Fin de juego*, 155.

28 Leticia Soler, *Historiografía uruguaya contemporánea (1985–2000)* (Trilce, 2000), 60.

29 Gerardo Caetano, 'Del primer batllismo al terrismo: crisis simbólica y reconstrucción del imaginario colectivo', *Cuadernos del CLAEH*, 49 (1989), 86.

30 Gerardo Caetano, 'Pasado-futuro: una polaridad crucial y resistente', in Caetano & Rodrigo Arocena (eds.), *Uruguay: Agenda 2020* (Santillana, 2007), 30–1.

31 Gerardo Caetano, 'Marco histórico y cambio político en dos décadas de democracia. De la transición democrática al gobierno de la izquierda (1985–2005)', in his *20 años de democracia*, 65.

32 See the notes in 'Pasado-futuro', 52–60.

33 Caetano, *20 años*, 9–11, his italics.

34 Batlle's Spanish word is 'desacralizar', which has overtones of 'secularise' and 'deconsecrate' given Batlle's robust anti-clericalism, though Caetano seems to give it more the idea of untying power from the political elite, of democratising it by snatching it down from Olympian heights.

35 Here, Caetano echoes Carlos Real de Azúa's highly influential critique of Batllismo, *El impulso y su freno* [1964].

36 Caetano, *20 años*, 38 and 72.

37 For an introduction to the Uruguayan context, see Maren & Marcelo Viñar, *Fracturas de memoria* (Trilce, 1993), Luis Roniger & Mario Sznadjer, 'The Legacy of Human Rights Violations and the Collective Memory of Redemocratized Uruguay', *Human Rights Quarterly*, 19 (1997), 55–77, Maren Ulriksen de Viñar (ed.), *Memoria social: fragmentaciones y responsabilidades* (Trilce, 2001), Aldo Marchesi, '¿"Guerra" o "terrorismo de estado"? Recuerdos enfrentados sobre el pasado reciente uruguayo', in Elizabeth Jelin (ed.), *Las conmemoraciones: las disputas en las fechas 'in-felices'* (Madrid, Siglo XXI, 2002), 101–47, and Eugenia Allier, 'The Peace Commission: A consensus on the recent past in Uruguay?', *European Review of Latin American and Caribbean Studies*, 81 (2006), 87–96.

38 In office at the time of the coup, Bordaberry was a key figure in providing a civilian facade for activities by the armed forces before and after the 1973 coup.

39 See Caetano, *20 años*, 15, and two years later, 'Pasado-futuro', 25, 41 and 43, his italics.

40 Gerardo Caetano, '"Nunca más" y no violencia: las exigencias de un "momento de verdad" y la construcción de una "memoria ejemplar"', in Constanza Moreira (ed.), *La hora de las reformas. Gobierno, actores y políticas en el Uruguay 2006–7* (Informe de coyuntura no. 7, Instituto de Ciencia Política/EBO, 2007), 21–36.

41 Caetano, '"Nunca más"', 21–2, 34–5, 26 and 36.

42 Caetano, '"Nunca más"', 26.

43 It seems that only the air force genuinely helped in uncovering the truth for Caetano's report, those most involved in the repression thus still effectively endorsing the national security doctrine expressed in *Las fuerzas armadas al pueblo oriental*, the military's two-volume act of self-justification dating from 1976–8. See Julián González,'La cuestión militar: tranquilidad en el frente y un gran desafío', in Moreira, *La hora*, 217. See also Caetano's disgust at an army general's defiant speech on the issue during 2006 ('"Nunca más"', 27–8).

44 Miranda is a university lecturer in law and a member of one of the organizations representing families of the 'disappeared'. See his 'Papelitos en los bolsillos (anotaciones para una agenda de derechos humanos)', in Caetano, *Uruguay: Agenda 2020*, 163–98.

45 Javier Miranda, 'Apuntes a mano alzada sobre políticas de derechos humanos en la coyuntura', in Moreira, *La hora*, 37–47.

46 Notably, *El joven Quijano 1900–1933* [1986], *Breve historia de la dictadura* [1987 and 2006] and *Historia contemporánea del Uruguay. De la colonia al MERCOSUR* [1994, revised and expanded 2005].

47 Significantly, Rilla joined his small party's leader in editing a book of papers on the ombudsman or public defender's office, public vetting of accounts and anti-corruption commissions, precisely those democratic institutions dedicated to enabling citizens to oversee the performance of state and politicians. See José Rilla & Pablo Mieres (eds.), *Transparencia y ciudadanía responsable* (CLAEH, 2007).

48 Rilla, 'Historia, memoria', 69–82.

49 José Rilla, 'Sobre la enseñanza de la historia reciente', in Moreira, *La hora*, 53–6.

50 Moreira, *Fin de juego*, 155.

51 For recent summaries of the sort space limitations prohibit here, see Caetano, 'Notas', 59–78, Gerardo Caetano & Adolfo Garcé, 'Ideas, política y nación en el Uruguay del siglo xx', in Oscar Terán (ed.), *Ideas en el siglo: intelectuales y cultura en el siglo xx latinoamericano* (Buenos Aires, Siglo XXI, 2004), 309–422, and Gustavo San Román, *Soy celeste. Investigación sobre la identidad de los uruguayos* (Fin de Siglo, 2007), 197–230. I return below to the last of these.

52 Alberto Methol Ferré, *¿Adónde va el Uruguay?* (no publ., 1958; published in Argentina as *La crisis del Uruguay y el imperio británico* [Buenos Aires, A. Peña Lillo, 1959]) and *El Uruguay como problema* (Diálogo, 1967).

53 Alberto Methol Ferré, 'Adiós, Sr. Nardone', *Marcha*, 1047 (24 February 1961), n.p. Benito Nardone was the leader of the Federación Ruralista (see also Chapter 1 above).

54   Alberto Methol Ferré, *El Uruguay como problema* (2nd ed., EBO, 1971).
55   Alberto Methol Ferré, *Uruguay como problema, y otros trabajos*, in *Electroneurobiología*, xv, 5 (2007), 3–104, available as PDF at http://electroneubio.secyt.gov.ar/index2.htm.
56   See, for example, Gustavo de Armas, 'De la sociedad hiperintegrada al país fragmentado. Crónica del último tramo de un largo recorrido', and Hugo Achugar, 'Veinte largos años. De una *cultura nacional* a un país fragmentado' in Caetano, *20 años*, 269–303 and 427–34, respectively. For a summary of current thinking on the subject, see Ariadna Islas & Ana Frega, 'Identidades uruguayas: del mito de la sociedad homogénea al reconocimiento de la pluralidad', in Ana Frega et al., *Historia del Uruguay en el siglo xx (1890–2005)* (EBO, 2007), 359–92. See below for further general comments on this important book.
57   Tabaré Vera (ed.), *Uruguay hacia 2000: desafíos y opciones* (Caracas, Nueva Sociedad, 1991).
58   Hugo Achugar (ed.), *Cultura(s) y nación en el Uruguay de fin de siglo* (Logos/FESUR, 1991).
59   Hugo Achugar (ed.), *Cultura Mercosur: políticas e industrias culturales* (Logos/FESUR, 1991).
60   Hugo Achugar & Gerardo Caetano (eds.), *Identidad uruguaya: ¿mito, crisis o afirmación?* (Trilce, 1992).
61   Hugo Achugar & Gerardo Caetano (eds.), *Mundo, región, aldea* (Trilce, 1994).
62   Gerardo Caetano (ed.), *Uruguay hacia el siglo XXI: identidad, cultura, integración, representación* (Trilce, 1994).
63   Alvaro Rico (ed.), *Uruguay: cuentas pendientes* (Trilce, 1995).
64   Hugo Achugar & Mabel Moraña (eds.), *Uruguay: imaginarios culturales, tomo 1: desde las huellas indígenas a la modernidad* (Trilce, 2000).
65   Oscar Brando (ed.), *Uruguay hoy: paisaje después del 31 de octubre* (Ediciones del Caballo Perdido, 2004).
66   See the preliminary remarks by Alvaro Portillo from the government and by 'the authors' as collective in Frega, *Historia del Uruguay*, 7–9 and 11–13.
67   Gabriel Peluffo Linari, 'Como el Uruguay no hay, o el país de la inmaculada concepción', in Hugo Achugar (ed.), *Como el Uruguay no hay* (Museo Municipal de Bellas Artes Juan Manuel Blanes, 2000), 15–22, quotes on p. 18.
68   I mention Rama's posthumous *La ciudad letrada* [1984] when discussing in the Introduction the changed role of intellectuals in the late twentieth century.
69   Hugo Achugar, '¿Cuál es la canción?', Gerardo Caetano, 'Entre el Parlamento y los ciudadanos. El espacio de la política y sus avatares en el imaginario de los uruguayos', Milita Alfaro, 'Imaginarios de la "ciudad iletrada". Notas acerca de la eficacia simbólica de las narrativas residuales', and Teresa Porzecanski, 'Indios, africanos e inmigrantes europeos: la búsqueda del origen en los nuevos discursos del imaginario uruguayo', in Achugar, *Como el Uruguay*, 9–11, 27–56, 61–79 and 83–103 respectively. There should seemingly have been an essay by Abril Trigo, but this has been replaced (pp. 107–9) by extracts from an interview between two Uruguayan expatriates related to his then still forthcoming book on the Uruguayan diaspora discussed at the end of this chapter.
70   Jorge Abbondanza, 'Sagrario criollo', in Achugar, *Como el Uruguay*, 6.

71 Isabela Cosse & Vania Markarian, *Memorias de la historia. Una aproximación a la conciencia histórica nacional* (Trilce, 1994).

72 San Román, *Soy celeste*. The author is himself an expatriate Uruguayan academic based in Edinburgh.

73 See Cosse & Markanian, *Memorias*, 45–60, 67 and 71, and San Román, *Soy celeste*, 50–61, 75.

74 San Román, *Soy celeste*, 61–74. Cosse & Markanian did not address this issue directly, but do imply, not surprisingly perhaps, that historical awareness is most widely absorbed through social and cultural phenomena accessible by all (see *Memorias*, 9).

75 See Cosse & Markanian, *Memorias*, 9–10, 36, 112, and San Román, *Soy celeste*, 77–80.

76 Caetano & Garcé, 'Ideas, políticas', 409.

77 Hugo Achugar, *La balsa de la Medusa. Ensayos sobre identidad, cultura y fin de siglo en Uruguay* (Trilce, 1994), 42. Further references to this book will appear in the text preceded by the letters *BM*.

78 Abril Trigo, *¿Cultura uruguaya o culturas linyeras? (Para una cartografía de la neomodernidad posuruguaya)* (Vintén, 1997), 160.

79 I do not consider Achugar's poetry here.

80 See especially Richard Rorty, *Philosophy and the Mirror of Nature* (Princeton UP, 1979).

81 Hugo Achugar, *Planetas sin boca* (Trilce, 2004), 124. Further page references will appear in the text, preceded by the letters *PSB*.

82 "Work in progress" is in English in the original.

83 Achugar's Spanish exploits the double meaning of 'ensayo' as 'essay' and 'rehearsal' as well as the ambivalence of the reflexive infinitive's reference to 'oneself' or 'itself': who or what undergoes constant change? Who or what undertakes this unceasing quest for meanings?

84 Hugo Achugar, *La biblioteca en ruinas. Reflexiones desde la periferia* (Trilce, 1994), 111. Further references to this book will appear in the text preceded by the letters *BER*.

85 Groucho, in a famous scene, responds 'Yes, please' to the question 'Tea or coffee?'. Both Žižek and Achugar are also aware, of course, of the echoes sounded by Groucho's surname.

86 Achugar's pivotal place in many of the collective volumes about Uruguayan national identity listed a few pages back illustrates further Achugar's predilection for forms of cultural production dependent on participation and discussion that result in provisional but stimulating proposals.

87 In this sense, the library is a particular but crucial example of the 'uncertain spaces' Achugar sees the modern 'errant intellectual' as condemned to occupy in the opening essay of the later *Planetas sin boca* (*PSB*, 23–4).

88 'After all, whose judgement? [¿el criterio de quién?]', he asks (*BER*, 23). Literary criticism as 'el ejercicio del criterio' is an idea of the nineteenth century Cuban poet, essayist and fighter for national independence José Martí. It was used as the title of a collection of literary journalism by Mario Benedetti in *El ejercicio del criterio* (Mexico, Nueva Imagen, 1981), where the book's epigraph acknowl-

edges the debt to Martí. How much of this is in Achugar's mind is difficult to establish, but the implied critique of the sovereign place accorded to a purely personal whim and taste hived off from wider social concerns is consistent with his general approach to the practice of literary and cultural commentary.

89 Recalling the "monologuismo" bemoaned by Arturo Sergio Visca in his *Un hombre y su mundo* [1960] to which I referred in my Introduction above.

90 See 'La nación entre el olvido y la memoria. Hacia una narración democrática de la nación', 'El lugar de la memoria', 'Monumentos, conmemoración y exclusion', 'Derechos de memoria. Sobre independencia y estados-nación en América Latina' (*PSB*, 115–78) and 'Territorios y memorias *versus* lógica del Mercado' (*PSB*, 217–28).

91 *Trilce*, 1990. Further references to this book will appear in the text, preceded by the initials *CEN*.

92 See, for example, Abril Trigo, 'De Artigas a Tabaré Vázquez, o de cómo se hace un imaginario (pos)nacional', at <www.henciclopedia.org.uy/autores/Trigo/ArtigasTabare.htm>.

93 Trigo would become co-editor, with Ana del Sarto and Alicia Ríos, of *The Latin American Cultural Studies Reader* (Durham/London, Duke UP, 2004), to which he also contributed the 'General Introduction' (1–14) and 'The 1990s: Practices and Polemics within Latin American Cultural Studies' (347–73). See also his 'Why do I do Cultural Studies?', *Journal of Latin American Cultural Studies*, ix, 1 (2000), 73–93.

94 *¿Cultura uruguaya o culturas linyeras?*, 9. Further references to this book will appear in the text preceded by the prefix *CU*.

95 Abril Trigo, *Memorias migrantes. Testimonios y ensayos sobre la diáspora uruguaya* (Rosario/Montevideo, Beatriz Viterbo/Trilce, 2003), 113. Further references to this book will appear in the text preceded by the initials *MM*.

96 In addition, the epigraph to the epilogue compares historians to theatre directors who emerge from behind the scenery to direct the work (*CEN*, 253), an apt description of Trigo's own combative approach to cultural and historical analysis.

97 These two neologisms are explained in the book's only concession to theoretical clarification, where Trigo's reading of Althusser, Lacan, Foucault, Castoriadis and their like is suggested but not acknowledged (*CEN*, 27, note 76). No theoretical writings are listed in a bibliography that contains an impressively long selection of readings from or about Uruguay. Subsequent books, however, will give Trigo's foreign sources equal prominence, an acknowledgement that parallels the increasing internationalisation of his idea of Uruguay.

98 Hugo Achugar, 'Una fotografía de mediados del año 2002', in Achugar (ed.), *Imaginarios y consumo cultural. Primer informe sobre consumo y comportamiento cultural, Uruguay 2002* (Trilce, 2003), 7–39, especially 10 and 38.

99 Nora Rabotnikoff, 'Memoria y política: compromiso ético y pluralismo de interpretaciones', *Revista Uruguaya de Ciencia Politica*, 9 (1996), 143–50.

Conclusion

1 Cited in José Luis de Diego, 'Intelectuales y política en los ochenta', *Hispamérica*, 103 (2006), 102.

2 After the Frente government indicated its intention to exploit holes in the existing impunity legislation to investigate unresolved 'disappearances' and start legal proceedings in cases of human rights abuse, the armed forces restated the justification for their actions in the 1970s. It is a profound irony that they selected the moment when soldiers stood guard as former Tupamaros guerrilla leader, now Senator, José Mujica took the oath of office from another already elected ex-MLN leader, as the triumphant completion of their task, after which they could at last 'return to barracks'. See Centro Militar/Centro de Oficiales Retirados de las Fuerzas Armadas, *Nuestra verdad: 1960–1980, la lucha contra el terrorismo* (Artemisa, 2007), 330–1.

3 In José 'Pepe' Mujica & Rodrigo Arocena, *Cuando la izquierda gobierne* (ed. Mario Mazzeo, Trilce, 2003), 12.

4 Carina Blixen, *Palabras rigurosamente vigiladas: dictadura, lenguaje, literatura. La obra de Carlos Liscano* (Ediciones del Caballo Perdido, 2006), 33–4.

5 Jaime Yaffé, 'Memoria y olvidos en la relación de la izquierda con el pasado reciente', in Aldo Marchesi et al, *El presente de la dictadura* (Trilce, 2004), 194.

6 Juan Flo, 'Problemas de la juventud en nuestro país', in Carlos Real de Azúa (ed.), *Problemas de la juventud uruguaya* (Marcha, 1954), 156. See the Introduction above.

BIBLIOGRAPHY

Only works quoted or referred to in the text or notes are listed. The key to abbreviations, acronyms and other conventions is on page vii. Place of publication for all books is Montevideo, unless otherwise stated.

Abbondanza, Jorge, 'Sagrario criollo', in Hugo Achugar (ed.), *Como el Uruguay no hay* (Museo Municipal de Bellas Artes Juan Manuel Blanes, 2000), 6.

Abella, Alcides (coord.), *1968 Uruguay 1985* (4 Vols, EBO, 2006–8).

Achugar, Hugo, 'Para un necesario debate sobre la cultura nacional', *Cuadernos de Marcha*, 3rd series, 11 (September 1986), 81–4.

——, 'Vanguardia y batllismo: el intelectual y el estado', *Río de La Plata*, 4–6 (1987), 419–30.

——, 'Entre dos orillas. Los puentes necesarios', in Saúl Sosnowski (ed.), *Represión, exilio y democracia: la cultura uruguaya* (EBO, 1987), 241–7.

——, 'Transformaciones culturales en el Uruguay del fin de siglo', *Hispamérica*, 59 (1990), 37–57.

——, *La balsa de la Medusa. Ensayos sobre identidad, cultura y fin de siglo en Uruguay* (Trilce, 1992).

——, *La biblioteca en ruinas. Reflexiones culturales desde la periferia* (Trilce, 1994).

——, '¿Cuál es la canción?', in his *Como el Uruguay no hay* (Museo Municipal de Bellas Artes Juan Manuel Blanes, 2000), 9–11.

——, 'Una fotografía de mediados del año 2002', in Achugar (ed.), *Imaginarios y consumo cultural. Primer informe sobre consumo y comportamiento cultural, Uruguay 2002* (Trilce, 2003), 7–39.

——, *Planetas sin boca. Escritos efímeros sobre arte, cultura y literatura* (Trilce, 2004).

——, 'Balances y desbalances culturales a comienzos del siglo xxi', in Marchesi, Aldo et al, *El presente de la dictadura* (Trilce, 2004), 209–13.

——, 'Veinte largos años. De una *cultura nacional* a un país fragmentado' in Gerardo Caetano (ed.), *20 años de democracia* (Taurus, 2005), 427–34.

—— (ed.), *Cultura(s) y nación en el Uruguay de fin de siglo* (Logos/FESUR, 1991).

—— (ed.), *Cultura Mercosur: políticas e industrias culturales* (Logos/FESUR, 1991).

—— (ed.), *Como el Uruguay no hay* (Museo Municipal de Bellas Artes Juan Manuel Blanes, 2000).

—— (ed.), *Imaginarios y consumo cultural. Primer informe sobre consumo y comportamiento cultural, Uruguay 2002* (Trilce, 2003).

—— & Caetano, Gerardo (eds.), *Identidad uruguaya: ¿mito, crisis o afirmación?* (Trilce, 1992).

Bibliography

—— (eds.), *Mundo, región, aldea* (Trilce, 1994).

—— & Moraña, Mabel (eds.), *Uruguay: imaginarios culturales, tomo 1: desde las huellas indígenas a la modernidad* (Trilce, 2000).

Acosta, Yamandú, 'Arturo Ardao: la inteligencia filosófica y el discernimiento del tercerismo en *Marcha*', in Horacio Machín & Mabel Moraña (eds.), *'Marcha' y América Latina* (Pittsburgh, Instituto Internacional de Literatura Iberoamericana, 2003), 123–61.

'AFS', 'Lo que no es y lo que es la Tercera Posición', *Marcha*, 580 (15 June 1951), 8.

Aguiar, César A., *Uruguay: país de emigración* (EBO, 1982).

—— & Cravotto, Antonio, *El Uruguay de nuestro tiempo, 4: población, territorio, ciudades* (CLAEH, 1983).

Aguirre Bayley, Miguel, *El Frente Amplio: historia y documentos* (EBO, 1985).

——, *Frente Amplio. "La admirable alarma de 1971"* (Cauce, 2005).

——, *Frente Amplio. Uno solo dentro y fuera de Uruguay en la resistencia a la dictadura* (Cauce, 2007).

Aharonián, Coriún, *Conversaciones sobre música, cultura e identidad* (Tacuabé, 2000).

Ainsa, Fernando, 'Catarsis liberadora y tradición resumida: las nuevas fronteras de la realidad en la narrativa uruguaya contemporánea', *Revista Iberoamericana*, lviii, 160–1 (1992), 807–25.

——, *Espacios de encuentro y mediación. Sociedad civil, democracia y utopia en América Latina* (Nordan Comunidad, 2004).

Albistur, Gerardo, 'Autocensura o resistencia. El dilema de la prensa en el Uruguay autoritario', in Alcides Abella (coord.), *1968 Uruguay 1985*, (Vol. 1, EBO, 2006), 111–36.

Aldrighi, Clara, *La izquierda armada. Ideología, ética e identidad en el MLN-Tupamaros* (Trilce, 2001).

Alfaro, Hugo, *Navegar es necesario: Quijano y el semanario* Marcha (EBO, 1984).

Alfaro, Milita, 'Con Rafael Bayce: "El Uruguay es un gran avestruz"', *Brecha* (22 September 1989), 2–3.

——, 'Imaginarios de la "ciudad iletrada". Notas acerca de la eficacia simbólica de las narrativas residuales', Hugo Achugar (ed.), *Como el Uruguay no hay* (Museo Municipal de Bellas Artes Juan Manuel Blanes, 2000), 61–79.

Allier, Eugenia, 'The Peace Commission: A consensus on the recent past in Uruguay?', *European Review of Latin American and Caribbean Studies*, 81 (2006), 87–96.

Alonso Eloy, Rosa & Demasi, Carlos, *Uruguay 1959–1968. Crisis y estancamiento* (EBO, 1986).

Alsina Thevenet, Homero, 'Presentación de Emir Rodríguez Monegal', in Lisa Block de Behar (ed.), *Diseminario. La deconsrucción: otro descubrimiento de América* (XYZ, 1987), 109–15.

Anon., 'Una declaración', *Marcha*, 1100 (23 March 1962), 15.

——, 'Crónica y moralidades', *El Popular* (7 July 1972), n.p.

——, *Artigas y el Movimiento de Liberación Nacional* (3rd ed., YOEA, 1987).

Appratto, Carmen et al., *El Uruguay de la dictadura (1973–1985)* (EBO, 2004).

—— & Artagaveytia, Lucila, 'La educación', in Carmen Appratto et al., *El Uruguay de la dictadura (1973–1985)* (EBO, 2004), 213–49.

Appratto, Roberto, *Se hizo de noche* (Amuleto, 2007).

Arana, Mariano & Destouet, Arturo (eds.), *5 vertientes de la izquierda* (EBO, 2004).

Arditi, Benjamín, 'Intelectuales y política. Una perspectiva socialista latinoamericana', *David y Goliath*, 56 (April 1990), 27–35.

——, 'Talkin' 'bout a Revolution: The End of Mourning', *Parallax*, 9, 2 (2003), 81–95, later expanded as chapter 5 in his *Politics on the Edges of Liberalism* (Edinburgh UP, 2007).

Ardao, Arturo, 'Segunda respuesta a un tercero', *Marcha* (20 January 1966), 8.

——, 'La independencia uruguaya como problema', *Cuadernos de Marcha*, 38 (1967), 83–96.

Ares Pons, Roberto, 'Aproximaciones a la problemática de nuestra juventud', in Carlos Real de Azúa (ed.), *Problemas de la juventud uruguaya* (Marcha, 1954), 45–69.

——, 'Es imposible un fascismo uruguayo', *Marcha*, 943 (26 December 1958), 7.

——, 'Sobre fascismo y ruralismo', *Marcha* 949 (27 February 1959), n.p.

——, *Uruguay: ¿provincia o nación?* (Buenos Aires, Coyoacán, 1961).

——, *La intelligentsia uruguaya y otros ensayos* (EBO, 1968).

Argones, Nelson & Mieres, Pablo, 'La polémica en el Frente Amplio, ¿pugna por contenidos organizacionales o institucionales?', *Cuadernos del CLAEH*, 49 (1989), 41–59.

Arismendi, Rodney, *Uruguay y América en los años 70* (Mexico, Ediciones de Cultura Popular, 1979).

Araujo, Ana María & Tejera, Horacio (eds.), *La imaginación al poder 1968–1988. Entrevistas a protagonistas de la insurrección juvenil de 1968* (FCU, 1988).

Astori, Danilo, 'La política económica de la dictadura', in Carmen Appratto et al., *El Uruguay de la dictadura (1973–1985)* (EBO, 2004), 147–77.

Avelar, Idelber, *The Untimely Present: Postdictatorial Latin American Fiction and the Task of Mourning* (Durham and London, Duke UP, 1999).

Bardanca, Héctor, 'Cultura nacional: los puntos sobre las jotas de joven y de jodido', *Cuadernos de Marcha*, 3rd Series, 13 (October 1986), 84–6.

Barros-Lémez, Alvaro, 'Uruguay: redemocratización, cultura, desexilio (¿se puede volver a casa?)', Saúl Sosnowski (ed.), *Represión, exilio y democracia: la cultura uruguaya* (EBO, 1987), 249–60.

——, *Intelectuales y política: polémicas y posiciones, años '60 y '70* (Monte Sexto, 1988).

——, 'La larga marcha de lo verosímil: narrativa uruguaya del siglo xx', *Casa de Las Américas*, 170 (1988), 40–50.

——, *Seregni* (Monte Sexto, 1989).

Baud, Michel & Rutten, Rosanne (eds.), *Popular Intellectuals and Social Movements: Framing Protest in Asia, Africa and Latin America*, in *International Review of Social History*, 49 (2004), Supplement 12.

Bauman, Zygmunt, *Legislators and Interpreters* (Ithaca, Cornell UP, 1987).

——, *Intimations of Postmodernity* (London and New York, Routledge, 1991).

Bayce, Rafael, 'La lógica del miedo 1968–1984: genesis y consolidación', *Relaciones*, 20–1 (January 1986), 7–9.

——, *Cultura política uruguaya. Desde Batlle hasta 1988* (FCU, 1989).

——, 'Legitimidad y crisis política. Microformas perversas de macrolegitimidad en el Uruguay', *Cuadernos del CLAEH*, 78/9 (1997), 349–73.

——, *5 tareas de Hércules. Para gobernar en el siglo xxi: Uruguay como ejemplo* (Trilce, 2005).

Benedetti, Mario, *El país de la cola de paja* (1st ed., Asir, 1960; 7th ed., Arca, 1968 and 8th ed., Arca, 1970).

——, *Literatura uruguaya siglo veinte* [1963] (4th. ed., Buenos aires, Seix Barral, 1997).

——, 'Un instante decisivo', *Pensamiento Crítico* (February 1970), 220–5.

——, 'Raúl Sendic: símbolo de una transformación' [1970], in Omar Costa, *Los Tupamaros* (Mexico, Era, 1971), 78–83.

——, 'La transformación empieza en las bases', *Cuadernos de Marcha*, 41 (1971), 25–7.

——, *Crónicas del 71* (Arca, 1972).

——, *Terremoto y después* (Arca, 1973).

——, *El escritor latinoamericano y la revolución posible* (Mexico, Nueva Imagen, 1974).

——, *Inventario* (5th ed., Buenos Aires, Alfa, 1974).

——, *El recurso del supremo patriarca* (8th ed., Mexico, Nueva Imagen, 1990).

——, *El ejercicio del criterio* (Mexico, Nueva Imagen, 1981).

——, *Primavera con una esquina rota* (Mexico, Nueva Imagen, 1982).

——, *El desexilio y otras conjeturas* (Madrid, El País, 1984).

——, *Escritos políticos (1971–1973)* (Arca, 1985).

——, *Yesterday y mañana* (Arca, 1987).

——, *Perplejidades de fin de siglo* [1993] (2nd pocket ed., Buenos Aires, Sudamericana, 2001).

——, *Memoria y esperanza. Un mensaje a los jóvenes* (Buenos Aires, Planeta, 2004).

Benvenuto, Luis et al., *Uruguay hoy* (Buenos Aires, Siglo XXI, 1971).

Berenguer, Amanda, 'Los signos sobre la mesa', in Saúl Sosnowski (ed.), *Represión, exilio y democracia: la cultura uruguaya* (EBO, 1987), 171–8.

Berocay, Roy, 'La música popular uruguaya en veinte años de democracia. Un país sonoro, creativo y cambiante', in Caetano, Gerardo (ed.), *20 años de democracia. Uruguay 1985–2005: miradas múltiples* (Taurus, 2005), 489–505.

Bértola, Luis, 'la dictadura, ¿un modelo económico?', in Aldo Marchesi et al., *El presente de la dictadura* (Trilce, 2004), 201–4.

Beverley, John, Oviedo, José & Aronna, Michael (eds.), *The Postmodernism Debate in Latin America* (Durham, Duke UP, 1995).

Bissio, Beatriz, 'Benedetti: reflexiones sobre los escombros que dejó la dictadura', *Cuadernos del Tercer Mundo*, 108 (1988), 58–64.

Blixen, Carina, *Palabras rigurosamente vigiladas: dictadura, lenguaje, literaura. La obra de Carlos Liscano* (Ediciones del Caballo Perdido, 2006).

Blixen, Samuel, *Seregni* (Ediciones de Brecha, 1997).

——, *Sendic* (Trilce, 2000).

Block de Behar, Lisa, 'Del silencio a la elocuencia: la resistencia crítica o los aspectos ambivalentes de un discurso en crisis', Saúl Sosnowski (ed.), *Represión, exilio y democracia: la cultura uruguaya* (EBO, 1987), 179–91.

—— (ed.), *Diseminario. La deconstrucción: otro descubrimiento de América* (XYZ, 1987).

Borges, Jorge Luis, 'Borges y Emir', in Lisa Block de Behar (ed.), *Diseminario. La deconsrucción: otro descubrimiento de América* (XYZ, 1987), 117–18.

Bottaro, José R., *25 años de movimiento sindical uruguayo* (Acción Sindical Uruguaya, 1985).

Brando, Oscar (ed.), *Uruguay hoy. Paisaje después del 31 de octubre* (Ediciones del Caballo Perdido, 2004).

'Brecha', 'La caída de los "socialismos reales" y el destino de la izquierda', *Brecha*, 333 (16 April 1992), a special Forum section page-numbered i–xx.

Brunner, José Joaquín, *América Latina: cultura y modernidad* (Mexico, Grijalbo, 1992).

Bruschera, Oscar, '¿Qué hacer?', parts 1–3, *Marcha*, (25 October, 1 and 8 November 1968).

——, 'Las líneas fundamentales del programa del Frente Amplio', *Cuadernos de Marcha* 47(1971), 3–7.

——, *Los partidos tradicionales* (Librosur, 1984).

——, *Las décadas infames* (Linardi y Risso, 1986).

Buquet, Daniel, 'Uruguay fin de siglo. Tiempos de coalición', *Nueva Sociedad*, 155 (May–June 1998), 6–14.

—— (ed.), *Las claves del cambio: ciclo electoral y nuevo gobierno 2004/5* (EBO, 2005).

—— (ed.), *¿Y ahora? El primer ciclo del gobierno de izquierda en Uruguay* (EBO, 2006).

Burity, Joanildo A., 'The Impertinence of Intellectuals. Democracy and Postmodernity in Latin America', *Angelaki*, ii, 3 (1997), 43–65.

Butazzoni, Fernando, 'Entre la subversion y la obediencia', Brecha (19 September 1986), n.p.

——, 'Una visión cultural del Uruguay de los 80', *Casa de las Américas*, 149 (July-August 1988), 44–55.

——, *Seregni-Rosencof, mano a mano* (Aguilar, 2002).

Caetano, Gerardo, 'Del primer batllismo al terrismo: crisis simbólica y reconstrucción del imaginario colectivo', *Cuadernos del CLAEH*, 49 (1989), 85–106.

——, 'Notas para una revisión histórica sobre la cuestión nacional en el Uruguay', *Revista de Historia*, 3 (1992), 59–78.

——, 'Entre el Parlamento y los ciudadanos. El espacio de la política y sus avatares en el imaginario de los uruguayos', in Hugo Achugar (ed.), *Como el Uruguay no hay* (Museo Municipal de Bellas Artes Juan Manuel Blanes, 2000), 27–56.

——, 'El árbol y el bosque en el Uruguay de la recesión', *Estudios Internacionales* [Chile], xxxv, 139 (October-December 2002), 107–18.

——, 'Democracia y cultura: reflexión en torno a algunos desafíos contemporáneos', in Hugo Achugar & Sonia D'Alessandro (eds.), *Global/local: democracia, memoria, identidades* (Trilce, 2002), 109–34.

——, 'Marco histórico y cambio político en dos décadas de democracia. De la transición democrática al gobierno de la izquierda (1985–2005)', in Caetano (ed.), *20 años de democracia* (Taurus, 2005), 15–73.

——, 'Pasado-futuro: una polaridad crucial y resistente', in Caetano & Rodrigo Arocena (eds.), *Uruguay: Agenda 2020* (Santillana, 2007), 13–60.

——, '"Nunca más" y no violencia: las exigencias de un "momento de verdad" y la construcción de una "memoria ejemplar"', in Constanza Moreira (ed.), *La hora de las reformas. Gobierno, actores y políticas en el Uruguay 2006–7* (Informe de coyuntura no. 7, Instituto de Ciencia Política/EBO, 2007), 21–36.

—— (ed.), *Uruguay hacia el siglo XXI: identidad, cultura, integración, representación* (Trilce, 1994).

Caetano, Gerardo & Garcé, Adolfo, 'Ideas, política y nación en el Uruguay del siglo xx', in Oscar Terán (ed.). *Ideas en el siglo: intelectuales y cultura en el siglo xx latinoamericano* (Buenos Aires, Siglo xxi, 2004, 309–422.

Caetano, Gerardo & Rilla, José, 'Izquierda y tradición en Uruguay', La Lupa section, *Brecha* (1 July 1988), n.p.

——, 'La juvenil madurez: conversación con José Pedro Barrán', in Fernando Pita (ed.), *Las brechas en la historia, 2: los temas* (Brecha, 1996), 135–47.

——, *Breve historia de la dictadura (1973–1985)* (2nd ed., EBO, 2006).

——, *Historia contemporánea del Uruguay: de la colonia al Mercosur* (2nd ed., Fin de Siglo, 2005).

Caetano, Gerardo, Gallardo, Javier & Rilla, José, *La izquierda uruguaya: tradición, innovación y política* (Trilce, 1995).

—— et al., *La hora de las reformas. Gobierno, actores y políticas en el Uruguay 2006–2007* (EBO, 2007).

'CaféAlaTurca', 'Rafael Bayce [entrevista]', *Café a la Turca*, 4 (1997), at <http://www.cafealaturca.8m.com/EntrBAYCE.htm> (accessed April 2005).

Calderón, Fernando (ed.), *Imágenes desconocidas: la modernidad en la encrucijada postmoderna* (Buenos Aires, CLACSO, 1988).

Calderón, Fernando & dos Santos, Mario R., 'Hacia un nuevo orden estatal en América Latina. Veinte tesis socio-políticas y un corolario de cierre', *Estudios Sociales Centroamericanos*, 53 (1990), 125–50.

Camp, Roderic A., *Intellectuals and the State in Twentieth Century Mexico* (Texas UP, 1985).

Campodónico, Miguel A., '"Escribir es para mí en realidad una función natural y es mi oficio" [entrevista con Mario Benedetti]', *Aquí*, 231 (1987), 12–13.

——, *Radicales y moderados: Danilo Astori. Vida y pensamiento político* (Linardi y Risso, 2004).

Canel, Eduardo, 'Municipal Decentralization and Participatory Democracy: Building a New Mode of Urban Politics in Montevideo City?', *European Review of Latin American and Caribbean Studies*, 71 (October 2001), 25–46.

Castañeda, Jorge G., *Utopia Unarmed: The Latin American Left After the Cold War* (New York, Knopf, 1993).

——, *Compañero: The Life and Death of Che Guevara* (London, Bloomsbury, 1997).

Castagnola, José Luis & Mieres, Pablo, 'La ideología política de la dictadura', in Carmen Appratto et al., *El Uruguay de la dictadura (1973–1985)* (EBO, 2004), 113–44.

Castro, Julio, 'La unión de las izquierdas', *Marcha* (30 September 1966), 6.

——, 'El Frente Amplio, un horizonte de esperanza', *Cuadernos de Marcha*, 53 (1971), 5–7.

——, 'Una larga marcha' [orig. *Marcha* (12 February 1971)], *Cuadernos de Marcha*, Tercera Epoca, i, 7 (1985), 53–5.

——, 'Una elección diferente' [orig. *Marcha* (1 October 1971)], *Cuadernos de Marcha*, Tercera Epoca, i, 7 (1985), 56–7.

——, 'La lucha recién empieza' [orig. *Marcha* (3 December1971)], *Cuadernos de Marcha*, Tercera Epoca, i, 7 (1985), 58–9.

Castro Urioste, José, 'Urgencias y rumores en la ensayística de Mario Benedetti: una lectura sobre *El país de la cola de paja*', *Anthropos*, 132 (May 1992), 82–8.

Castro Vega, Jorge, 'Con humildad y sin permiso', *Aquí*, 183 (9 December 1986), 15.

——, 'Con los pies en la tierra', *La Revista del Sur*, 1 (Suplemento) (August 1987), 77.

——, 'Hacia una cultura de la restauración', *Cuadernos de Marcha*, 3rd series, 28 (February 1988), 63–8.

Caula, Nelson, (ed.), *El diario de Enrique Erro. La cárcel, el exilio y la transición* (Rosebud, 1998).

—— & Machín, Hugo (eds.), *¿Izquierda?* (Rosebud, 1994).

—— & Silva, Andrés, *Alto el Fuego: Fuerzas Armadas y Tupamaros* (5th ed., Monte Sexto, 1988).

Centro Militar/Centro de Oficiales Retiradas de las Fuerzas Armadas, *Nuestra verdad: 1960–1980, la lucha contra el terrorismo* (Artemisa, 2007).

Centro Uruguay Independiente , *CNT: 1964–1965. Documentos sindicales*, I (CUI, 1984).

——, *CNT: programa y estatutos* (CUI, Documentos Sindicales No. 2, 1984).

——, *El pueblo delibera. El Congreso del Pueblo veinte años después* (CUI, 1985).

Chavez, Daniel, 'Del Frente Amplio a la Nueva Mayoría. La izquierda uruguaya ante la perspectiva del gobierno', in César A. Rodríguez Garavito et al., *La nueva izquierda en América Latina* (Bogotá, Norma, 2005), 147–90.

Ciganda, Juan Pedro, *Sin desensillar . . . y hasta que aclare. La resistencia a la dictadura, AEBU, 1973–1984* (Cauce, 2007).

Clericetti, Julio L., *Historia política uruguaya 1938–1972* (n. publ., 1984).

Cogorno, José L., 'Visión organizativa a través del análisis histórico del PDC', in INDAL, *Democracia Cristiana y la formación del Frente Amplio* (2nd ed., INDAL, 1973), 103–10.

Collazo, Ariel, 'El Uruguay no es excepción', *Pensamiento Crítico* (July 1967), 83–109.

Comité Ejecutico de la Unión Popular, 'Llamamiento al pueblo urugayo', *Marcha* (24 August 1962), 2.

Comité Ejecutivo Nacional del Partido Socialista, 'Declaración', *El Popular* (2 September 1963), n.p.

Congreso del Pueblo, 'Programa de soluciones a la crisis', *El Popular*, 3062 (16 August 1965), 9.

——, 'Llamado al pueblo uruguayo', *El Popular*, 3062 (16 August 1965), 10.

Conteris, Híber, 'El Uruguay postmoderno y la pérdida de la memoria', in Adrina J. Bergero & Fernando Reati (eds.), *Memoria colectiva y políticas del olvido: Argentina y Uruguay, 1970–1990* (Buenos Aires, Beatriz Viterbo, 1997), 89–114.

Corbo Longuiera, Baniel J., *El plebiscito constitucional de 1980* (Puerta del Sol, 2006).

Cores, Hugo, 'La lucha de los gremios solidarios', *Brecha* (11 August 1989), 15–18.

——, *El 68 uruguayo. Los antecedentes. Los hechos. Los debates* (EBO, 1997).

Coronil, Fernando, 'El estado de América Latina y sus Estados', *Nueva Sociedad,* 210 (2007), 203–15.

Cortázar, Julio, 'Politics and the Intellectual in Latin America', in Jaime Alazraki and Ivan Ivask (eds.), *The Final Island: The Fiction of Julio Cortázar* (Oklahoma University Press, 1978), 37–44.

Cosío Villegas, Daniel, 'El intelectual mexicano y la política', in Careaga, G, (ed.), *Los intelectuales y el poder* (Mexico, Sepsetentas, 1972), 115–34.

Cosse, Gustavo, 'Acerca de la democracia, el sistema político y la movilización social: el caso del "ruralismo" uruguayo', *Estudios Rurales Latinoamericanos,* v, 1 (1983), 77–100.

Cosse, Isabel & Markarian, Vania, *Memorias de la historia. Una aproximación a la conciencia histórica nacional* (Trilce, 1994).

——, *1975: Año de la Orientalidad. Identidad, memoria e historia en dictadura* (Trilce, 1996).

Costa Bonino, Luis, *Crisis de los partidos tradicionales y movimiento revolucionario en el Uruguay* (EBO, 1985).

Cotelo, Ruben, 'Repentinismo y mito', *El País* (9 January 1961), 16.

——, *Los contemporáneos*, Capítulo Oriental 2 (CEDAL, 1968).

——, 'Introducción: dramatis personae', in Carlos Real de Azúa, *Tercera posición, nacionalismo revolucionario y tercer mundo* (Cámara de Representantes de la República Oriental del Uruguay, 1997), Vol. 3, 813–24.

Couriel, Alberto, *Globalización, democracia e izquierda en América Latina* (EBO, 1996).

——, *La izquierda y el Uruguay del futuro* (2nd ed., EBO, 2004).

——, 'Uruguay: basic criteria for a left project', *Diplomacy, Strategy & Politics,* 3 (2005), 144–70.

Cultelli, Andrés, *La revolución necesaria. Contribución a la autocrítica del MLN* (Buenos Aires, Colihue, 2006).

Da Rosa, Julio C., *Civilización y terrofobia: apuntes de campo y ciudad* (Diálogo, 1968).

Dagnino, Evelina, 'Culture, Citizenship and Democracy: Changing Discourses and Practices of the Latin American Left', in Sonia E. Alvarez, Evelina Dagnino & Arturo Escobar (eds.), *Cultures of Politics and Politics of Cultures. Revisioning Latin American Social Movements* Boulder, Westview Press, 1998), 33–63.

D'Auria, Verónica & Guerra, Silvia, *Conversaciones oblicuas entre la cultura y el poder. Entrevistas a diez intelectuales uruguayos* (Ediciones Caracol al Galope, 2001).

Debray, Regis, *The Revolution on Trial* (London, Penguin, 1978).

Delgado Aparaín, Mario, 'Reflexiones sobre una generación desgeneracionada', *La Hora* (1 November 1986), 8–9.

D'Elía, Germán, *El Uruguay neo-Batllista* (EBO, 1983).

Demasi, Carlos, 'La dictadura militar: un tema pendiente', in Hugo Achugar (ed.), *Uruguay: cuentas pendientes. Dictadura, memorias y desmemorias* (Trilce, 1995), 29–49.

—— (ed.), *El regimen cívico-militar (1973–1980)* (FCU, 2004).

——, Rico, Alvaro & Rossal, Marcelo, 'Hechos y sentidos de la política y la pospolítica: Transición y postransición democrática', in Oscar Brando (ed.), *Uruguay hoy: Paisaje después del 31 de octubre* (Ediciones del Caballo Perdido, 2004), 7–77.

Derrida, Jacques, 'Nacionalidad y nacionalismo filosófico' and 'Psyché: invenciones del otro', in Lisa Block de Behar (ed.), *Diseminario. La deconsrucción: otro descubrimiento de América* (XYZ, 1987), 27–106.

de Armas, Gustavo, 'De la sociedad hiperintegrada al país fragmentado. Crónica del último tramo de un largo recorrido', Gerardo Caetano (ed.), *20 años de democracia* (Taurus, 2005), 269–303.

—— & Garcé, Adolfo, *Uruguay y su conciencia crítica: intelectuales y política en el siglo xx* (Trilce, 1997).

—— (eds.), *Técnicos y política* (Trilce, 2000).

de Armas, Gustavo, Garcé, Adolfo & Yaffé, Jaime, 'Introducción al estudio de las tradiciones ideológicas de los partidos uruguayos en el siglo xx', *Política y Gestión*, vii, 5 (2003), 77–101.

de Diego, José Luis, 'Intelectuales y política en los ochenta', *Hispamérica*, 103 (2006), 101–8.

de Sierra, Gerónimo, 'La izquierda de la transición', in Gillespie, Charles et al., *Uruguay y la democracia* (EBO, 1984), I, 149–60.

de Sierra Nieves, Carmen, 'Intelectuales y universitarios uruguayos frente a la "Guerra Fría" y la "Tercera Posición"', *Ciclos*, viii, 16 (1998), 125–41.

de Torres Wilson, José, *La conciencia histórica uruguaya* (Feria del Libro, 1964).

di Candia, César, 'Reportaje a Mario Benedetti', *Búsqueda* (5 January 1989), 31.

——, *Tiempos de tolerancia, tiempos de ira* (Fin de Siglo, 2005).

——, *Memoria: el camino de la violencia uruguaya (1940–1973)* (6 vols., El País, 2006).

Díaz, José Pedro, 'Heridas de nuestra cultura', *Cuadernos de Marcha*, 3rd series, 12 (October 1986), 71–5.

——, 'La cultura silenciosa', in Saúl Sosnowski (ed.), *Represión, exilio y democracia: La cultura uruguaya* (EBO/University of Maryland, 1987), 201–19.

Donas, Ernesto, & Milstein, Denise, *Cantando la ciudad: Lenguajes, imaginarios y mediaciones en la canción popular montevideana (1962–1999)* (Nordan Comunidad, 2003).

Draper, Susana, 'Cartografías de una ciudad posletrada: La república de Platón (Uruguay, 1993–1995)', *Revista Iberoamericana*, lxix, 202 (January–March 2003), 31–49.

Draper, Susana & Betancor, Orlando, 'Filosofía, ¿crítica cultural? Un diálogo con Ruben Tani', *Relaciones*, 206 (2001), 4–5.

Duran, Manuel, 'The Beleaguered Latin American Intellectual', *Ventures*, 7 (Fall, 1977), 55–60.

Dutrénit Bielous, Silvia, 'Se cruzan los relatos: memoria personal y reconstrucción histórica', *Estudios Sociales*, 25 (2003), 119–46.

Eco, Umberto, *Apocalypse Postponed* (ed. Robert Lumley, London, Flamingo, 1995).

'El Popular', 'Mesa redonda de escritores en el FIDEL', *El Popular* (10 August 1963), n.p.

——, 'La hora de la unidad ha sonado', *El Popular* (9 July 1963), 3.

——, 'Ahora sí, el pueblo sabe cuál es el camino', *El Popular* (10 August 1971), 7.

Escanlar, Gustavo, González, Rosario & Muñoz, Carlos, 'Arte en la lona. Un cross a la mandíbula', *Cuadernos de Marcha*, 3rd series, 31 (1988), 75–8.

Espinosa, Gustavo, 'Trampas para cazar al otro', <www.henciclopedia/org.uy/autores/Espinosa/Trampas/htm>.

Esquivel, Daniel, *Tabaré Vázquez: seductor de multitudes* (Fin de Siglo, 1997).

Falero, Alfredo & Vera, Angel, 'Transformaciones sociales y campo popular en Uruguay: construcción de alternativas y escenarios posibles', in Oscar Brando (ed.), *Uruguay hoy. Paisaje después del 31 de octubre* (Ediciones del Caballo Perdido, 2004), 145–64.

Faroppa, Luis A., *Políticas para una economía desequilibrada: Uruguay 1958–1981* (EBO, 1984).

Fasano Mertens, Federico, *Después de la derrota. Un eslabón débil llamado Uruguay* (Mexico, Nueva Imagen, 1980).

Ferman, Claudia, 'In Defence of Modernity: Its Utopian idea, its Revolutionary Memory, and its Cultural Criticism. An Interview with Nicolás Casullo', in Ferman (ed.), *The Postmodern in Latin and Latino Cultural Narratives* (New York and London, Garland, 1996), 63–76.

Fernández, Nelson, *Quién es quién en el gobierno de la izquierda* (Fin de Siglo, 2004).

Fernández, Pablo, 'El poder de la irreverencia', *Brecha*, 920 (17 July 2003), 25.

Fernández Huidobro, Eleuterio, *La tregua armada* (TAE, 1989).

——, *Historia de los tupamaros* (vol. 3, TAE, 1990).

——, *Artigas el olvidado* (EBO, 2000).

Fernández Retamar, Roberto, 'Conversación con Mario Benedetti', *Cambio*, ii, 5 (1976), 23–30.

FIDEL, 'Un llamado a la unidad', *El Popular* (1 July 1963), 1.

Figueredo, María, *Poesía y canción popular: su convergencia en el siglo xx, Uruguay 1960–1985* (Linardi y Risso, 2005).

Filguiera, Carlos H. (ed.), *Movimientos sociales en el Uruguay de hoy* (EBO, 1985).

Filgueira, Fernando et al., 'Los dos ciclos del Estado uruguayo en el siglo xx', Instituto de Ciencia Política, *El Uruguay del siglo xx: la política* (EBO, 2003), 173–204.

Finch, M. H. J., *A Political Economy of Uruguay since 1870* (London, MacMillan, 1981).

Fink, Leon, *Progressive Intellectuals and the Dilemmas of Democratic Commitment* (Cambridge [MA], Harvard UP, 1997).

Flo, J., 'Problemas de la juventud en nuestro país', in Carlos Real de Azúa (ed.), *Problemas de la juventud uruguaya* (Marcha, 1954), 143–56.

Fornet, Ambrosio (ed.), *Recopilación de textos sobre Mario Benedetti* (Havana, Casa de Las Américas, 1976).

Franco, Jean, *The Decline and Fall of the Lettered City: Latin America and the Cold War* (Cambridge [MA], Harvard UP, 2002).

Franco, Rolando, *Democracia a la uruguaya* (El Libro Libre, 1984).

—— (ed.), *Sociología del desarrollo, políticas sociales y democracia* (Mexico, Siglo XXI, 2001).

Frega, Ana et al., *Historia del Uruguay en el siglo xx (1890–2005)* (EBO, 2007).

Galeano, Eduardo, 'Los partidos obreros resisten el impacto', *Marcha*, 942 (19 December 1958), 6 [under full surname 'Hughes Galeano].

——, 'Nueva parte del tema', *Marcha*, 943 (26 December 1958), 6 [under full surname 'Hughes Galeano'].

——, '¿El partido socialista nace de nuevo?', *Marcha* (30 March 1962), n.p.

Gallo, Alberto, 'Jóvenes jóvenes I (en literatura)', *Brecha* (21 June 1989), La Lupa section, n.p.

Ganón, Isaac., *Estructura social del Uruguay* (Editorial As, 1966).

Garcé, Adolfo, 'Tres fases en la relación entre intelectuales y política en Uruguay (1830–1989)', in Gustavo de Armas & Adolfo Garcé (eds.), *Técnicos y política* (Trilce, 2000), 55–83.

——, *Ideas y competencia política en Uruguay (1960–1973): Revisando el 'fracaso' de la CIDE* (Trilce 2002).

——, *Donde hubo fuego* (Fin de Siglo, 2006).

—— & Yaffé, Jaime, *La era progresista* (Fin de Siglo, 2004; 2nd ed., Fin de Siglo, 2005).

Gargiulo, Martin, 'The Uruguayan Labor Movement in the Post-Authoritarian Period', in Edward C. Epstein (ed.), *Labor Autonomy and the State* (Boston, Unwin Hyman, 1991), 219–46.

Garretón, Manuel A., 'From Authoritarianism to Political Democracy: A Transition That Needs Rethinking', in Luis Albala-Bertrand (ed.), *Democratic Culture and Governance* (New York/Gaithersberg, UNESCO/Hispamérica, 1992), 21–33.

——, 'Modelos y liderazgos en América Latina', *Nueva Sociedad*, 205 (2006), 102–13.

Gatto, Hebert, 'Izquierda tradicional y nueva izquierda', *Zeta*, 15 (May 1987), 14–19.

——, 'Democracia y revolución', *Cuadernos de Marcha*, 3rd series, 43 (May 1989), 43–9.

——, *El cielo por asalto. El Movimiento de Liberación Nacional (Tupamaros) y la izquierda uruguaya (1963–1972)* (Taurus, 2004).

Gelman, Juan, 'Mario Benedetti: "el escritor es un trabajador como tantos"', *Crisis*, ii, 19 (1974), 40–50.

Gillespie, Charles, *The Breakdown of Democracy in Uruguay: Alternative Political Models* (Washington, Wilson Center Latin American Program Working Paper No. 143, 1984).

——, *Negotiating Democracy: Politicians and Generals in Uruguay* (Cambridge UP, 1991).

—— et al., *Uruguay y la democracia* (3 vols., EBO, 1984).

Gillespie, Charles and González, Luis E., 'Uruguay: the Survival of Old and Autonomous Institutions', in Larry Diamond, Juan J. Linz and Seymour Lipset, (eds.), *Democracy in Developing Countries, Vol. 4: Latin America* (Boulder, Lynne Reimer/London, Adamantine, 1991), 207–45.

Giménez, Fabián & Villagrón, Alejandro, *Estética de la oscuridad: posmodernidad, periferia y mass media en la cultura de los noventa* (Trazas, 1995).

Goicoechea Pérez, Gastón, 'El recurso del miedo', in Abella, Alcides, *1968 Uruguay 1985*, (Vol. 3, EBO, 2006), 45–59.

Goldfrank, Benjamin, 'The Fragile Flower of Local Democracy: A Case Study of Decentralization/Participation in Montevideo', *Politics & Society*, xxx, 1 (2002), 51–83.

González, Guillermo, 'El Uruguay, su impulso y su freno', *Brecha* (7 August 1992), 3.

González, Julián, 'La cuestión militar: tranquilidad en el frente y un gran desafío', in Constanza Moreira (ed.), *La hora de las reformas. Gobierno, actores y políticas en el Uruguay 2006–7* (EBO, 2007), 214–20.

González, Luis, *Uruguay: una apertura inesperada* (CIESU/EBO, 1984).

González Bermejo, Ernesto, 'Encuentro de compañeros y la unidad crítica', *Marcha*, 1575 (24 December 1971), 10–11 and 19.

——, 'Al término de un banquete interminable', *Brecha* (4 December 1992), 15–17.

González Sierra, Y., *Cronología histórica del movimiento sindical uruguayo. Hechos, resoluciones políticas y eventos sindicales, 1870–1984* (CIEDUR, 1989).

Graceras, Ulíses, *Los intelectuales y la política en el Uruguay* (El País, 1970).

Graham-Yooll, Andrew, *After the Despots: Latin American Views and Interviews* (London, Bloomsbury, 1991).

Gregory, Stephen, 'Bourgeois Contentment and the Defeat of Utopian Desire in Mario Benedetti's *Primavera con una esquina rota*', *Anales* [Sydney], i, 2 (1992), 81–96.

——, 'Uruguay as a Problem and the National Book Industry, 1960–1973', *Anales* [Sydney], iii, 2 (1994), 43–58.

——, 'The Road or The Inn? Mario Benedetti as Activist and the Movimiento de Independientes 26 de Marzo', forthcoming in *Journal of Iberian and Latin American Research* [Melbourne].

Gutiérrez, Carlos M., 'La ilusión frentista, 1: la propuesta del PDC', *Marcha* (28 June 1968), 8–9.

——, '¿Hacia un tercer partido?', *Marcha* (18 October 1968), 11.

Halperin Donghi, Tulio, *El espejo de la historia. Problemas argentinos y perspectivas hispanoamericanas* (Buenos Aires, Sudamericana, 1987).

Hamed, Amir, *Retroescritura* (Fin de Siglo, 1998).

——, 'Uruguay versus los buenos: minmanual para evadir toda emergencia' [speech given in December 2002], at <www.henciclopedia.org.uy/autores/Hamed/Emergente.html>.

Handelman, Howard, 'Labor-Industrial Conflict and the Collapse of Uruguayan Democracy', *Journal of Interamerican Studies and world Affairs*, xxiv, 4 (1981), 371–94.

Harnecker, Marta (ed.), *Frente Amplio: los desafíos de una izquierda legal* (4 vols., La República, 1991).

Hopenhayn, Martin, *No Apocalypse, No Integration: Modernism and Postmodernism in Latin America* (trans. Cynthia M. Tompkins and Elizabeth R. Horan, Durham, Duke UP, 2001).

Iglesias, Enrique, *Uruguay: una propuesta de cambio* (Arca, 1966).

INDAL, *Partido Comunista del Uruguay y la formación del Frente de Izquierda* (2nd ed., Heverlee-Louvain, INDAL, 1972).

——, *Democracia cristiana del Uruguay y la formación del Frente Amplio* (2nd ed., Caracas, INDAL, 1973).

——, *El Frente Amplio del Uruguay y las elecciones de 1971* (Heverlee-Louvain, INDAL, 1973).

Instituto de Ciencia Política, *El Uruguay del siglo xx: la política* (EBO, 2003).

Intendencia Municipal de Montevideo, 'Presupuesto participativo ciclo 2007' at <www.montevideo.gub.uy>.

Islas, Ariadna & Frega, Ana, 'Identidades uruguayas: del mito de la sociedad homogénea al reconocimiento de la pluralidad', in Frega et al., *Historia del Uruguay en el siglo xx (1890–2005)* (EBO, 2007), 359–92.

Jacob, Raúl, *Benito Nardone: El Ruralismo hacia el poder* (EBO, 1981).

——, *El Uruguay de Terra, 1931–1938* (EBO, 1983).

Junta de Comandantes en Jefe, *Las Fuerzas Armadas al pueblo uruguayo* (2 vols., Junta de Comandantes en Jefe, 1976 and 1978).

Labrousse, Alain, *The Tupamaros* (London, Penguin, 1973).

Laclau, Ernesto & Mouffe, Chantal, *Hegemony and Socialist Strategy. Towards a Radical Democracy* (2nd ed., London, Verso, 2001).

Lagos, Marta, 'A apearse de la fantasía: Hugo Chávez y los liderazgos en América Latina', *Nueva Sociedad*, 205 (2006), 92–101.

Laguarda, Manuel, 'Reflexiones acerca de la ruptura', *Alternativa Socialista* (30 March 1989), n.p.

——, 'Socialismo o reformismo desde lo alto', *Cuadernos de Marcha*, 3rd series, 44 (June 1989), 59–65.

——, 'Socialismo o reformismo desde lo alto (segunda parte)', *Cuadernos de Marcha*, 3rd series, 45 (July 1989), 27–30.

Lamolle, Guillermo, *Cual retazo de los suelos. Anécdotas, invenciones y meditaciones sobre el Carnaval en general y la murga en particular* (Trilce, 2005).

Lanza, Edison & Tulbovitz, Ernesto, *Tabaré Vázquez: misterios de un liderazgo que cambió la historia* (Alcierre, 2005).

Lanzaro, Jorge (ed.), *La izquierda uruguaya entre la oposición y el gobierno* (Fin de Siglo, 2004).

Larsen, Neil, *Reading North by South. On Latin American Literature, Culture and Politics* (Minneapolis, Minnesota UP, 1995).

Lasca, Moisés, 'Los artistas e intelectuales en el Frente Amplio', *Estudios*, 59 (1971), 93–7.

Lechner, Norbert, *Estado y política en América Latina* (2nd ed., Mexico, Siglo XXI, 1983).

——, 'De la revolución a la democracia. El debate intelectual en América del Sur', *Opciones*, 6 (1985), 57–72.

——, *La democratización en el contexto de una cultura postmoderna* (Santiago, FLACSO, Documento de Trabajo no. 292, 1986).

——, 'In Search of the Lost Community', in Luis Albala-Bertrand (ed.), *Democratic Culture and Governance* (New York/Gaithersberg, UNESCO/Hispamérica, 1992), 63–8.

Leicht, Fernando, *Cero a la izquierda. Una biografía de Jorge Zabalza* (Letraeñe, 2007).

Lepro, Alfredo, *Refrescando la memoria: Jorge Pacheco Areco, Presidente de la República, 1967–1972* (no publ., 1983).

Lerin, Francois & Torres, Cristina, *Historia política uruguaya (1873–1980)* (Ed. Del Nuevo Mundo, 1987).

Lessa, Alfonso, *La revolución imposible* (Fin de Siglo, 2003).

Linn, Tomás, 'El turno de las nuevas generaciones: ¿Parricidas éstos o filicidas aquéllos?', *Cuadernos de Marcha*, 3rd series, 28 (February 1988), 69–71.

——, 'La necesaria mudanza interior', *Cuadernos de Marcha*, 3rd series, 35 (September 1988), 3–6.

Liscano, Carlos, *Conversaciones con Tabaré Vázquez* (Ediciones del Caballo Perdido, 2003).

Lockhart, Washington, *El Uruguay de veras* (Alfa, 1969).

Luna, Juan Pablo, *La política desde el llano. Conversaciones con militantes barriales* (EBO, 2004).

Macadar, Luis (ed.), *La crisis uruguaya y el problema nacional* (CINVE/EBO, 1984).

Machado Carlos, *Historia de los orientales, Tomo III: De Batlle a los '70* (EBO, 1997).

—— (ed.), *Izquierdas y derechas en América Latina. Documentos* (Editorial Patria Grande, 1968.

Machado Ferrer, Martha and Fagúndez Ramos, Carlos, *Los años duros: cronología documentada (1964–1973)* (Monte Sexto, 1987).

Maggi, Carlos, *El Uruguay y su gente* [1963] (3rd ed., Alfa, 1967).

——, *Gardel, Onetti y algo más* (Alfa, 1964).

——, *Sociedad y literatura en el presente: el "boom" editorial*, Capítulo Oriental 3 (CEDAL, 1968).

——, *Los militares, la televisión y otras razones de uso interno* (Arca, 1986).

——, *El Uruguay de la tábula rasa* (Fin de Siglo, 1992).

Maidanik, Mauricio, 'Por un diálogo militante', *Marcha*, 1279 (5 November 1965), 30–1.

Mántaras Loedel, Graciela, 'La generación del 45', *Prólogo*, 1 (1968), 13–22.

Marchesi, Aldo, '¿"Guerra" o "terrorismo de estado"? Recuerdos enfrentados sobre el pasado reciente uruguayo', in Elizabeth Jelin (ed.), *Las conmemoraciones: las disputas en las fechas 'in-felices'* (Madrid, Siglo XXI, 2002), 101–47.

—— et al., *El presente de la dictadura. Estudios y reflexiones a 30 años del golpe de estado en Uruguay* (Trilce, 2004).

Markarian, Vivian, *Left in Transformation: Uruguayan Exiles and the Latin American Human Rights Networks* (London and New York, Routledge, 2005).

Martínez, Virginia, *Tiempos de dictadura 1973/1985* (EBO, 2007).

Martínez Moreno, Carlos, 'Crepúsculo en Arcadia: la institucionalidad y su derrumbe a la uruguaya', in Luis Benvenuto et al., *Uruguay hoy* (Buenos Aires, Siglo XXI, 1971), 405–55.

Martorelli, Horacio, *La promesa de las ciencias sociales* (CLAEH, 1983).

Masliah, Leo, 'La música popular. Censura y represión', in Saúl Sosnowski (ed.), *Represión, exilio y democracia* (EBO, 1987), 111–25.

Massera, José L., 'Libertad y democracia: contraseña unificadora', *Estudios*, 48 (1968), 49–53.

Maurada, Lauro, 'Revistas "subte" sin subterfugios', *Brecha* (22 April 1988), 30–1.

Mazzeo, Mario, *Charlando con Pepe Mujica* (Trilce, 2002).

——, *MPP: orígenes, ideas y protagonistas* (Trilce, 2005).

Mazzuchelli, Aldo, 'Los auténticos decadentes', <www.henciclopedia.org.uy /autores/Mazzuchelli/Benedetti.htm>.

——, 'El país' como sujeto de frases vacías', <www.henciclopedia.org.uy/autores/ Mazzuchelli/Frases.htm>.

MB [ME?], 'Fascismo y otras yerbas', *Marcha* 950 (6 Marcha 1959), 2.

Melgar, Alicia and Cancela Walter, *El desarrollo frustrado: 30 años de economía uruguaya, 1955–1985* (CLAEH/EBO, 1986).

Methol Ferré, Alberto, *¿Adónde va el Uruguay?* (no publ., 1958).

——, 'La parroqia entra en la historia', *Marcha* 940 (5 December 1958), 6.

——, '¿Quién gana las elecciones?', *Marcha* 941 (12 December 1958), 6 and 10.

——, 'Terciarios y moralismo', *Marcha* 942 (19 December 1958), 6 and 10.

——, 'Otra vuelta de tuerca', *Marcha* 943 (26 December 1958), 6–7.

——, *La crisis del Uruguay y el imperio británico* (Buenos Aires, A. Peña Lillo, 1960).

——, 'Adiós, Sr. Nardone', *Marcha* 1047 (24 February 1961), n. p.

——, *El Uruguay como problema* (Diálogo, 1967; [EBO, 1971 and Buenos Aires, A. Peña Lillo, 1973]).

——, 'La pérdida de un visible sistema de referencias', *Diplomacia en Acción*, i, 1 (1991), 37–40.

——, *Uruguay como problema, y otros trabajos*, in *Electroneurobiología*, xv, 5 (2007), 3–104, available as PDF at http://electroneubio.secyt.gov.ar/index2.htm.

Midaglia, Carmen, *Las formas de acción colectiva en Uruguay* (CIESU, 1992).

Mieres, Pablo, 'La reforma constitucional de 1996 en Uruguay y sus posibles efectos sobre los partidos y el sistema de partidos', *Cuadernos del CLAEH*, 80 (1997), 5–29.

Milán, Eduardo, 'Pequeñas notas sobre una gran depression cultural', *Cuadernos de Marcha*, 3rd series, 11 September 1986), 78–80.

Miller, Nicola, *In the Shadow of the State: Intellectuals and the Quest for National Identity in Twentieth Century Latin America* (London, Verso, 1999).

Miranda, Javier, 'Papelitos en los bolsillos (anotaciones para una agenda de derechos humanos)', in Gerardo Caetano (ed.), *Uruguay: Agenda 2020* (Taurus, 2007), 163–98.

——, 'Apuntes a mano alzada sobre políticas de derechos humanos en la coyuntura', in Constanza Moreira (ed.), *La hora de las reformas. Gobierno, actores y políticas en el uruguay 2006–7* (EBO, 2007), 37–47.

Moraña, Mabel, *Memorias de la generación fantasma. Crítica literaria 1973–1988* (Monte Sexto, 1988).

—— & Machín, Horacio (eds.), *MARCHA y América Latina* (Biblioteca de América, 2003).

Moreira, Constanza, *Democracia y desarrollo en Uruguay: una reflexión desde la cultura política* (Trilce, 1997).

——, *Final de juego. Del bipartidismo tradicional al triunfo de la izquierda en Uruguay* (Trilce, 2004).

—— (ed.), *La hora de las reformas. Gobierno, actores y políticas en el Uruguay, 2006–7* (Observatorio Político, Informe No. 7, Instituto de Ciencia Política/EBO, 2007).

Moreiras, Alberto, 'Postdictadura y reforma del pensamiento', *Revista de Crítica Cultural*, 7 (November 1993), 26–35.

Motta, Sara, 'Utopias Re-imagined: A Reply to Panizza', *Political Studies*, 54 (2006), 898–905.

Movimiento Revolucionario Oriental [MRO], 'Habla el MRO', *Marcha* (10 November 1961), n. p.

Mudrovcic, M. E., *Mundo Nuevo: cultura y guerra fría* (Rosario, Beatriz Viterbo, 1997).

Mujica, José 'Pepe' & Arocena, Rodrigo, *Cuando la izquierda gobierne* (ed. Mario Mazzeo, Trilce, 2003).

Munck, Ronaldo, 'After the Transition: Democratic Disenchantment in Latin America', *European Review of Latin American and Caribbean Studies*, 55 (1993), 7–19.

Muñoz, Carlos & Escanlar, Gustavo, 'Uruguay: ¿algo más que rock and roll?', *Cuadernos de Marcha*, 3rd series, 30 (April 1988), 65–6.

Murillo, César, 'Para una teoría de la mediocridad uruguaya', *Graffiti*, 31 (July 1993), 8–13.

Myers, Scott, *Los años oscuros. Uruguay 1967–1987* (Editorial Latina, 1997).

Nahum Benjamin, *Breve historia del Uruguay independiente* (EBO, 2003).

——, *Manual de historia del Uruguay, Tomo II: 1903–2000* (17th ed., EBO, 2003).

—— et al., *Historia uruguaya, Tomo 7: Crisis política y recuperación económica, 1930–1958* (EBO, 1989).

——, *Historia uruguaya, tomo 8, 1959–1973: El fin de la era liberal* (EBO, 1992).

Nattero, Víctor, 'Viviendo en Uruguay', at <http://www.freewebs. com/rockuruguayo80/Nattero.htm> (accessed December 2007).

Notaro, Jorge, *La política económica en el Uruguay 1968–1984* (EBO, 1984).

Núñez, Sandino, *Disneywar. Apuntes sobre violencia territorial en la aldea global* (Lapzus, 2006).

Oreggioni, Alberto (ed.), *Diccionario de literatura uruguaya*, vols. I and II (Arca/ Credisol, 1987); vol. III (Arca, 1991). Revised as *Nuevo diccionario de literatura uruguaya* (2 vols., EBO, 2003).

Palacios Videla, Ignacio, 'Conversación con Methol Ferré: un profeta realizado - del Uruguay opulento al Mercosur', *Todo es Historia*, xxv, 297 (1992), 33–47.

Panizza, Francisco, *Uruguay: Batllismo y después* (EBO, 1990).

——, 'Unarmed Utopia Revisited: The Resurgence of Left-of-Centre Politics in Latin America', *Political Studies*, 53 (2005), 716–34.

Partido Comunista del Uruguay, 'Llamado a todas las fuerzas antimperialistas, democráticas y avanzadas del país', *Estudios*, 18 (December 1960), 9–12.

P[artido] D[emócrata] C[ristiano], 'Una salida hacia el Uruguay nuevo', INDAL,

Democracia cristiana cristiana del Uruguay y la formación del Frente Amplio (2nd ed., Caracas, INDAL, 1973), 99–102.

Payssé González, Eduardo, 'Vivián Trías: la crisis y la unidad de las izquierdas', *Marcha* (20 October 1961), 7 and 22.

——, 'Ariel Collazo: "Artigas no era Blanco ni Colorado"', *Marcha* (8 December 1961), 8 and 26.

Peirano Basso, Luisa, *'Marcha' de Montevideo* (Buenos Aires, Javier Vergara, 2001).

Peláez, Fernando & Peveroni, Gabriel, *Rock que me hiciste mal. El rock uruguayo desde los 60 a nuestros días* (EBO, 2006).

Peluffo Linari, Gabriel, 'Como el Uruguay no hay, o el país de la inmaculada concepción', in Hugo Achugar (ed.), *Como el Uruguay no hay* (Museo Municipal de Bellas Artes Juan Manuel Blanes, 2000), 15–22.

Perelli, Carina, *Someter o convencer: el discurso military* (EBO, 1987).

——, 'Youth, Politics and Dictatorship in Uruguay', in Corradi, Juan E., Wiess Fagen, Peter & Garretón, Miguel A. (eds.), *Fear at the Edge: State Terror and Resistance in Latin America* (California UP, 1992), 212–35.

Perelli, Carina & Rial, Juan, *De mitos y memorias políticas: la represión, el miedo y después* (EBO, 1986).

Pérez, Romeo, 'La izquierda en la fase post-autoritaria', in Gillespie, Charles et al., *Uruguay y la democracia* (EBO, 1984), I, 129–47.

Petras, James, *The Left Strikes Back: Class Conflict in Latin America in the Age of Neoliberalism* (Boulder, Westview, 1999).

Petras, James & Morley, Morris, *US Hegemony under Siege: Class, Politics and Development in Latin America* (London and New York, Verso, 1990).

Petruccelli, José L., 'Consequences of Uruguayan Emigration: Research Note', *International Migration Review*, xiii, 3 (1979), 519–26.

Peveroni, Gabriel, 'Rock que me hiciste mal', at <www.henciclopedia.org.uy/Peveroni/Rockuruguayo.html>.

Pino, Mirian, 'El semanario *Marcha* de Uruguay: una genealogía de la crítica de la cultura en América Latina', *Revista de Crítica Literaria Latinamericana*, xxviii, 56 (2002), 141–56.

Pisani, Carlos O., *Sistema político-electoral del Uruguay, siglo XXI* (Arca, 2004).

Porzecanski, Teresa, 'Ficción y fricción de la narrativa de imaginación escrita dentro de fronteras', Saúl Sosnowski (ed.), *Represión, exilio y democracia: la cultura uruguaya* (EBO, 1987), 221–30.

——, 'Indios, africanos e inmigrantes europeos: la búsqueda del origen en los nuevos discursos del imaginario uruguayo', in Hugo Achugar (ed.), *Como el Uruguay no hay* (Museo Municipal de Bellas Artes Juan Manuel Blanes, 2000), 83–103.

'Praxis' Editorial Board, 'De redacción', *Praxis*, 1 (1967), 3–5.

Prego, Omar, *Reportaje a un golpe de estado* (La República, 1988).

——, '¿Hacia una cultura de la degradación?', *Cuadernos de Marcha*, 3rd series, 29 (March 1988), 59–63.

Queirolo, Rosario, 'Entrevista al edil Jorge Zabalza', in Luis E. González, *Los partidos políticos uruguayos en tiempos de cambio* (FCU, 1999), 115–16.

——, 'La tradicionalización del Frente Amplio: ¿pugna por contenidos organizacionales o institucionales?', in Luis E. González, *Los partidos políticos uruguayos en tiempos de cambio* (FCU, 1999), 87–127.

'Quidam', 'Fascismo uruguayo', *Marcha*, 942 (19 December 1942), 2.

Quijano, Carlos, 'Todos somos prisioneros', *Brecha* (12 June 1992), 32.

Quijano, José M., 'La ilusión frentista, 2: entre diálogo y represión', *Marcha* (28 June 1968), 9–10.

Rabotnikoff, Nora, 'Memoria y política: compromiso ético y pluralismo de interpretaciones', *Revista Uruguaya de Ciencia Política*, 9 (1996), 143–50.

Rama, Angel, "Testimonio, confesión y enjuiciamiento de historia literaria y nueva literatura uruguaya", *Marcha* (3 July 1959), 17B-22B, 30B.

——, 'El escritor y su país', *Marcha* (16 December 1960), n. p.

——, 'Los nuevos compañeros', *Marcha*, 1186 (27 December 1963), 2–4.

——, *La generación crítica 1939–1969* (Arca, 1972).

——, 'Otra vez la utopía, en el invierno de nuestro desconsuelo', *Cuadernos de Marcha*, 2nd Series, 1 (1979), 75–81.

——, 'La lección intelectual de *Marcha*', *Cuadernos de Marcha*, 2da Epoca, 19 (1982), 53–8.

——, *La ciudad letrada* (Hanover, Ediciones del Norte, 1984); in English as *The Lettered City* (trans. John C. Chasteen, Duke UP, 1996).

Rama, Carlos M., '¿Es posible un fascismo uruguayo?', parts 1 and 2, *Marcha*, 941 (12 December 1958), 6 and 10; 947 (13 February 1959), 6.

——, 'Es posible un fascismo uruguayo', *Marcha*, 951 (13 March 1959), 6.

——, *Sociología del Uruguay* (Buenos Aires, Eudeba, 1965).

——, *Uruguay en crisis* (El siglo Ilustrado, 1969).

——, 'Historia del movimiento obrero y social uruguayo', *Cuadernos Americanos*, ccxix, 4 (1978), 129–45.

Rama, Germán W., *El club político* (Arca, 1971).

——, *La democracia en Uruguay* (Buenos Aires, Grupo Editor Latinoamericano, 1987).

Ramírez Gallegos, Franklin, 'Mucho más que dos izquierdas', *Nueva Sociedad*, 205 (2006), 30–44.

Real de Azúa, Carlos, '¿Adónde va la cultura uruguaya?', *Marcha*, 885 (25 October 1957), 22–3.

——, 'Partidos políticos y literatura en el Uruguay', *Tribuna Universitaria*, 6–7 (1958), 101–35.

——, *Tercera posición, nacionalismo revolucionario y tercer mundo* [1963] (3 vols., Cámara de Representantes de la República Oriental del Uruguay, 1996–1997).

——, 'Legatarios de una demolición', *Marcha*, 1186 (27 December 1963), 7–8.

——, *El impulso y su freno* (EBO, 1964).

——, *Partidos, política y poder en el Uruguay (1971 – coyuntura y pronóstico)* (Universidad de la República, 1988), originally in Luis Benvenuto et al., *Uruguay hoy* (Buenos Aires, Siglo XXI, 1971), 143–321.

—— (ed.), *Problemas de la juventud uruguaya* (Marcha, 1954).

—— (ed.), *Antología del ensayo uruguayo contemporáneo*, (2 vols., Universidad de la República, 1964).

Remedi, Gustavo, 'Theorising Popular Culture Studies in Uruguay', *Studies in Latin American Popular Culture*, 15 (1996), 85–97.
——, *Carnival Theater. Uruguay's Popular Performers and National Culture* (trans. Amy Ferlazzo, Minneapolis, Minnesota UP, 2004 [Spanish original, 1996]).
Rey Tristán, Eduardo, *A la vuelta de la esquina: la izquierda revolucionaria uruguaya 1955–1973* (Fin de Siglo, 2005).
Reyes Daglio, César, 'El Congreso del FIDEL y los caminos de la unidad total de las izquierdas', *Estudios*, 26 (1963), 62–4.
Rial, Juan, *Partidos políticos, democracia y autoritarismo* (2 vols., CIESU/EBO, 1984).
——, 'El imaginario social. Los mitos políticos y utopías en el Uruguay. Cambios y permanencias durante y después del autoritarismo', in Saúl Sosnowski (ed.), *Represión, exilio y democracia: la cultura uruguaya* (EBO/University of Maryland, 1987), 63–89.
——, 'Makers And Guardians of Fear: Controlled Terror in Uruguay', in Juan E. Corradi, Peter Wiess Fagen, Miguel A. Garretón (eds.), *Fear at the Edge: State Terror and Resistance in Latin America* (California UP, 1992), 90–103.
Ribeiro, Ana, *Historia e historiadores nacionales (1940–1990)* (Academia Nacional de Letras, 1991).
Rico, Alvaro, 'El orden de los simulacros y el orden social en la restauración democrática' in his *Uruguay: cuentas pendientes. Dictadura, memorias y desmemorias* (Trilce, 1995), 63–120.
——, *Cómo nos domina la clase gobernante* (Trilce, 2005).
—— (ed.), *Uruguay: cuentas pendientes. Dictadura, memorias y desmemorias* (Trilce, 1995).
—— et al., *15 días que estremecieron al Uruguay: golpe de estado y huelga general* (Fin de Siglo, 2005).
Rilla, José, 'Uruguay 1980: transición y legitimidad plebiscitaria', *Nueva Sociedad*, 150 (1997), 77–83.
——, 'Cambiar la historia. Historia política y elite política en el Uruguay contemporáneo', *Revista Uruguaya de Ciencia Política*, 11 (1999), 107–27.
——, 'Historia, memoria y ciudadanía', in Gioscia, Laura (ed.), *Ciudadanía en tránsito. Perfiles para el debate* (EBO, 2001), 69–82.
——, *La actualidad del pasado. Usos de la historia en la política de partidos del Uruguay [1842–1972]* (Debate, 2008).
—— & Mieres, Pablo (eds.), *Transparencia y ciudadanía responsable* (CLAEH, 2007).
Roballo, Alba, 'Para salvar al Batllismo, me voy del Batllismo', *Cuadernos de Marcha*, 46 (1971), 67–71.
Rocca, Pablo, '35 años en *Marcha*: escritura y ambiente literario en *Marcha* y en el Uruguay, 1939–1974', *Nuevo Texto Crítico*, vi, 11 (1993), 3–151.
Rodríguez, Hector, 'El Congreso del Pueblo', *Marcha*, 1263 (16 July 1965), 6–7.
——, 'El elefante y la caja de fósforos', *Marcha*, 1268 (23 August 1965), 6–7.
——, *Nuestros sindicatos (1865–1965)* (Ediciones Uruguay, 1965).
——, *Sindicatos: participación y negociación* (FCU, 1985).
Rodríguez, Universindo et al., *El sindicalismo uruguayo* (Taurus, 2006).
Rodríguez Monegal, Emir, *Literatura uruguaya del medio siglo* (Alfa, 1966).

———, *Narradores de esta América* (Arca, 1969).

———, *El boom de la novela latinoamericana* (Caracas, Tiempo Nuevo, 1972).

———, *Jorge Luis Borges. A Literary Biography* (New York, Dutton, 1978).

———, 'Borges/De man/Derrida/Bloom', in Lisa Block de Behar (ed.), *Diseminario. La deconsrucción del otro: otro descubrimiento de América* (XYZ, 1987), 119–23.

Roland, Eduardo, *Contra cualquier muro: graffiti de la transición 1985–1989* (Ediciones de UNO/Vintén, 3rd ed., 1990).

Roniger, Luis & Sznadjer, Mario, 'The Legacy of Human Rights Violations and the Collective Memory of Redemocratized Uruguay', *Human Rights Quarterly*, 19 (1997), 55–77.

Rorty, Richard, *Philosophy and the Mirror of Nature* (Princeton UP, 1979).

Rosencof, Mauricio, *De puño y letra* (Tafalla, Txalaparta, 1998).

Rubio, Enrique, *La izquierda del futuro* (Marcha, 1999).

———, *Saber y poder. La cuestión democrática en la sociedad del conocimiento* (2003).

———, *Izquierdas y derechas en la mundialización* (EBO, 2007).

———, de Souza, Hebert & Pereira, Marcelo, *Coyuntura: respuesta y cambio* (CUI, 1985).

——— & Pereira, Marcelo, *Utopía y estrategia; democracia y socialismo* (Trilce, 1994).

Ruffinelli, Jorge, 'El país de adentro y el país de afuera', Saúl Sosnowski (ed.), *Represión, exilio y democracia: la cultura uruguaya* (EBO, 1987), 261–6.

———, 'Uruguay: dictadura y redemocratización. Un informe sobre la literatura 1973–1989', *Nuevo Texto Crítico*, 5 (1990), 37–66.

Ruz F., Mauricio, 'Doctrina de seguridad nacional: contribución a un debate', *Mensaje* [Chile], 261 (August 1977), 418–26.

Salinas, Julio A., 'La ofensiva ruralista de la década del 50 y las relaciones entre el estado y la sociedad uruguaya', *Estudios Rurales Latinoamericanos*, ii, 1 (1979), 56–76.

San Román, Gustavo, 'La *Enciclopedia Uruguaya*: nacionalismo paradójico', *Río de la Plata*, 26/7 (2003), 89–102.

———, *Soy celeste. Investigación sobre la identidad de los uruguayos* (Fin de Siglo, 2007).

Santi, Enrico Mario, 'Politics, Literature and the Intellectual in Latin America', in David W. Foster & Daniel Altamiranda (eds.), *Theoretical Debates in Latin American Literature* (New York, Garland, 1997), 335–52.

Sarlo, Beatriz, *Escenas de la vida posmoderna. Intelectuales, arte y videocultura en la Argentina* (Buenos Aires, Ariel, 1995). Also in English: *Scenes from Postmodern Life* (trans. Jon Beasley-Murray, Minneapolis, Minnesota UP, 2001).

Saunders, Frances Stonor, *Who Paid the Piper? The CIA and the Cultural Cold War* (London, Granta, 1999).

Scheletto, Salvador, 'Por el ojo de una cerradura. Una mirada sobre la experiencia de gobierno municipal de la izquierda en Montevideo (1990–2004)', in Jorge Lanzaro (ed.), *La izquierda uruguaya entre la oposición y el gobierno* (Fin de Siglo, 2004), 381–434.

Schwartz, Niko, 'La unión de las izquierdas', *Marcha*, 942 (19 December 1958), 3.

Semino, Miguel A., *Partidos políticos y elecciones en el Uruguay*, (FCU, 1984).

Sempol, Diego, 'La historiografía blanca sobre el pasado reciente: entre el testimonio y la historia', in Alcides Abella (coord.), *1968 Uruguay 1985* (Vol. 2, EBO, 2006), 23–8.

Seregni, Liber, *La autoridad del pueblo* (ed. Germán Wettstein, Indice, 1984).

——, *Una línea coherente, I* (Libros para la Patria Nueva, 1988).

Servicio Paz y Justicia [SERPAJ], *Uruguay nunca más* (SERPAJ, 1989).

Silva, Alberto, *Profesor Juan José Crottogini. Una vida alumbrando vida* (La Rueda de Amargueando, 2004).

Solari, Aldo, *Estudios sobre la sociedad uruguaya*, (2 Vols., Arca, 1964–5).

——, *El tercerismo en el Uruguay* (Arca, 1965).

——, *El desarrollo social del Uruguay en la postguerra* (Alfa, 1967).

——, *Uruguay: partidos políticos y sistema electoral* (El Libro Libre/ FUCCYT, 1988).

Soler, Leticia, *Historiografía uruguaya contemporánea (1985–2000)* (Trilce, 2000).

Sosa, Gabriel, *Qué difícil es ser de izquierda en estos días y otras historias de amor* (Planeta, 2004).

Sosnowski, Saúl (ed.), *Represión, exilio y democracia: la cultura uruguaya* (EBO, 1987).

Stolowicz, Beatriz, 'El desprestigio de la política: lo que no se discute', *Política y cultura*, 17 (2002), 165–92.

Tagliaferro, Gerardo, *Fernández Huidobro. De las armas a las urnas* (Fin de Siglo, 2004).

Tapia Valdés, Jorge, 'La doctrina de la seguridad nacional y el rol político de las fuerzas armadas', *Nueva Sociedad*, 47 (1980), 23–46.

Terra, Juan Pablo, 'En los comienzos del Frente', *Cuadernos de Marcha*, 46 (1971), 45–9.

——, 'El Partido Demócrata Cristiano y las Raíces del Frente', *Cuadernos de Marcha*, 47 (1971), 13–17.

——, '¿Por qué impulsamos el Frente?', in INDAL, *Democracia Cristiana* (2nd. ed., Caracas, INDAL), 155–6.

——, *Mística, desarrollo y revolución* (Librosur, 1985).

Therborn, Göran, *What Does The Ruling Class Do When It Rules?* [1978] (London, Verso, 2008).

'Today' [Escanlar, Gustavo], 'Sobre una entrevista', *Aquí* (16 December 1987), 4.

——, 'Carta', *Cuadernos de Marcha*, 3rd series, 29 (March 1988), 76–8.

Torres, Jorge, *La derrota en la mira* (Fin de Siglo, 2002).

——, *Cuba y el che: la ruta mágica* (Fin de Siglo, 2007).

Touron, Luis, 'La brega unitaria: una constante del Partido Comunista', *Estudios*, 57 (1970), 47–59.

Trigo, Abril, 'Contracultura del insilio (1973–1985)', *Revista Hispánica Moderna*, xliii, (1990), 228–38.

——, *Caudillo, estado, nación. Literatura, historia e ideología en Uruguay* (Gaithersburg, Hispamérica, 1990).

——, 'Joven narrativa uruguaya', *Hispamérica*, 58 (1991), 87–112.

——, Poesía uruguaya actual (los más jóvenes)', *Hispamérica*, 64/65 (1993), 121–47.

——, *¿Cultura uruguaya o culturas linyeras? (Para una cartografía de la neomodernidad posuruguaya)* (Vintén, 1997).

——, 'Why Do I Do Cultural Studies?', *Journal of Latin American Cultural Studies*, ix, 1 (2000), 73–93.

——, 'De Artigas a Tabaré Vázquez, o de cómo se hace un imaginario posnacional', at <www.henciclopedia.org.uy/autores/Trigo/ArtigasTabare.htm>.

——, *Memorias migrantes. Testimonios y ensayos sobre la diáspora uruguaya* (Rosario/Montevideo, Beatriz Viterbo/Trilce, 2003).

——, 'El proyecto cultural de *Capítulo Oriental* y *Enciclopedia Uruguaya* (Reflexiones sobre las publicaciones en fascículo de los años 60)', *Hispamérica*, 94 (2003), 13–24.

——, 'The Politics and Anti-Politics of Uruguayan Rock', in D. Pacini Hernández, E. Zolov, H. Fernández L'Hoeste (eds.), *'Rockin' Las Américas: The Global Politics of Rock in Latin/o America* (Pittsburgh UP, 2004), 115–41.

——, del Sarto, Ana & Ríos, Alicia (eds.), *The Latin America Cultural Studies Reader* (Durham and London, Duke UP, 2004).

Turiansky, Vladimir, *El movimiento obrero uruguayo* (Pueblos Unidos, 1973).

Ulriksen de Viñar, Maren (ed.), *Memoria social: fragmentaciones y responsabilidades* (Trilce, 2001).

'Unión Popular', 'Llamamiento al pueblo uruguayo', *Marcha* (24 August 1962), 2.

Uricoechea, Fernando, *Intelectuales y desarrollo en América Latina* (Buenos Aires, CEDAL, 1969).

Urioste Braga, Fernando, 'La gran tarea del Frente', *Cuadernos de Marcha*, 47 (1971), 66–9.

Valenti, Esteban, 'Un alegato optimista de Quijano', *Brecha* (10 July 1992), 10.

Varela, Gonzalo, *De la república liberal al estado militar: Uruguay 1968–1973* (Ediciones del Nuevo Mundo, 1988).

Vázquez, Tabaré, *El gobierno del cambio* (La República, 2004).

Vera, Tabaré (ed.), *Uruguay hacia 2000: desafíos y opciones* (Caracas, Nueva Sociedad, 1991).

—— & Chávez, Hugo, 'Carta a los presidentes de América Latina', *Diplomacia Estrategia Política*, i, 3 (2005), 194–8.

Verdesio, Gustavo, Peveroni, Gabriel & Roland, Eduardo, 'La movida de los 80: la ruptura cultural en Uruguay', parts I and II, <www.henciclopedia.org.uy/autores/Verdesio/Movida80.htm> and <www.henciclopedia.org.uy/autores/Verdesio/Movida80II.htm>.

Vescovi, Rodrigo, *Ecos revolucionarios. Luchadores sociales, Uruguay 1968–1973* (Nóos, 2003).

Viera, Eduardo, *La crisis económica uruguaya* (Ed. Pueblos Unidos, 1971).

Vilas, Carlos M., 'La izquierda latinoamericana. Búsquedas y desafíos', *Nueva Sociedad*, 157 (1998), 64–75.

Viñar, Maren & Marcelo, *Fracturas de memoria* (Trilce, 1993).

Visca, Arturo S., *Un hombre y su mundo* (Asir, 1960; revised and expanded edition, Ministerio de Educación y Cultura, 1978).

Wachendorfer, Achim (ed.), *La izquierda uruguaya frente a la crisis del socialismo real* (FESUR, 1991).

Waksman, Guillermo, 'La izquierda avanza hacia el gobierno', *Nueva sociedad*, 148 (March–April 1997), 12–19.

Weinstein, Martin, *Uruguay: The Politics of Failure* (New Brunswick, Transition, 1979).

——, *Uruguay: Democracy at the Crossroads* (Boulder, Westview, 1988).

Weschler, Lawrence, *A Miracle, A Universe. Settling Accounts with Torturers* (Chicago, Chicago UP, 1998).

Winn, Peter & Ferro-Clérico, Lilia, 'Can a Leftist Government Make a Difference? The Frente Amplio Administration of Montevideo, 1990–1994', Chalmers Douglas A. et al., *The New Politics of Inequality in Latin America* (OUP, 1997), 447–68.

Wojciechowski, Gustavo, 'Tics culturales', *La Revista del Sur*, 1 (Suplemento) (August 1987), 87–8.

Yaffé, Jaime, 'Izquierda, historia y tradición en Uruguay. La tradicionalización del Frente Amplio y el nacimiento de la tercera divisa', *Cuadernos del CLAEH*, 86/87 (2003), 155–92.

——, 'Del Frente Amplio a la Nueva Mayoría. La izquierda uruguaya (1971–2004)', *Secuencia* [Mexico], 60 (September–December 2004), 175–210.

——, 'Memoria y olvidos en la relación de la izquierda con el pasado reciente', in Aldo Marchesi et al., *El presente de la dictadura* (Trilce, 2004), 184–98.

——, *Al centro y adentro* (Linardi y Risso, 2005).

——, 'Réquiem para el "Réquiem para la izquierda". El triunfo del FA: de la competencia interpartidaria al desempeño electoral', in Daniel Buquet (ed.), *Las claves del cambio: ciclo electoral y nuevo gobierno 2004/5* (EBO, 2005), 43–62.

——, 'El insospechado papel de las "aspirinas blancas"', in Alcides Abella (coord.), *1968 Uruguay 1985*, (vol. 3, EBO, 2007), 87–106.

Yáñez, Ruben, '1971: un salto cualitativo en la cultura uruguaya', *Estudios*, 62 (1972), 90–3.

Yúdice, George, Franco, Jean & Flores, Juan (eds.), *On Edge: the Crisis of Latin American Culture* (Minneapolis, Minnesota UP, 1992).

Zabalza, Jorge, *El miedo a la democracia* (TAE, 1989).

——, *El tejazo y otras insurrecciones* (TAE, 1995).

——, *La estaca* (Ediciones del Cerro, 1998).

Zibechi, Raúl, 'La izquierda sorprendida', *Brecha*, 16 December 1994), 3–5.

——, *La revuelta juvenil de los '90* (Nordan Comunidad, 1997).

Zubillaga, Carlos, 'Historiografía y cambio social: el caso uruguayo', *Cuadernos del CLAEH*, 24 (1982), 23–47.

——, *La democracia atacada* (EBO, 1988).

——, 'Luchas populares y cultura alternativa en Uruguay', *Siglo XIX*, iii, 6 (1989), 11–39.

——, *Historia e historiadores en el Uruguay del siglo xx* (Facultad de Humanidades y de Ciencias de la Educación, 2002).

—— & Pérez, Romeo, *Los partidos políticos* (CLAEH, 1983).

Zum Felde, Alberto, *Proceso intelectual del Uruguay* (3 vols., Librosur, 1985).

CONTENTS